THE CHARM OF THE COTSWOLDS

THE CHARM OF THE COTSWOLDS

Published by The Reader's Digest Association Limited

LONDON • NEW YORK • SYDNEY • MONTREAL

THE COTSWOLDS: the name evokes idyllic villages of golden stone, and country lanes whose only traffic consists of horses clip-clopping past on a morning ride and tractors buzzing about their rural business. It speaks of peaceful, picturesque towns with historic market squares, antique shops and tearooms. The reality can be a little different, particularly in the tourist season, but no less fascinating and infinitely more varied—as in bustling Cirencester, Regency Cheltenham or the oriental splendour of Sezincote.

In the introduction to this book, travel writer John Kahn sets the scene quite literally from above, surveying the area first from the window of a tiny Cessna plane, and later with the aid of a magical balloon ride. In the main part of the book, 'A Year in the Cotswolds', journalist and Cotswold resident John Hudson takes the reader to the heart of Cotswold life, meeting local characters, visiting great houses and witnessing centuries-old village traditions. Finally, the 'Highlights' section, with its useful map, is the Digest's own choice of the very best places to visit and things to do, be it on a day trip or a more leisurely ramble through this most unspoilt corner of England.

THE CHARM OF THE COTSWOLDS was edited and designed by The Reader's Digest Association Limited, 11 Westferry Circus, Canary Wharf, London E14 4HE
www.readersdigest.co.uk

Reprinted with amendments 2004

A Year in the Cotswolds Original full-length version by John Hudson, first published by Alan Sutton Publishing Limited, 1995
© John Hudson, 1995
British condensed version © The Reader's Digest Association Limited, 1999

CONTRIBUTORS

Series Editor Steve Savage

Volume Editor Charlotte Rundall

Assistant Editor/Researcher Miriam Sharland

Associate Editors David Blomfield, Hugo de Klee

Copy Editors Morag Lyall, Barbara Roby

Editorial and Picture Research Assistant Kate Michell

Art Editor Karen Stewart

Designer Carl Meek

Picture Researcher Helen Ashford

Additional material by Michael Bird, James Harpur, Joe Henson, John Kahn, Mark Lewis, Tim Locke, Jane Philipson

Cartography Anthony Sidwell (page 9), Malcolm Porter (pages 150–51)

Index Brian Amos

FRONT COVER *The River Eye meanders past stone cottages in the tranquil village of Upper Slaughter.*
BACK COVER (TOP) *A surprise sight in rural England: Sezincote, an Indian-style palace near Moreton-in-Marsh.*
BACK COVER (BOTTOM) *Country children dance round the Maypole, a tradition kept alive in the Cotswolds.*
TITLE PAGE *The tiny church of St Michael's at Duntisbourne Rouse dates back to Saxon times.*

THIS PAGE *Tetbury's 17th-century Market House, built for weighing wool, is the focal point of the town.*
PAGES 6–7 *The yellow stone houses of Chipping Campden bask drowsily in the summer sun.*
PAGES 24–5 *A cottage in the High Street of Broadway is hung with cascades of wisteria blooms.*
PAGES 148–9 *Racegoers get a final view of runners and riders at Cheltenham before placing their bets.*

CONTENTS

EXPLORING

THE COTSWOLDS

with John Kahn

THE COTSWOLDS

with John Kahn

I T STRUCK ME RECENTLY that my long acquaintance with the Cotswolds was actually no more than a nodding acquaintance, based on quick forays into the region: day-trips from Oxford, or deliberate detours while en route to Wales or Bristol.

What I had glimpsed on those forays was the way in which one could feel far from modern city life. In the Cotswolds it is the village that sets the tone, and the pace. People stop to talk to you; you find yourself driving more slowly; the days seem longer somehow. And the look of things—that too seems of another age: scarcely a building of more than three storeys (the only high-rise being the occasional church spire), and a marked lack of satellite dishes and neon signs. Such characteristics hold good, it is true, for dozens of rural regions throughout the country. What is distinctive about the Cotswolds is the pervasiveness of this unspoilt quality: how widely and uninterruptedly it prevails across the region, how consistently it permeates the villages, and how harmonised these villages are with one another; how all of a piece the entire region seems to be.

My own impression, however, was piecemeal, and I felt the time had come to attempt an assessment of the region as a whole. To do that, it would make sense to begin with some kind of overview. Why not a literal one, then, by means of a flight over the area? Very well, but what kind of flight? Light aeroplane, or balloon? In the event, it turned out to be both.

A BIRD'S-EYE VIEW

The experts I consulted all came down in favour of the plane. A plane would cover far more of the countryside; the route would be of my own choosing rather than at the whim of the wind; and so on. One phone call was all it took. A flying

school, based near Gloucestershire Airport at Staverton, was happy to oblige. A tiny Cessna would be at my disposal in two days' time (complete with pilot, I hasten to add), for an hour in the early afternoon.

From the low-lying runway, a nearby limestone ridge was visible, zigzagging in a northeastward direction. This ridge is the Cotswold scarp or Cotswold edge (hence the names of such villages as Wotton-under-Edge and Aston-sub-Edge). The pilot, to my relief, approached it obliquely rather than head-on: you want to have plenty of height before venturing near it.

The altimeter registered 2,200 feet. For a flight altitude, that may not sound particularly impressive, but the view it affords from the cockpit, at least on such a clear and sunny afternoon, sweeps from the cooling towers of Didcot power station in one direction to the mountains of Wales in the other. And when two small salvos of Red Arrows streaked across our path, they were actually flying at a level well below our own. (Of all the unplanned and unexpected experiences sprung on me during my various travels, watching the Red Arrows from above must rate as one of the oddest.)

At 2,200 feet, you can see virtually all of the Cotswolds at a single glance. And your perspective on the region changes dizzyingly. The once-imposing ridge now appears to flatten out, and becomes distinguishable not by its contours but by its colour: a long green stripe formed by the grassy slopes alongside the ridge and the intermittent golf courses on its rim, set off from the varied shades of browns and yellows assumed by the high-summer fields on either side of it. Or consider how distance seems to shrink: on the ground, a tiresome drive separates the four famous market towns of Chipping Campden, Moreton-in-Marsh, Stow-on-the-Wold and Bourton-on-the-Water; from the air, they line up obligingly like four small stepping stones, separated by a mere hop, step and jump. Bourton itself, now a scattering of doll's houses, proves how closely, after all, it resembles its 'perfect replica', the miniature Model Village which is perhaps its favourite tourist attraction.

A MANUFACTURED BEAUTY

Among such a multitude of enchantments, however, a disenchantment or two is bound to lurk. And the main one here is, curiously, the overall impression of the region as seen from above. The popular image of the Cotswolds is, in part, of a nature haven, accessible yet somehow unspoilt—a place where jaded town dwellers from the Midlands or the Southeast can get back in touch with nature, or at least get somehow close to nature. Indeed, the region enjoys the official designation of AONB—Area of Outstanding Natural Beauty. Yet viewed from the air, untamed nature seems very much sidelined. Apart from the lush, steep valleys around Stroud, the pale green fringe along the ridge and the occasional dark green patch of woodland, the view is overwhelmingly of fields— that mosaic of yellows and browns (in August at any rate), with dry-stone walls

ABOVE *This 'natural' landscape of rolling hills around Winchcombe is, in fact, the product of centuries of carefully managed farming.*

or hedgerows as the grouting. There is a beauty to it, certainly, but does it really qualify as *natural* beauty? For the people who live in the region rather than just visit it, the landscape is certainly a working landscape, given over to the serious business of agriculture rather than to the gratification of nature-loving tourists.

The statistics bear out this impression. In 1935 some 40 per cent of the Cotswolds was covered by permanent grassland. Today that grassland accounts for just 1.5 per cent of the area. And yet, for all that, nature somehow still seems remarkably robust and vivacious in the Cotswolds, and its constant presence is one of the memories you take away with you when you return home. Wild flowers, birdsong and butterflies abound disproportionately. And above every river valley perch a dozen prominences yielding wonderful views along or across it. They are wonderful in a genial rather than a dramatic way, since the landscape rolls fairly gently, and they are rustic rather than wild views, since the scenery consists mostly of farmland, studded with a distant village or two or an elegant manor house, perhaps. As you take the stiffish walk up to Belas Knap—the intriguing Stone Age burial mound—for instance, you keep turning round and looking back across pastures or cornfields at the ever-widening panorama below, with Sudeley Castle and the pretty town of Winchcombe balancing the composition as unobtrusive embellishments.

More memorable still are the views *from* the Cotswolds, down the grassy slopes of the limestone ridge, northwards over the Vale of Evesham or westwards across the glinting Severn to the Malvern Hills and the hazy Welsh mountains in the far distance. You can't hike very far along the Cotswold Way, the famous 100-mile walk tracing more or less the edge of the ridge, without finding a spellbinding lookout point. From Dover's Hill or Fish Hill in the north to Tog Hill in the south, and all points in between, with their evocative names to add to the charm: Cleeve Cloud, Crickley Hill, Birdlip Hill, Painswick Beacon, Coaley Peak, Nibley Knoll…

However little of the truly natural survives, such views have all the feel of 'Outstanding Natural Beauty', and have the same strange, unmistakable effect on the spirits, at once calming and uplifting. Perhaps, then, AONB is not really a serious misnomer after all.

UNBOUNDED COUNTRYSIDE

The Cotswold AONB is the largest of the forty-one AONBs in England and Wales. The function of the designation here, as of its counterparts elsewhere, is broadly speaking to protect the landscape (though, unlike a National Park Authority, it can only advise and educate—not regulate). The landscape in question is a single, distinctive landscape, hence not just the AONB's great size but its strange jagged borders as well. The basis of that landscape is limestone, and the unifying effect it has on the scenery.

This limestone is quite different in character from the easily dissolved limestone of, for example, the Mendips or the Peak District; it is the tougher oolitic ('egg-rock') limestone, packed with roe-like granules—and many marine

ABOVE *Marine fossils such as this abound in Cotswold limestone, and date from the Jurassic period, when the region was covered in sea.*

fossils suggestive of its undersea origins. An ancient formation of it extends in an arc from the Dorset coast up to the North York Moors. Its most conspicuous elevated stretch, forming that Cotswold ridge or escarpment, looms over Bath and Broadway alike. The 'wolds' of the Cotswolds are the uplands formed by the limestone. They are rolling or hilly uplands rather than a plateau, thanks to 'outliers', such as Bredon Hill, and to the aeons of carving performed by the local rivers—the Windrush, the Coln, the Evenlode and others. Though clearly delineated on the west by the Cotswold ridge, the uplands have no obvious eastern boundary, fading gently as they do into the flat expanses of Oxfordshire.

Where do the Cotswolds begin and end, then? Historically, the range of the term 'Cotswolds' has expanded greatly from humble beginnings. The *wolds* element perhaps referred originally to woods rather than uplands; the *cot* element probably derives from Cod (pronounced 'code'), the name of a Saxon chieftain of about AD 800, who lived along the upper reaches of the Windrush. (A rival derivation, from *cotes* in the sense of 'sheep stalls', is now considered doubtful.) The Cotswolds, then—'the woodlands or high lands of chief Cod'—probably referred at first to a limited area near the Windrush's source. Over the centuries, the name came to apply to a larger and larger area, absorbing the Stroud valley little more than 100 years ago. Since then, it has slowly continued its move downwards towards Bath, though the popular image seems reluctant to follow it there.

BELOW *Daybreak reveals a light icing of wintry frost on the banks of the meandering River Evenlode.*

The popular image of the area is fairly conservative. Imagine, deep within the bounds of the M4, M5 and M40 motorways, a kind of triangle (with bulging sides) linking Chipping Campden in the north, Stroud in the southwest and Burford in the southeast. That would enfold the 'essential Cotswolds' as popularly understood.

But such attempts to define the borders are ultimately futile. The prosaic truth is that, as with so many British regions—'the Highlands', 'the Lake District' and so on—the heartland is clear but the outskirts are not. The boundaries are disputable, but why bother to dispute them? Within reason, you can draw them to your own specifications. If a village looks and feels like a Cotswold village, if it has that indefinable Cotswold spirit and that entrancing old-world appearance, that's qualification enough.

THE HALLMARK OF THE COTSWOLDS

The village: for visitors to the Cotswolds, it is the village more than anything else that distinguishes the region, almost symbolises it. (A fairly liberal definition of the term 'village' prevails in the Cotswolds, covering anything from a tiny hamlet to a fair-sized market town.) The very words 'Cotswolds' and 'village' seem to fit together in a natural and lilting combination. And what distinguishes a Cotswold village in turn, first and foremost, is Cotswold stone, the selfsame oolitic limestone that lies beneath the village's foundations. It is a remarkable building material. For the quarryman and mason, it is relatively soft and easy to work. For the builder and home owner, it is robust and resilient, since it hardens once exposed to the air and properly weathered. One other engaging quality: its colour varies from district to district, in proportion to the iron content. Compare the façades of my two favourite market towns: the honey and apricot shades of Chipping Campden in the north with the greyish beige of more southerly Painswick.

Not that the Cotswold villages and market towns have a monopoly on Cotswold stone. The majestic cathedral of Gloucester provides a further local showcase; further afield, several Oxford colleges benefit from the unique glow it seems to confer, and Blenheim Palace and Windsor Castle too; and in London, St Paul's and the Houses of Parliament serve as the ultimate monuments to its strength and versatility.

In a Cotswold village its appeal seems more than visual—it exudes a mellow warmth and sense of calm that you can almost feel. And such qualities apart, it impresses any passer-by with its sheer quantity. Not just the walls but the lichened roofs; not just the church but the churchyard's table-top tombs; not just the cottages and almshouse terraces but the manor house too, and the occasional terrace of elegant Georgian townhouses; not just the barns but the dovecotes; not just the garden paths but the clapper bridge across the stream. Look at an old sepia photograph of Stanway or Naunton or Duntisbourne Leer, say, and you could almost be looking at a full-colour photo taken of the same scene today on a late autumn afternoon.

ABOVE *In the Cotswolds even the most functional buildings are beautiful, such as this dovecote on the edge of Blockley.*

LEFT *Stanton, restored in the early 20th century by Philip Stott, is one of the loveliest of Cotswold villages.*

Those with an eye for such things will identify several characteristic features of Cotswold architecture— distinctive gables or mullions, for example—but to an eye as inexpert as mine, the one constant theme is the steep pitch of the roofs. It's all to do with the roof tiles. They were traditionally made by leaving waterlogged limestone slabs to freeze in the winter and thereby to split along the grain. The resulting tiles not only were thicker and heavier than slate tiles of the same size but also, being so porous, required more overlapping in order to prevent leakage. So the weight of roofing material was huge, and only steep-angled rafters could hope to distribute and support such a heavy load. The effect of the stone is to blend the buildings into the countryside, so much so that they seem to grow out of the landscape rather than intrude on it. They belong there. The best of the villages appear utterly right in their settings, as venerable and dignified and almost as natural as a great oak.

ABOVE *A stonemason puts the final touches to limestone roof tiles during repairs to Chastleton House.*

HISTORY INTO LANDSCAPE

How did it happen that so much of the region retains this wonderful antique look, the appearance almost of being frozen in time two or three centuries ago? The answer lies in a severe downturn in the region's fortunes from the late 18th century to the early 20th. The Cotswolds' long heyday as a wool-producing and cloth-milling region began to wane in the face of heavy taxation and competition from Yorkshire and abroad. As the crisis deepened, with families migrating and even starving, the local economy drew in its horns, and the construction industry of the time wound down and went into an extended recession.

When demand for housing eventually resumed in earnest, it proved a fairly easy matter to restore the old buildings, no matter how long-deserted and derelict, thanks to the resilience of the limestone with which the walls were built. And the restorations have usually been tasteful and convincing. That is due, in part, to the planning regulations of recent decades, but before then it would have been due to the local residents' own proud appreciation of their unique architectural heritage. And it has paid off, in some senses anyway. By resolutely failing to modernise their appearance, the villages can boast an aesthetic simplicity and a nostalgic glow very much in keeping with current taste, and the resulting tourist influx has restored prosperity to the region.

Earlier generations of Cotswold inhabitants have left their mark on the landscape too, to a greater or lesser extent. Tantalising hints remain of various prehistoric peoples, dating back as many as 7,000 years. There are the mysterious Rollright Stones, a kind of mini-Stonehenge just north of Chipping Norton. There are dozens of burial mounds, from the Stone Age onwards, the best known being—if only for their splendid names—Belas Knap and Hetty Pegler's Tump.

The Roman presence in the region still exerts a subtle influence: drive out of Cirencester along the A417 or the A429, and you are tracing one or other of the country's main Roman roads—Ermine Street (northwestwards towards Gloucester) and the Fosse Way (northeastwards into Warwickshire). Cirencester (Corinium) itself was a major Romano-British town and regional capital, second in size and importance only to Londinium (London). In a park on its outskirts, a grassy crater represents the remnants of an ancient Roman amphitheatre. Did gladiators really once fight their gory duels in front of cheering crowds here in the peaceful heart of England? For a more formal evocation of Roman Cirencester, be sure to visit the Corinium Museum in the centre of town. The Orpheus mosaic there is a wonder, bettered only perhaps by the mosaics of Chedworth Roman Villa, a remarkable archaeological site a few miles to the north.

With the end of Roman rule, it was the Saxons' turn to impose their authority on the region. In 577, at the bloody Battle of Dyrham, just north of Bath, they made their intentions clear, crushing three Romano-British chieftains, the kings of Bath, Gloucester and Cirencester. Saxon churches, however much

ABOVE *The Corinium Museum in Cirencester is a treasure trove of Roman artefacts, such as this gravestone of a Roman cavalryman.*

RIGHT *Roman remains in the Cotswolds are not confined to museums: this mosaic, buried for centuries, was uncovered at a Winchcombe farm.*

restored, are still in evidence, as at Duntisbourne Rouse and Winstone. But all in all, the Saxons' remnants, as elsewhere in England, are less conspicuous and probably less extensive than those of their Roman predecessors. Chief Cod may have bequeathed his name to the Cotswolds, but he left nothing else of note.

When the Normans replaced the Saxons as local overlords a few centuries later, the era of church-building began in earnest. And not just churches—cathedrals and abbeys too. In addition, the region's main economic resources—wool and cloth—at last received their rightful recognition. Exports to Europe grew prodigiously. The opportunity was there for the taking, whether by feudal lord, enterprising merchant or monastic house. When Hailes Abbey near Winchcombe, for instance—today consisting of haunting ruins—was flourishing in the 13th to 16th centuries, it was being sustained, in part at least, by wool money.

The landscape changed accordingly. Woods succumbed to the demand for pastureland; dry-stone walling later began to filigree the grassy slopes and valley floors. The local breed of sheep, the so-called Cotswold Lion, proved extraordinarily productive, yielding a heavier fleece than any other British breed. The Cotswolds became the major contributor to the nation's principal source of income. Even the Crown became heavily reliant on wool tax. Wool duly acquired a symbolic stature, to the point that the Lord Chancellor's official seat in the House of Lords took the form of a woolsack.

In the Cotswolds, great fortunes were acquired by landowners, wool merchants or brokers, and later cloth-mill owners. It is thanks to their investments or largesse that much of the region's familiar architecture came into being: manor houses, market halls, charitable almshouses and schools, terraces of workers' cottages, churches. In Chipping Campden, for instance, the majority of the famous buildings—William Grevel's House, Woolstaplers' Hall, Market Hall, the almshouses, manorial gatehouse and church—were financed by wool money.

ABOVE *R. Whitford's painting shows proud Northleach farmers with their Cotswold Lion sheep. This particular flock stole the laurels at the Royal Show in 1861.*

As connoisseurs of old churches will tell you, the Cotswolds offer some of the richest pickings in the country, from village gems as in North Cerney or Oddington, to the bold 18th-century Gothic Revival church in Tetbury, or the magnificent 15th- to 16th-century Perpendicular-style 'wool churches' of Cirencester, Northleach, Fairford, Lechlade, and so on, complete with their stained glass, fine carvings and memorial brasses.

In the Age of the Golden Fleece, as it came to be known, the architectural landscape of the Cotswolds was expanding and changing constantly. Then, as the Industrial Revolution progressed, the demand for local wool and cloth collapsed in district after district, and time froze.

THE REGION'S ALLURE

What lures so many visitors to the region today? There are perhaps 9 million a year, 80 per cent of them day-trippers. For some, particularly those with children, it's the specialist tourist attractions: the Cotswolds Falconry Centre near Moreton-in-Marsh, or the Cotswolds Water Park south of Cirencester, a conglomeration of over 100 lakes offering a range of leisure pursuits from birdwatching to jet-skiing. For others, it's the auctions and antique shops in Burford or Stow-on-the-Wold, or the country customs—morris dancing and woolsack races, craft fairs and steam rallies.

And then there are the stately homes: Stanway House, for instance, a beautiful 'Jacobethan' manor—built between 1590 and 1630, and exhibiting both Elizabethan and Jacobean characteristics—garnished with a medieval tithe barn; or Sudeley Castle, together with its romantic ruins and its gorgeous sequence of traditional gardens. And the two great eccentricities of the region: Snowshill Manor, with its bewildering collection of antique bric-a-brac, and Sezincote, a lavish mansion built in 1805 in the style of a Mogul palace, which inspired in part the design of Brighton Pavilion. And there are other magnificent Cotswold gardens: Painswick Rococo Garden, for example, or Batsford Arboretum.

For ramblers, it's not just the famous Cotswold Way and the challenge of getting from Chipping Campden to Bath within ten days, but the Macmillan Way too, and the Warden's Way and the Windrush Way, the Heart of England Way and the Oxfordshire Way, and the countless footpaths through farms and woodlands.

But for most visitors, the favourite activity is exploring villages—village-tasting, or village-sampling, as it's sometimes known. It consists typically of driving (unfortunately but often unavoidably) to a village, then inspecting it on foot—studying the layout, admiring the village square and the cottage gardens, inspecting the church, taking tea perhaps, wandering along the river banks and (unconsciously but unavoidably) awarding points.

Several Cotswold villages could lay claim to being 'the most beautiful village in England', on the basis of receiving that accolade from some guidebook or celebrity: Snowshill, Blockley, or Bourton-on-the-Hill, all of them more than usually hilly; Stanton, with its uncharacteristic sprinkling of thatched roofs; Bibury, Broadway, Bisley, Burford; Upper Swell and Lower Slaughter; Great Rissington and Little Barrington. Any regular visitor is likely to harbour a particular favourite, and liable to press its case with surprising strength of feeling when discussing the day's village-sampling afterwards with companions in the pub.

Unspoilt though the Cotswolds try to remain, they can hardly hope to exclude the 20th century. The trick, then, when village-sampling, is to try to filter out the modern elements, especially motor vehicles. In that way, you get a purer sense of how things were in bygone times. Some villages, sad to say, seem less susceptible to such filtering. On a busy weekend, it's difficult to view Stow-on-the-Wold as a traditional market town rather than as an antiques bazaar. When Burford and Bibury and Bourton-on-the-Water become too self-conscious of their charms, and too eager to meet the wishes of coach-party tourists, they forfeit their authentic character and become theme-park versions of themselves.

Painswick, on the other hand, retains its dignity even when most bustling. And Chipping Campden seems to hush and sober its hordes of sightseers, the way a cathedral might. Its glorious High Street ('the most beautiful village street now left in the island', according to the historian G. M. Trevelyan) has long been renowned for magically harmonising so many buildings of different centuries and styles; perhaps it somehow contrives to harmonise human impulses, too.

In the course of my own village-sampling over the years, my allegiance has shifted regularly from one favourite to another. On this recent visit of mine, a new candidate emerged to stake its claim. It is (thank goodness) unheralded by the guidebooks. I had scarcely known of its existence before, let alone seen it. How could I have overlooked it? Its charms apart, it seems to have the distinction of containing all the essential ingredients of a Cotswold village. Not that there could be such a thing as a typical Cotswold village, of course, but this one certainly impressed me as somehow epitomising 'Cotswold-ness'.

It was a hot afternoon, towards the end of my visit, when I chanced upon it. I was driving to the Cotswold Farm Park, with the intention of seeing a Cotswold Lion in the flesh. The road brought me in sight of a hamlet, basking in the sunlight. Its name, according to the road map, was Guiting Power. I slowed the car to a dawdle. Hollyhocks and climbing roses paraded on the garden walls of the outlying cottages. A village green, and then another. Just a few cars at the road-side—easily filtered out of the picture, and not even necessary in the case of a gleaming Austin Six, backed onto a sloping parking bay and proudly displaying its running boards and antique wheels.

A friendly passer-by gave me my bearings. The village's curious name? Guiting rhymes with 'fighting', and is probably an old word for 'gushing', in reference to the formerly sprightly river or to some spring in the vicinity, though possibly derived from the name of a Saxon landowner again; and the Power element is derived from the name of the village's owners in the 13th century, the Le Poer family.

Today the village has about 300 residents. Farming and quarrying provide most of the work. The school

BELOW *Guiting Power has two village greens. This one is graced with a medieval-style war memorial (and a passing feline visitor).*

has closed down, but a strong sense of community persists, with two friendly pubs to choose from, and a lively (though modern and ugly) village hall. A hundred years ago, by contrast, the village had been in a pitiful state of depression and decay. The main church was finally repaired and refurbished in 1903 (rather too inventively for the liking of the purists), and the village slowly smartened up, culminating in a superb restoring of the village centre once a new owner took over the manor in 1958. Today the double green looks almost like a film set for some costume drama, and it's all too easy to imagine yourself transported back to some idyllic (and never-existing) era of rural English life.

ABOVE *The Norman Church of St Michael in Guiting Power was restored in 1903, but kept its original impressive doorways.*

The village nestles in the innermost Cotswolds, close to the upper Windrush and one of its tributaries. A few minutes' stroll in one direction along a lane and foot-path takes you to a wooded valley and across a small bridge into fine walking country. In the other direction runs the lane to the village church. On the left of the lane is the manor house—modest but handsome—and adjoining it, apparently serving as an extended front garden, is a field of sheep. If you cross to the middle of the field, you can scrutinise a twin archaeological site: the foundations of a tiny Saxon church alongside a prehistoric mound, probably the remains of a Bronze Age tomb. And then, at the end of the lane, St Michael's Church and its peaceful churchyard. Lovingly maintained, they show no signs of the dereliction they suffered from a century ago. The church retains two original Norman doorways. Above one of them is an amusing stone carving of a head with its tongue sticking out—presumably in scorn of those who criticised the restoration designs for taking too many liberties. Beyond the church, a footpath leads ramblers out along another stretch of the quiet and delightful Warden's Way, towards Naunton. Most of them, though, must surely loiter much longer than planned in Guiting Power itself, to get their fill of its own quiet delights.

The same holds true for motorists. I never did get to see the Cotswold Farm Park.

A PROVIDENTIAL WIND

'You're a lucky man,' a voice assured me over the phone. I had rung a balloon-tours office, thinking it might be worth attempting another overview of the Cotswolds. That flight on the Cessna a few days earlier had failed to do the trick. The problem lay, on reflection, with the incongruity of it: the jarring contrast between the roaring, rattling, thrilling tumult of the flight and the gentle, languorous landscape it was intended to display. It is a landscape for rambling or trotting or floating over, for lingering over, certainly not for buzzing over pell-mell. What about a balloon ride, then? That ought to hit the right note. The pace seems so much more in keeping with that of the region.

'Yes, definitely very lucky,' the voice on the phone continued cheerfully. 'A berth has just become available on tomorrow morning's sailing.' Lucky? A 5.30 wake-up call, to get to the launching site by 6am! That's lucky? What about a little later in the day, I suggested. The owner of the voice explained, perhaps not for the first time in his life, that balloon flights take place in the early mornings and early evenings only. Too hazardous during the rest of the day: thermals. Very well, I said, an evening flight then, please. 'Certainly,' the voice replied, 'if you care to wait another five weeks for the next available ticket.'

Six in the morning is not an hour of the day that I am particularly familiar with, or wish to be, but it seemed worth braving in the circumstances, and I duly presented myself at Cheltenham racecourse, the agreed take-off venue, just as dawn was breaking. Mist still hovered about, but a bright day was in prospect. Fair stood the wind for—where exactly? Part of the fun of a balloon ride is not knowing where you're headed.

A quick roll call and safety lesson as the balloon inflates; nervous laughter as eleven passengers clamber into the giant laundry basket; a last sustained whoosh of the burners, and we're off.

The few low clouds or straggler mist patches part to make way for us. Cheltenham, in its Regency splendour, stretches luxuriously as it wakes. Gloucester

BELOW *A 'balloon's eye' view of Cheltenham, with its elegant park and Regency buildings, and the famous racecourse beyond.*

Cathedral becomes visible briefly, only to recede as we sail slowly away towards the rising sun. In the fields, the straw bales—cylindrical rather than rectangular these days—cast long morning shadows over the stubble.

Our altitude apparently is only slightly lower than that of my Cessna five days before, but today's flight is so much slower that everything seems in sharper focus.

We drift serenely over farmhouses, a quarry, a stretch of woodland where we spot a deer darting across a clearing. Field after field. But not a single village.

Where are we? A glance at our pilot yields no hint. He scans his chart, but keeps his own counsel. A tree-ringed farmstead passes below now, part of a stud farm. At last a small village inches into view. Another glance at the pilot, in hopes of enlightenment.

'Village ahoy!' he announces laconically. 'Nice place. Name of Guiting Power. Worth visiting.'

There it sprawls, shimmering in the limpid air, like some fairy encampment that has overslept and neglected to disperse before daybreak. The twin village greens, apparently deserted; archaeological remnants exhibited with beautiful clarity in the field beside the manor house; church and churchyard solemnly marking the end of the lane.

To see the jewel-like village of Guiting Power unexpectedly from the air, just a day or two after unexpectedly wandering into it by road, was a double benediction. It felt as if…some Guiding Power had been at work, rather than just a random breeze, in wafting the balloon along this exact route on that lovely Cotswold morning.

INTRODUCING
A YEAR IN THE COTSWOLDS

For an overview of a quite different kind, read the book that follows, slightly condensed for this volume. John Hudson, a regional reporter of great experience and a long-term resident of the hilltop village of Chalford Hill, east of Stroud, tells of his life in the Cotswolds over the course of one year. The book traces different strands of local life as they weave in and out of his everyday experience, and the resulting record of his observations gradually forms a kind of impressionistic portrait of the region itself. In compiling it, he brings all his journalist's skills to bear: stylistic flourish, indefatigable curiosity, affection without condescension, scepticism without cynicism, an eye for detail, an ear for anecdote.

The portrait is of a place very much caught between the new and the old. The Cotswolds so lyrically evoked by Laurie Lee in his much-loved reminiscence of childhood, *Cider With Rosie*—that Cotswold world is no more. Yet echoes of it do still sound faintly in the Cotswolds of today—at village festivals, in eccentric characters, on deserted hillsides, and so on—and John Hudson, being so attuned to the region, has managed to discern them and relay them vividly to his readers.

OPPOSITE *A vibrant balloon glides dreamily through the Cotswold hills. In this the author found the perfect mode of transport.*

A YEAR IN THE COTSWOLDS

A condensation of the book by John Hudson

CHAPTER ONE

CELEBRATIONS AND SNOWDROPS

ABOVE *The author, John Hudson, who recorded the year-round delights of his local Cotswolds.*

THIS BOOK AIMS TO TELL of life today in the Cotswolds, but does not record any particular year. What it is, after my nineteen years of living in the village of Chalford Hill, is a book that sets out to portray something of the life of the Cotswolds and their people and places throughout the seasons; and, since we are all moulded by our past, I have contrived to find ample opportunity to look back and reflect on the area's rich history.

Just as the places and events are real, so are the people. Most real of all are members of my family who flit in and out of these pages: my wife Linda, who teaches part-time at the primary school in Cranham; my son Dan, who is nine and a pupil at the village school here in Chalford Hill; and my daughter Rose, aged twenty, at university in Sussex, so now only an occasional traveller along our Cotswold byways.

A WINTER WALK

It is New Year's morning, and across the valley, somewhere towards Minchinhampton, some bright spark has discovered that he can wish the whole neighbourhood a Happy New Year by setting off fireworks so loud that they sound like nautical maroons. I speculate on whether some hapless lifeboat is responding to the Minchinhampton false alarm, nudging its earnest way through the lock on the Stroudwater Canal at Eastington; if so, the rowdy one might find himself in a spot rather more confined than the lofty Hampton heights by the time the next new year rolls around. Then I reflect that this is an uncharitable line of thought, my resolution to be more tolerant of others being less than fifteen minutes old.

It is warm enough to stand in front of the house with a drink and watch how our little corner of the Golden Valley takes to growing a year older. By and large it accepts it quietly, with not too many post-midnight drams before turning in for the night. Up at France Corner there is a teenage get-together at Gill and Aubrey Watson's big mill house of a home. A car horn toots on Cowcombe Hill. Dogs howl in the kennels at Skaiteshill Farm. An old donkey brays far below. Perhaps he knows a thing or two about what is in store this year, but what is he trying to tell us? Linda and I give up wondering and close the door: what with him and the dogs, it's getting rowdy out there all of a sudden.

We are not the first out walking in Cirencester Park later in the day. In fact we are never the first out doing anything, unless you count work that keeps me in Bristol until late at night and often sees me bringing the day's first sign of human life to the lonely stretch of the Bath–Stroud road between Dunkirk and Nailsworth. What am I doing here, I ask, when through the length and breadth of the dark,

ABOVE *Clothed in crisp, white frost, the evocatively named Golden Valley, where the author lives, loses none of its appeal.*

damp Cotswolds all sensible folk are abed—dozing in Dursley, snoozing in Stow-on-the-Wold, nodding off in Naunton, kipping in Condicote?

Not this morning, however, not on New Year's Day. Instead, the world and his dogs are streaming through the gates of Cirencester Park. The Earl of Bathurst has a front garden quite large enough to be shared with one and all, some two and a half thousand acres of it. It is a splendid facility, and not one to be taken for granted. On a bench near the gatehouse, two middle-aged couples are enjoying the contents of a flask that appears to contain coffee with an added festive kick, judging from their giggles. A horse clops by under a new blanket, and an Airedale

RIGHT *Cirencester Park extends for five miles beyond Cirencester to Sapperton, and provides great walks, rides and views for the town's inhabitants. A 40-foot-tall yew hedge—one of the tallest in the world— maintains the privacy of the Earl of Bathurst.*

in a smart tan jacket shows interest in the trunk of one of the earl's horse chestnuts. Christmas gifts now come to all manner of creatures, whether or not they kneel in their stalls and kennels at midnight on the holy eve.

Warm clothes are needed, since for all the mildness of a few hours ago, there is frost in the air and the turf is crisp and firm. I once saw Prince Charles fall off his polo pony on the great lawn here, and if he were to do so today he would be even less favourably impressed by the experience than he was then. As it is, it is Dan who slips on the grass, scuttling away from a dog whose acquaintance he has no wish to make, and from then on the walk towards that little stone pavilion known as Pope's Seat becomes an uphill task both literally and metaphorically.

Whoever designed Cirencester Park—and names most often quoted include Alexander Pope, aided and abetted by Congreve, Gay and Prior, as if it were the most natural thing in the world for a who's who of early 18th-century literature to custom-make great swaths of countryside—obviously paid little heed to the morale of late 20th-century nine-year-olds who see walking for pleasure as a contradiction in terms. True, when you turn round, the tower of St John Baptist parish church, at the town end of the Roman-straight Broad Ride, grows distant quickly; but the way ahead, with no focal point, must seem interminable from a viewpoint four feet nine inches above ground level. 'Crisps in the car, Dan,' we say. 'We'll be there in five minutes.' He is not convinced, but looking on the bright side, it is plain that the new year can only improve for him after this.

CITY OF SURPRISES

As a child growing up a long way away from here in the 1950s, I knew Cirencester as 'Ciceter' ('sisseter'), as surely as Beauchamp was 'Beecham' and Featherstone-haugh was 'Fanshaw'. On moving here, however, it was soon quite apparent that for almost everyone, Cirencester was Cirencester, or 'Ciren' if you knew it more intimately than I shall ever presume to do.

In *Cotswold Days* in 1937, Colin Howard, a truthful chronicler of everyday life, reported: 'I have always heard Cirencester pronounced "Ciceter" by the inhabitants, whom you might fairly expect to have some say in the matter.' Yet by the early 1980s, the town guide was observing 'the pronunciation "Ciceter" is still used in the *Standard* newspaper and by some lawyers and solicitors', which is a very different matter, especially since the *Standard*'s use of it was deliberately anachronistic, as the title of a long-running column that is now no more.

My view is that 'Ciceter', clearly a dialect pronunciation, was taken up by the nobs and has now been discarded by them. At the same time, while working folk in the Cotswolds still speak with a rich local accent, they are no longer immersed in the dialect of prewar times that talked of Painswick as 'Pannick', Randwick as 'Runnick', or, indeed, Cirencester as 'Ciceter'. With 'Ciren', or 'Zoiren', they are even saving themselves a syllable.

The gentrification of 'Ciceter' doubtless owes much to Shakespeare (in *Richard II*):

> *... the rebels have consumed with fire*
> *our town of Ciceter in Gloucestershire.*

But not too many of us are Shakespearean scholars any more and, on a more positive note, we are no longer willing to put up with mannerisms of speech that strike us as mere affectations. The footballer and manager Gordon Strachan is simply Strachan to the thousands on the terraces, though the pronunciation 'Straun' lived on in the Stroud textile mill until the company was taken over.

A neighbour who has lived here for a dozen years, and has visited Cirencester every couple of weeks for most of that time, has only just today discovered the wonderful Coxwell Street, between Dollar and Thomas Streets at the north end of town. How has she gone for all these years, she asks herself, without having any inkling of this most Continental of old thoroughfares, the great old clothier's Coxwell Court standing like some Italian merchant's *palazzo*? She feels ashamed that for all her visits in the past she has been locked tight into a grid that has taken her from Tesco to the Brewery Arts Centre, into Cricklade Street and back to the car.

You need to know Cirencester for years before it ceases to surprise. For instance, it took me a long time to discover the Roman amphitheatre, the grassy Bull Ring, from the peaks of which you can currently enjoy the best view in town of the building of the new Waitrose supermarket. Apart from topographical surprises, however, there is obviously something about the people. 'The money here,' said a market trader I found myself sharing a table with in Viner's Café, 'it's something else.' He explained that he worked two other big Cotswold markets, the Tuesday one that turns Moreton-in-Marsh's broad and elegant High Street into a weekly bazaar and the even larger one at Carterton, over by RAF Brize Norton in Oxfordshire, which is a magnet for families in Fairford and Lechlade and their surrounding villages. (West Cotsallers have no idea of the impact of this Forces town on the local economy of their neighbours to the east.) 'You can't say there's a lot of cash sloshing round Carterton, what with the defence cuts at the air bases,' my companion explained. 'Trade is pretty flat at Moreton, too, but here folk seem fireproof. There's nowhere like it.'

ABOVE *The 2nd-century amphitheatre in what was known as Corinium is one of the largest and best preserved in the country. Its size reflects the town's status as the second city after London during the Roman occupation.*

It reminded me of something Linda said after her last supermarket trip to Cirencester, an experience that always leaves her feeling low for forsaking poor old struggling Stroud. 'It's oozing money. In Cheltenham people are looking in the shop windows on the Promenade wishing they'd got money and sometimes pretending they have. Stroud is, well, just Stroud. Cirencester's packed with people who know of a recession only through reading about it in the *Telegraph*. I don't know whether they spend their money, but they've certainly got it.'

My table mate could confirm that they spend it as well—on carrots, swedes and potatoes, if nothing else. An hour or so later I saw him back at work and looking cheerful, his stall dwarfed by the parish church's great battlemented south porch and humbled by the majestic sweep of the marketplace façades. Just yards away from him, the Barnett family's fishmonger's and the gourmet's paradise next door were putting on a mouth-watering display of fare from the very top bracket, with prices to match.

The wealth of much of the population of Cirencester and its surroundings, along with the perception that everyone is equally blessed with cars, mobility and resources, makes the lot of less-privileged people all the more difficult. It means that Jane Winstanley finds she can never let up in her role as head of Cirencester and District Volunteer Bureau. 'There's real hardship out there, real poverty in the most unlikely places, the Coln villages, everywhere,' she says.

Cirencester's unique role in history as a Roman town to which all roads led can be seen at its own Corinium Museum. Mosaic pavements were the greatest triumph of Roman art in the Cotswolds—there is a vast one (buried for safety) at Woodchester, near Stroud, and others can be seen, along with so much more of everyday life nearly 2,000 years ago, at the National Trust's Chedworth Roman Villa—but nowhere can they be better viewed, in all their satisfying earth tones of browns and greys, than at the Corinium. One of them, portraying a hare, was discovered in the town shortly before the museum reopened in 1974, and became its symbol. But if David Viner, who masterminded the award-winning design of the museum, is pressed to name his favourite exhibit, he will tell you it is the five-line acrostic found in a piece of wall plaster from the Roman town:

```
R   O   T   A   S
O   P   E   R   A
T   E   N   E   T
A   R   E   P   O
S   A   T   O   R
```

It is an enigmatic piece of work, but it is surely no coincidence that eleven of the letters can be rearranged to form the Christian symbol PATERNOSTER, together with the A and O of Alpha and Omega, the first and last letters of the Greek alphabet.

'Scratch Gloucestershire and find Rome, as sure as God's in Gloucestershire.'

ABOVE *The impressive church of St John Baptist towers over the busy marketplace at the heart of prosperous Cirencester.*

BELOW *This fine mosaic pavement depicting a hare is one of the prize Roman artefacts on display in the Corinium Museum.*

ROCOCO REVIVAL

Lord Dickinson, who owns the Rococo Garden at Painswick, thought he knew a thing or two about the ways of nature, but, along with the rest of us, he cannot make out winters that scarcely begin before the new year and then meander into spring with just the occasional diversion of electric storms that remind you of firework night, and hailstones so large, and hurled down with such ferocity, that to go out in them would be to risk injury. He used to open up daily at snow-drop time in late February and early March, but this year the show has been brought forward a full month, and after a balmy November there were a couple of weeks when it seemed as if even this might be too late. 'Fortunately, December did turn colder, and that slowed the snowdrops' growth,' he says. 'Nevertheless, I do wonder what has happened to our seasons.'

What has happened in the restoration at Painswick in recent years, and what is continuing to happen, is a story of national importance in gardening circles, but it seems that the snowdrops have been there in the woodlands below the pond and alongside the stream for generations. There is a picture taken 100 years ago of an elderly woman and some children sitting among drifts of them in the woods, and the plants are so prolific it is easy to believe they were there a century before that. There was a craze for growing snowdrops in the Cotswolds in the last century, with the villages around Stroud at the heart of it. One of the master growers, James Atkins, lived in Painswick, and his *Galanthus nivalis* 'Atkinsii' is one of several varieties flourishing in the Rococo Garden.

LEFT *Snowdrops have become synonymous with the Rococo Garden at Painswick: these harbingers of spring appear to have flowered there for generations.*

BELOW *The 18th-century artist Thomas Robins's painting of Painswick in 1748 inspired the Dickinsons to restore the Rococo Garden to its former glory.*

Snowdrops are one of the great survivors at Painswick. Many other species there have returned after decades, and, in some cases, centuries, of absence only as a result of the efforts of Lord and Lady Dickinson, and more recently the charitable trust of which he is chairman.

Lord Dickinson inherited Painswick House and the estate that went with it in 1955. Later, a romantic picture of how the garden had been—or at least, how Lord Dickinson's ancestor Benjamin Hyett had wished it to look—more than 200 years earlier was found in the house. Painted by Thomas Robins of Cheltenham in 1748, at around the time of Hyett's completion of the garden, it showed a scene so remote from that of the 1950s that Lord Dickinson was not alone in seeing it merely as an attractive heirloom and a fascinating historical document.

Robins depicted serpentine paths, tree-lined vistas, pools, little pavilions in the classical and Gothic styles and a large, formal kitchen garden, the kind of combination of the aesthetic and the edible now best seen at Rosemary Verey's famous garden at Barnsley House, near Cirencester. Lord Dickinson knew that some of these features still existed, but felt they were beyond reach—literally, in the case of the Gothic pavilion at the end of the beech walk, since there was simply no way through to it. The plunge pool and the rustic grotto around its source spring were equally obscured by ash and elder saplings, and besides, there was something so otherworldly and dreamlike about the Robins painting, with its broad border of seashells and delicate flowers and foliage, its liberties with scale and perspective, that it was hard to imagine such a scene ever existed in the chilly Cotswolds.

BELOW *The rococo period in garden design flourished briefly during the transition from 17th-century formal gardens to the more fluid shapes of the 18th century; this exedra (in classical architecture, a meeting place for discussion) at Painswick is typical of the rococo style.*

AN ENGLISH COUNTRY GARDEN

THE ENGLISH have been creating gardens out of nature's surrounding wilderness for centuries, combining usefulness (herbs, vegetables and fruit for the kitchen and medicine cabinet) and pleasure (flowers, ponds and walks) for their own purposes. Pleasure gardens as a feature of the country house first appeared during the Elizabethan period. This flowering of interest was accompanied by the first gardening literature, notably by Thomas Hill, whose books included designs for knot gardens—square gardens quartered by flower beds in interlacing geometric patterns.

Garden design underwent a revolution in the early 18th century, spearheaded by Lancelot Brown, royal gardener at Hampton Court. His nickname of Capability derived from his habit of assuring clients that their grounds revealed great 'capability of improvement'. He spurned the layout of the geometric Renaissance garden in favour of a more 'natural' parkland effect. Working with new elements— lawns, lakes, winding avenues, slopes, groves and encircling woods—he aimed for a unified composition and a maximum of harmonious panoramas. Well over 100 estates were landscaped to his designs.

In the late 18th century, fashion changed again. Some designers took the natural look in a more dramatic

ABOVE *Capability Brown spurned formal gardens in favour of natural-looking parks with trees and lakes.*

LEFT *The grounds of Blenheim Palace, Woodstock, were, by consensus, Brown's greatest achievement.*

BELOW *Bright flowerbeds at Rosemary Verey's Barnsley House epitomise the country-garden style.*

direction; others favoured a more exotic or picturesque style. Humphry Repton reintroduced some classical elements, such as balustraded terraces. He also designed the gardens at Sezincote in the Cotswolds, with oriental touches which reflected the Mogul architecture of the house.

The world-renowned gardens to be found in the Cotswolds include classic examples that both predate and postdate that heyday. The formal terraced gardens of Owlpen Manor, featuring topiary yews and box parterres, date back to the 16th and 17th centuries. The unique Rococo Garden at Painswick, originally laid out in 1748, has been lovingly restored. Sudeley Castle has an astonishing array of old-fashioned gardens: the latest addition here is the Knot Garden, inspired by the pattern on a dress worn by Elizabeth I. Rosemary Verey, one of the present generation of garden designers, has also incorporated a knot garden into the

grounds of Barnsley House. As an adviser on royal gardens—for Prince Charles's nearby Highgrove estate—she can be considered one of the spiritual heirs of Capability Brown himself.

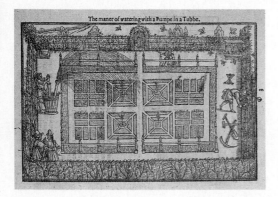

The maner of watering with a Pumpe in a Tubbe.

ABOVE *Thomas Hill pioneered gardening literature with* The Gardener's Labyrinth, *published in 1580.*

The rococo style in gardening is characterised by a combination of the geometrical and formal, winding paths and woodland features, typical, in fact, of the transitional period between the symmetry of the Tudor and Stuart approach and the man-made landscapes of the later 18th century, the 'nature embellished' of Capability Brown. The seashells picked out by Robins in his border were a typical decorative device in such gardens, where shady grottoes were a popular feature. It is even possible that Robins was the designer of the six acres at Painswick, and that his painting was as much a plan for the original builders as it eventually turned out to be for the restorers.

It was in the early 1980s, when the architectural historians Roger White and Tim Mowl were preparing a paper on Painswick, which was eventually published in the *Journal of Garden History*, that Lord Dickinson realised exactly what treasures lay in his own back yard and decided to accept the challenge of restoring Benjamin Hyett's pleasure grounds to their former glory. With the Robins painting as a guide and the benefit of some expert help, Lord and Lady Dickinson set about the practical task in October 1984. Two years and £50,000 later they had done more than enough to whet the appetites not just of gardening enthusiasts but of growing numbers of local people, who recognise that there is something extraordinary going on at Painswick, a task that will take decades to complete but will equally be remembered for generations to come. Now the Painswick Rococo Garden Trust has taken the financial strain off the Dickinsons alone, but on open days Lord Dickinson can still occasionally be found selling tickets at the door of the bright shop and tearooms in the coach house at the entrance to the garden.

While new work goes on constantly, there is already about the pleasure grounds an air of well-rounded permanence that will strengthen as the years go by. As for those snowdrops, they need no help from the conservationists to multiply and delight the eye, even though, if the weather trends continue, they will soon be doing so in late November.

BLESSED BY A BYPASS

If a town can resemble a ship, that is Northleach this bitter morning. Not any ship, but the lost, abandoned *Mary Celeste*, with frost clothing the square and trees like cobwebs, and not a living soul to be seen up and down the street. I would call it a village street except that Northleach, of course, is a proud Cotswold town. Besides, until the bypass was built north of the community in the mid-1980s, this was the A40, the Queen's highway between London and Fishguard or, from a more local perspective, between Cheltenham and Oxford. Northleach would not have looked like the *Mary Celeste* ten years ago today, but it is incomparably better off now.

Dropping down the Fosse Way to Northleach from the bypass roundabout, the first change you notice is the way the town has grown in the past few years—some 300 new houses, they say, and not outrageously expensive-looking ones at that. Before the bypass the planners were reluctant to release new land for building, since access to the major road caused serious safety problems. An apparent downside of the bypass is that besides the acres of countryside swallowed up by four and a half miles of new road, yet more fields are being lost to housing estates. But to the outsider it seems that the town can take it, with its historical heart unaltered; and what is far more to the point, most of the residents are happy too.

Community spirit is flourishing, the result of an influx of mainly young newcomers, most of them anxious to settle. It also does much for the frame of mind when you can sleep at night, and that was rarely the case when the juggernauts were rumbling through at all hours. Old-timers living on or close to the High Street talk happily of not having to sleep with ear-plugs in any more; of being able to open the front windows without fear of noise and pollution; of being able to park their cars in relative safety; and of simply being able to open the door and cross the road.

There are many other benefits, most of them stemming from the two sides of the street coming together into a harmonious whole. The string of old inns—the Wheatsheaf, the Union, the Red Lion and the rest—can truly market themselves as country hotels, quiet retreats in a town that sleeps soundly at night. It is easy for visitors to go by foot between Northleach's several attractions. The 15th-century Church of St Peter and St Paul is one of the great Cotswold wool churches—'the

THE AGE OF THE GOLDEN FLEECE

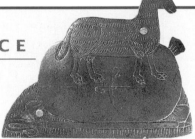

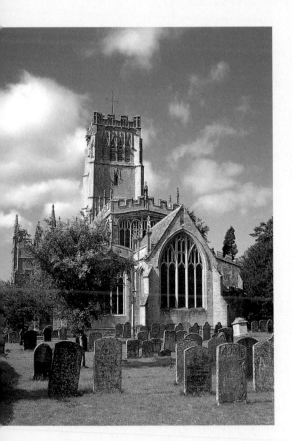

THE COTSWOLDS seem to have been custom-designed to support a prosperous wool industry. The limestone grassland once nurtured large sheep, and the exposed terrain encouraged a heavy fleece on them. The central location allowed for easy transportation of wool and cloth, and the presence of fast-flowing streams to power mills promoted a large-scale cloth industry.

Cotswold wool was prized in Europe, especially from the 14th century onwards. Merchants from the Low Countries vied to buy the raw wool and the homemade cloth. At its peak, the English wool trade accounted for almost half of the nation's total income, and to symbolise its importance a woolsack was used for the Lord Chancellor's seat.

The wool economy's influence on the region is still visible today in its heritage of architecture: the great barns that

ABOVE *At the foot of wool merchant John Taylour's tomb in Northleach church is a brass sheep on a woolpack.*

originated as wool warehouses; the famous Perpendicular-style 'wool churches', endowed by rich merchants, at Cirencester, Northleach, and so on; the stately homes of cloth manufacturers; and the market halls, such as that at Tetbury.

As the Industrial Revolution dawned, the Cotswolds' heyday waned. Sheep farms and cloth mills alike went bankrupt. Competition from Yorkshire wool, mechanised factories, industrial unrest—they all contributed to crushing the Cotswold economy. The long 'Age of the Golden Fleece' was over. But there was a silver lining: urban development came to a virtual halt, so the antique architecture was preserved, to the delight of today's residents and visitors.

LEFT *The church of St Peter and St Paul in Northleach was rebuilt in the 15th century with riches from the wool trade.*

cathedral of the Cotswolds', in the eyes of some—founded on the wealth of the Forteys and Midwinters, Busshes and Taylours, whose memorial brasses still glow as one of the region's most fascinating historical features. Interestingly, the chief benefactor, John Fortey, is described as being a renovator of roads, as well as of churches.

A couple of hundred years after his time, the Gloucestershire woollen trade had moved to the Stroud valleys, leaving Northleach bereft until the stagecoach age. Even then it was late on the uptake, for it was not until around 1830 that the main road was diverted through town. Ironically, the Gloucester–London turnpike had earlier been built to bypass it, and the imaginative will tell you that on dark and stormy nights you can still see spectral coaches bumping along its long-lost route, to the west of the Fosse Way, not far from the Puesdown Inn. After the coming of the railways Northleach itself returned to being something of a ghost town, for this was one of the Cotswold communities that suffered most from the agricultural depression and drift from the land of Victorian times.

What else is there to see here today? The Cirencester-based District Council's Cotswold Countryside Collection benefits mightily by having its own ample parking space and being on the Fosse Way at its junction with the old A40, just a well-signposted couple of minutes' drive from the bypass roundabout. Opened in 1982, it is an expertly and thoughtfully presented country-life display built around a collection of Gloucestershire wagons and farming implements put together over many years by Olive Lloyd-Baker, a member of one of the old-established county landowning families.

The first time I saw these grand vehicles was shortly after the death in 1975 of Miss Lloyd-Baker, who had kept them in sheds, in a deteriorating state of repair, at the family home at Hardwicke, in the Severn Vale near Gloucester. She had inherited the estate from her father, and made a point of rescuing these bygones from her tenanted farms all over the county as mechanisation made them obsolete. It was a marvellous feat, but many people were worried about their future in this remote and vulnerable place. A carelessly tossed-away cigarette end could have accounted for the carts—all with subtly differing characteristics of build and colour, depending upon their district of origin—in a matter of minutes.

What to do with them? The Treasury announced that it would accept them in lieu of death duty, but only if they could be kept together and put on show somewhere in Gloucestershire. Even so, when David Viner of Cirencester's Corinium Museum first told me of his local authority's plans to make a showpiece of them at a historic building in Northleach, which was in equal need of tender loving care, it still seemed too glib an answer. I should have known better. Few people have a better eye than David Viner for presenting history in a way that combines interest with integrity, or have a greater knack for getting things done.

The building in and around which the collection is housed is the old Northleach House of Correction, completed in 1791 and one of a number designed for Gloucestershire by a leading enlightened architect of the day, William Blackburn. The name with which it is forever linked, however,

BELOW *Legacy of a bygone era, this beautifully crafted harvest wagon is one of a collection on display at the museum in Northleach.*

is that of Sir George Onesiphorus Paul, county high sheriff and dedicated prison reformer, whose virtues are extolled on his memorial in Gloucester Cathedral. The original cell blocks and courtyard were demolished in the interwar years, and the building was a considerable white elephant until its new age of splendour dawned. However, a few cells survived from a later block of 1844, and some have been restored to an approximation of how they would have looked then, complete with an iron bed, barred window, and a somewhat miffed-looking jailbird reflecting on his hard life, attired almost as a clown in a parti-coloured suit and pointed white cap.

Back in the centre of Northleach, the other main visitor attraction is the restorer Keith Harding's award-winning World of Mechanical Music, with a shop in front and beyond it a beautifully presented museum of antique clocks, musical boxes, automata and mechanical musical instruments. These are now great collectibles, many combining fine cabinet-making with Victorian engineering ingenuity, and by the time they have been made like new by Mr Harding they will bring out the musician in even the least artistic of us: ask the price of some of them and the answer will make you whistle.

ROADS AND TOADS

There is snow on Pancake Day morning, three or four inches of it overnight and more heavy flurries, on and off, until noon. I am due in Bristol in the afternoon, and I am in my usual winter quandary—to stay put, or to work like a dervish to break free? Best of all are the days when seven or eight inches blanket the village overnight, cutting us off from the world in a way that brooks no argument. Then we turn back the clock to all the pre-motorised centuries of history, and the only sounds to be heard are those of neighbours padding through the soft white lanes, garden paths being scraped and brushed by the efficient and safety-conscious, and the excited shouts of children sent home from school almost before they have arrived. By eleven o'clock everyone is out sledging.

Snowfalls like today's are rather more troublesome. I knew this one was on its way because the television

ABOVE *A snowfall in Chalford Hill presents the author with a familiar quandary.*

news had been absolutely certain of the fact. I am well aware that rather than bringing my car right home through the sharp angles and steep little pitches of the heart of the village, I could more sensibly have left it down in the valley on the main road or at least up beside the pub, where a slither along Abnash is usually rewarded by escape down the well-gritted, tree-shaded Old Neighbourhood hill. The truth is that, though knowing I had to be in Bristol this afternoon, I took neither of these commonsense options and now find myself blocked in enough to make it tiresomely difficult to get out. Even so, Harry the milkman ploughed through in his four-wheel drive this morning, and as usual my neighbour John

Ballinger, the best part of a generation older than I am, has put me to shame by clearing his steep drive while I am still in bed. The last I hear of him he is slithering and burning rubber and roaring away down Puddeny Pie Lane, where a sideways slide of just a couple of inches will leave a coat of your car's paint on John and Judith Flint's dry-stone wall.

I have no stomach for any of this, and telephone Bristol to cry off. 'That's funny,' says the voice of authority at the other end of the line. 'Nothing at all down here. Dry as a bone.' Any incredulity in the voice—and there is incredulity by the bucketful—seems to stem not from wondering awe at a climate that can deal such contrasting hands to neighbouring communities, but from barely concealed exasperation that I should be spinning the old 'snowed-in' line once again. This is mid-February: it must be spring—toads are on the mating march.

He is right. Usually they are everywhere around this time, oblivious to traffic and ill-placed feet and resolute in their assaults on dry-stone walls six feet thick; they seem certain that in the end they will prevail and a way will open up for them to cool waters beyond. Not many of us can claim to be fond of toads, but it seems that the sight of scores of them being wiped out as they cross the road is distressing to large numbers of people. It must be twenty years since the Department of Transport first put up 'Toads Crossing' signs at Dowdeswell Reservoir between Andoversford and Charlton Kings. Those signs were quite a talking point at the time, but they were no nine-day wonder, and all over the Cotswolds, and indeed far beyond, the idea has been copied not only by wildlife professionals but by groups of well-wishers with a simple desire to help nature take its course. If you live in a sensitive area, you can even borrow portable triangles from the Gloucestershire Wildlife Trust.

This year they are taking action for the first time at Ruscombe, in the wooded uplands northwest of Stroud, where common toads are on the move. The sign shows a rather fed-up-looking toad peering out from a red triangle, but the villagers' efforts do not stop there. 'One resident went out with a bucket and filled it with the creatures,' says an organiser of the venture. 'Hundreds of toads are coming from the hillside in search of any water they can find in the village.'

Another enthusiast is Daphne Neville, an actress who lives in another village near Stroud, with a river, canal and good-sized lake of her own all close at hand. She is most often to be seen in public with an otter draped over her shoulder, for she loves the creatures, and has done more to interest children in them than any number of nature lessons at school. At this time of year, however, she and her family and friends are on toad patrol, escorting thirty-plus across the lane on a mild, damp night, and mourning the squashing of perhaps twenty more.

SLATES AND STONES

A householder in Duntisbourne Leer is in trouble with Cotswold District Council for reroofing his home with artificial slates. They must come down, says the local authority. Not knowing any of this, I drove through the village a couple of weeks

ABOVE AND BELOW
Sandra Jeans of Dowdeswell campaigned successfully for the 'Toads Crossing' signs, enabling the creatures to cross the roads in greater safety during their annual migration.

ago, glimpsed the obviously expensive work from the other side of the ford, and thought how magnificent the roof looked, the new slates glimmering in the winter sun with an almost ethereal sheen. It also struck me that this sight was a rare treat, for in a couple of years' time they would be as weathered and lichened and mossy as all their neighbours—exactly the point the desperate owner of the property is making in the newspapers this week.

The problem with natural materials is the price. Cotswold District Council is adamant that barns should not be reroofed with artificial slates, and there is strong evidence that, faced with crippling costs, farmers and landowners are simply leaving roofs that are in need of attention to rot, rather than bankrupting themselves over them. One farmer quotes £9,000 to reroof in imitation stone, £45,000 for the real thing. One of the council's arguments is that by insisting on natural products, the market for them will grow, new quarries will open and competition will force the price down. There are merits in this point of view in terms of long-term strategy, but it seems of little comfort to the man with the £45,000 bill. There are even the iconoclasts who wonder whether fakes are not the better bet, after

HIGHGROVE: CHANGING THE FACE OF FARMING

IN A QUIET CORNER of Gloucestershire stands a handsome, pale-grey stone house, built by an 18th-century merchant and now home to HRH the Prince of Wales. But this is no fairytale palace: Highgrove is a working estate, encompassing the Duchy Home Farm, where Prince Charles has put into practice his philosophy of farming and conservation.

The prince is famously opposed to the development of genetically modified food and well known for his enthusiasm

ABOVE *Prince Charles is as committed to the organic ethos in his gardens as he is on his farm, and takes a hands-on approach.*

for traditional and sustainable methods of agriculture. On moving into Highgrove in 1980, he was determined to run the estate using organic methods. He began with his garden, and then set aside a small area for organic cultivation on the farm in 1985. This proved so successful that by 1990 he had decided to convert

ABOVE *In front of the house, Highgrove's herd of organic Aberdeen Angus beef cattle graze on pastures untreated by chemicals.*

the whole farm. The estate is now fully organic: in place of artificial fertilisers a traditional crop-rotation system is used, and well-rotted manure adds nutrients to

all. There is some wonderful lore surrounding Cotswold stone slates—smallest to the top, broadest to the bottom, and so on—but we all know that the steeply pitched roof is one of the most typical features of our vernacular architecture because local stone is porous.

Barns are quite an issue in a variety of ways. The council's policy is for them to be converted for a use that provides employment, while owners of redundant farm properties and their developers know that the real money is to be made out of conversions into dream houses. The Country Landowners' Association has argued that the cost of repairing historic buildings to statutory standards is now so high that the owners must be allowed to put them to the most commercially viable use. In the meantime, Cotswold District Council is sticking to its guns, and at least some of the wealthiest estates have been able to put its theory into practice. Leading the way with a typically thorough conversion, no expense spared, has been the Prince of Wales's estate, which for several years has had well-established workshops for a number of crafts and trades in farm buildings at Doughton, a short walk across the fields from Highgrove. Nearer Cirencester, there has also

LEFT *The prince is particularly proud of the thyme walk, which he planted in 1991. This tapestry of herbs contains all the varieties of thyme in the world.*

the soil. In the kitchen garden, nature's own balancing mechanism is allowed to work in place of pesticides—flowers and vegetables grow side by side, and the blossoms attract aphid-eating ladybirds and hover flies.

In 1998 the farm started an experimental plan to grow organic vegetables at Highgrove for sale to families in the local area. A box scheme was set up by which supplies of fresh produce were delivered door to door, with vegetables such as carrots, potatoes, beans, cabbages and onions all receiving the royal seal of approval.

With growing public awareness that intensified agriculture has led to the radical transformation of much of the British countryside, together, it would seem, with

a rise in the number of food scares such as BSE, or mad-cow disease, demand for a more sensitive method of farming has risen and organic produce has grown in popularity. Prince Charles has been at the forefront of this change in public mood, and is now probably the highest-profile organic farmer in the country. At Highgrove he is putting into practice his vision of sustainable agriculture, and among many welcome effects of this has been the reappearance on the estate of skylarks and wild partridge, whose numbers have decreased dramatically elsewhere in Britain.

BELOW *Highgrove's kitchen garden provides a bountiful harvest of organic fruit and veg. for consumption in the house.*

been success on the Bathurst and Chester-Master estates and out at Barnsley, but such enlightenment is not an option open to everyone.

If you are in the market, there is certainly scope to acquire the natural building materials. A few years ago the commercial supply of roofing slates, in particular, seemed all but spent, but now they are to be had in profusion from quarries in Naunton, Andoversford and Tetbury, at least in the form of 'presents', or slabs to be found already formed to a suitable width. Frost-split slates of the type once produced in the hills can still be had at Collyweston, near Stamford, that handsome limestone town that seems for all the world like a little outpost of the Cotswolds in Lincolnshire, and this is one instance when the district council is quite happy to turn a blind eye to imports. Indeed, the spirit of European unity being upon us, we are now even free to bring in our 'Cotswold stone' slates from France, with companies from Devizes, Northleach and Foxcote, near Andoversford, making the connection. This is presumably limestone from around Locronan in Brittany, a little town often fancifully promoted as the Cotswold village of France.

We are also lucky enough to have half a dozen busy quarries producing dressed building stone in the whole spectrum of Cotswold hues. Four to the north—at Fish Hill, near Broadway, at Upton Wold on the Northwick estate near Moreton-in-Marsh, and two at Temple Guiting—produce the classic rich orange stone that built Broadway, Chipping Campden and Stanway, as well as delicious cream-coloured slabs for use in the central towns and villages. Farmington Quarry, near Northleach, is another major supplier of this paler material, now that there is no longer quarrying at Minchinhampton and Painswick, while Veizey's Quarry, near Tetbury, turns up pale grey stone well suited to the South Cotswolds, its upper strata abounding in fossilised shells. Planners believe that to go golden in Tetbury or grey in Campden is almost as reprehensible as using reconstituted stone, and in the light of an attempt to introduce northern stone to a corner of the Stroud valleys in recent times, this is one area in which I cannot fault them. It is hard to explain

RIGHT *Cotswold towns and villages are built from distinctively coloured local stone. In Chipping Campden the stone has a warm golden hue.*

LEFT *Pale-coloured limestone has been quarried at Veizey's Quarry near Tetbury for centuries. At one time most Cotswold villages had their own quarry.*

BELOW *Cotswold stone lends itself perfectly to building: when first quarried the limestone is soft and easy to shape, but it hardens after long exposure to sunlight.*

why stone so like gingerbread that you could eat it in Campden simply strikes you as rusty in moist Chalford, but that is the truth of the matter. Not that I would wish to be the one to sign the order for the demolition of the two otherwise well-built and doubtless well-loved houses in question.

Meanwhile Peter Seccombe, the officer responsible for the Cotswold Area of Outstanding Natural Beauty (AONB), is concerned that the hills too should go into the next century in the best possible heart. The 20th century has certainly taken its toll. Stone walls are deteriorating and disappearing; permanent grassland has fallen from two-fifths of the total area sixty years ago to less than a fiftieth today; woodlands are being neglected; and villages are losing their schools, shops, pubs, post offices and buses. Community shops, volunteer bus services, even a post office in a pub in one village, are hopeful signs and trends to be built upon, as is the work of the more than 200 voluntary Cotswold wardens who turn their hand to everything from coppicing, clearing footpaths and

rebuilding walls to leading guided walks and talking to the unconverted. A local partnership, the AONB joint advisory committee, coordinates their efforts and those of the paid rangers, with input from the Cheltenham-based Countryside Commission, the score of local authorities with land in the AONB and a number of other organisations.

'We all know we live somewhere rather special,' says Mr Seccombe. 'We have the task of making people fully aware of what makes it so special.'

CHAPTER TWO

DAFFODILS AND FRIDAY FISH

WITH A CLEAR ROAD you can be off the Cotswold tops and into Wales in half an hour. If you enter by the southern route, over the Severn Bridges, you can enjoy the sensation of crossing the water to another country. Yet for all the narrowness of that stretch of water, for all the convenience of the M5's Ross Spur road to the north, Welsh people in the Cotswolds can still feel far from their roots when Dewi Sant's day rolls around. One such expat is Bill Morris, a retired headmaster who was an unpaid clergyman at the Anglican churches at France Lynch and Chalford until recent times. The passing years and indifferent health have meant that he is not so busy there these days, but we keep up the tradition he started of a St David's Day service at Chalford on the first Sunday after March 1.

The congregation is already into the first hymn as I walk beside the church towards the door at the far end, and it scarcely seems to be raising the roof with that legendary *hwyl*, or fervour, with which the Welsh are supposed to give voice. They built walls thick when Christ Church was going up in the 1720s, however, and as I click open the hefty door's latch I find myself in a room full enough of song and people—dozens of adults and an equal number of Cubs and Scouts— who seem intent on honouring St David at least as cheerfully as they will be honouring St George in a few weeks' time.

With the church bare for Lent, the posies of daffodils at the pew ends are little beacons of life and colour in the sunshine streaming through the high windows. Chalford church contains work by many of this century's finest Cotswold crafts-men, among them Norman Jewson, William Simmonds, the locally based Peter Waals, and Edward Payne, the stained-glass artist whose open studio days at his

LEFT AND BELOW
*Picturesque Keble's
Bridge spans the River
Leach and links the
hamlets of Eastleach
Martin and Eastleach
Turville. It was probably
named after John Keble,
a leading light in the
Oxford Movement and
a popular curate of the
two Eastleach parishes.*

home in Box, beside Minchinhampton Common, continued almost until his death. This worthy work and much else besides make Christ Church a place of interest for Arts and Crafts enthusiasts, yet the parable of the glory of the lilies of the field was never more clearly illustrated than by these little bunches of garden daffs in their cheap earthenware pots.

The guidebooks will tell you to visit the Eastleach villages at daffodil time, but you must be prepared to be a week too early or too late, unless your intelligence network is spot-on and you are able to drop what you are doing instantly and head out to that gentle country east of Cirencester. It is the same with the snow-drops at Painswick or around the Tortworth Chestnut, with the old roses at Kiftsgate Court and Sudeley Castle, the magnolias at Batsford Park, the acers at Westonbirt: only a hot line to nature and a flexible timetable, or serendipity, will ensure your being in the right place at exactly the right time.

The daffodils at Eastleach are the tall, golden, garden kind, not the pale little *Narcissus pseudonarcissus*, daffy-down lilies or Lent lilies, that used to adorn the fields around Dymock and its neighbouring villages in the northwestern corner of Gloucestershire and still flourish in the oak woodlands there. There is nothing so spontaneous about the Eastleach daffs. They were clearly planted, generations ago, to glorify the greens and public spaces, churchyards and, most of all, river banks of this pretty, wooded and undulating spot in the midst of rich but featureless farmland.

Apart from their springtime splendour, what most of us remember about the twin villages of Eastleach Turville and the smaller Eastleach Martin are their two churches, a couple of minutes' walk from each other on either side of the Leach, and the bridge of flat paving stones, with no protective parapet or handrail, that links the two communities at the spot where the daffodils grow in greatest profusion.

It is known as Keble's Bridge. The scholarly explanation is that this is in memory of the Keble family, who owned the manor of Eastleach Turville for five generations from the 16th century, rather than in tribute to John Keble, the

Oxford Movement cleric who was curate of the two parishes from his ordination in 1815 until 1823, when he took up the curacy of Southrop for a brief spell. To attribute the naming of the bridge to a succession of dull squires centuries ago, rather than to a local celebrity who became one of the most talked-about men in Victorian Britain, is the way of many scholars who seek obscurity where none exists.

Certainly Canon William Wright, a keen historian, rector of the joint parishes from 1903 to 1929 and curate for twenty-one years before that, was prepared to believe the John Keble explanation. After all, in the early years of his ministry Wright was surrounded by elderly parishioners who had first-hand recollections of this inspiring priest, and an old lady from one of the big houses in Eastleach Turville recalled her father entertaining Keble on endless Sunday afternoons. 'It may have received this name from the many times he crossed it, especially when he came down from the old house on the hill,' Wright concluded. Keble was a largely absentee curate, spending his weeks in study and debate as a fellow of Oriel College, Oxford. But when he was down at the weekend, dashing hither

THE OXFORD MOVEMENT

LEFT *John Henry Newman in 1845, the year he converted to Roman Catholicism; he later attained the office of cardinal.*

BASED IN OXFORD during the 1830s and 40s, and led by the churchmen John Keble, John Henry Newman, R. H. Froude and E. B. Pusey, the Oxford Movement aimed to restore High Church rituals and traditions to the Church of England. Fearing that the Anglican ship was drifting into a mist of liberalism in an increasingly secular society, the movement's supporters sought to emphasise the Church's links with pre-Reformation Christianity and uphold the authority of bishops.

The movement began officially in July 1833 when Keble, a Gloucestershire-born priest, preached a sermon in the University Church of St Mary, attacking the government's interference in Church affairs. Later that year, Newman and Pusey published the first *Tracts for the Times*—a highly influential series of 90 treatises that earned its authors

the sobriquet 'Tractarians'. While many Anglicans were attracted to their perspective, those on the Church's liberal wing saw the Tractarian path as the slippery slope to Rome and papistry.

Their worst fears seemed to be realised in 1841, when Newman's notorious *Tract 90* tried to show that the Thirty-Nine Articles—Anglican statements of doctrine—were close to Catholic teachings. Newman was widely denounced for his views and in 1842, in a state of disillusionment, he withdrew from Oxford to a semi-monastic community. After profound reflection, he joined the Roman Catholic Church in 1845. That year also marked the official end of Tractarianism. But Keble and Pusey continued to give leadership to those with High Church leanings, and the movement's influence continued to affect the ritual and worship of Anglo-Catholics—those members of the Church of England who incline towards the Roman Catholic Church.

and thither on his duties and necessary social rounds on either side of the river, it is not hard to imagine that he found that old bridge a vital working tool.

What the guidebooks also tell us is that this is a clapper bridge, though none of my dictionaries is equal to the task of defining 'clapper' in the context of bridges, paving stones or whatever. Some years ago we were walking along towards Eastleach Turville church when a toddler began straying over the unprotected flagstones and her dad was forced to leap after her and scoop her to safety. He returned to his family on the road cradling her in his arms. 'Oi 'ad to run loike the clappers to catch the little moite,' he laughed. I doubt, though, whether many earnest historians would accept that explanation of the term 'clapper bridge'.

Eastleach Turville's church is dedicated to St Andrew, and Eastleach Martin's, now redundant but well loved, to St Michael and St Martin. Those with a rudimentary

knowledge of ancient land ownership will not find it hard to understand how two lords of the manor with their estates divided by a river could find themselves building churches in close proximity, and the down-to-earth Canon Wright had no time for the tale that the churches were commissioned by rival sisters who had quarrelled. Both date from Norman times and, since each was glorified considerably in the 13th century, we can surmise there was at least a certain amount of keeping up with the Joneses along this stretch of the Leach valley 700 or more years ago. The Norman south doorway of Turville church is a real treasure, but its surroundings and its well-used interior seem almost tamed by modern times compared with the Martin building, on low land closer to the river and much more hauntingly a thing of the past. There was apparently another element of rivalry when the Sunday bells rang out, St Martin's three chiming 'we ring best' while across the way St Andrew's pair insisted 'we too, we too'.

Eastleach Turville, on three levels, is by far the more populated and livelier community, especially at Whitsuntide, when there are sports and fancy-dress parades for the children, and a 'bob-apple' contest for the village youngsters on the green outside the Victoria pub. This involves chunks of bread soaked in treacle and suspended from tree branches and, while everyone wins a prize, there are special ones for those who eat the most bread or come out of the competition the messiest-looking, given that they are wearing protective plastic sacks.

Locally, Eastleach Martin is better known as Bouthrop or 'Butherup', as distinct from neighbouring Hatherop or Southrop's 'Sutherup'. Also in the parish, and another winner in the funny name stakes, is Macaroni Downs Farm, on the cold uplands across which the Bibury Races were run in the 18th century. There was a

ABOVE *St Andrew's Church in Eastleach Turville also serves the parishioners of Eastleach Martin these days, following the closure in 1982 of the once-rival Church of St Michael and St Martin.*

BELOW *Fred Archer of Prestbury poses here with his principal patron, Lord Falmouth. Archer had a brilliant yet tragically short career as a flat-race jockey, committing suicide in 1886 at the age of just 29.*

grandstand out here—a preposterous thought, given the remote scene today—and this was the spot to which all the fops, dandies and, yes, macaronis with feathers in their caps, flocked to view the action. From playboys gambling, the scene has reverted to lambs gambolling: who says we are not making progress?

CHELTENHAM FEVER

Some mistake: it is the first day of the National Hunt Festival at Cheltenham, yet the sun is ablaze and glinting off acre after acre of windscreens down at Prestbury Park as I descend Cleeve Hill towards town. An astonishing sight, this, not just the absence of the snow, sleet and hail that so often beset the racegoers over the three days, but these cars and coaches and helicopters that have homed in from far and wide, not to mention much activity over to the west in the skies above Staverton Airport. If all the students of the turf currently getting lit up in the ninety or so racecourse bars were laid end to end, you would be left with an extremely fluid line stretching right over to Dublin and halfway back across the Irish Sea.

I turn into Prestbury's main street just in time to catch hordes of last-minute punters disgorging from the King's Arms (once home to the 19th-century wonder jockey Fred Archer) and waving their arms in vain for passing taxicabs. If Cheltenham Festival week lore could be relied upon, I would now take aboard two priests and a trainer's brother from Limerick, and end up with £100 in used fivers stuffed in my top pocket and spot-on tips for 20–1 winners over the next three days. The trouble is, such lucky breaks usually happen only to friends of friends.

Just one of my acquaintances, a Bristol publisher named Dougal Templeton, claims first-hand experience of Emerald Isle munificence at Cheltenham. A couple

LEFT *Cheltenham is Britain's premier steeplechase venue. Horses have to be at the peak of fitness to make it round the arduous course, jumping fences that are over four feet six inches high.*

of years ago he had been queuing at a bar at the racecourse for about ninety minutes, and when his turn finally came he was irritated when an Irishman tapped him on the shoulder and asked him to be good enough to get them in for him and his mates, too. Soon poor old Dougal was manhandling crates of Guinness back to the thirsty crew, but life took a turn for the better when a wad of notes was thrust into his hand and he was told to keep the change. That turned out to be more than forty pounds, which helped bring joy to a widening circle of bookmakers as the afternoon wore on.

The only time I ever stood in that scrum of damp and pungent tweed, corduroy and waxed cotton, I did not even end up with a drink. That was in the usually genteel Queen's Hotel, which is rather a different place when the sporty types are in town. Not that it is just the Queen's: every hotel, guesthouse and bed and breakfast in the Cotswolds is crammed, and indeed three-quarters of them have been booked since the end of last year's festival. In Broadway, earlier on today, the Lygon Arms had no room for us for morning coffee. 'If you're going to Cheltenham, take your own sandwiches,' I was once told by Rodger Farrant, clerk of the course at Chepstow. You will hear worse tips than that at Prestbury Park in Festival week.

Those Irishmen who buy Rolls Royces from Broughton's with their winnings on their way home, those priests who put their last tenner on a combination of outsiders from their home patch and jet back with suitcases of money to reroof the village hall: they are all at the heart of the Cheltenham legend—though I have never discovered which came first, the Irish flocking to Cheltenham because the Gold Cup meeting falls on or near March 17, or the timing of the meeting to

ABOVE *A tick-tack man uses a system of sign language—tick-tack—to relate the odds to other bookmakers at race meetings. White gloves ensure that his hand movements can be clearly seen.*

coincide with St Patrick's Day to lure them over. Whichever, it has produced an event with a very special chemistry, a National Hunt showpiece joyfully more intimate and rural in spirit than Liverpool's Grand National, for all the whirring helicopters and those acres of cars.

The Cotswolds are such rich pastures for breeding and training horses—that patient, unglamorous, one-day-at-a-time grind—that many of the four-legged stars are familiar neighbours as they exercise through our villages and lanes. Even in our steep, hillside Chalford—hardly the Cotswolds of the rolling acres—we are well used to the heads of Graeme Roe's lads and girls bobbing along beyond our side wall, out for the morning from his stables across the valley at Hyde.

These local links are another part of the Cheltenham magic, and while the Irish might come over having been given one or two tips from the horse's mouth back home, so punters from Cheltenham's doorstep can feel they know a thing or two about David Nicholson's bright hopes from Temple Guiting, or perhaps like the look of what Tom George is doing with the horses in his yard at Slad.

A DAY AT THE RACES

RACING IS TO CHELTENHAM what stone is to the Cotswolds. Indeed, since the early 19th century jockeys have run flat races on the excellent turf at Cleeve Hill and, most famously, Prestbury Park. From flat-racing Cheltenham went on to host steeplechases: this exhilarating sport evolved from the hunting field, taking its name from the days when horses were raced across country between two church steeples, jumping anything that barred their way.

The National Hunt organisation is at the heart of steeplechasing, and each March the National Hunt Festival is held at Prestbury Park. Some 20 races are run during this three-day extravaganza, including the prestigious Cheltenham Gold Cup. When it was first held in 1924, the Gold Cup commanded only £685 in prize money; today—thanks to inflation and the race's growing reputation—the winnings exceed £200,000. Over the

ABOVE Jockeys urge their horses to the finishing line at Cheltenham in 1826; today's jockeys race for the coveted Gold Cup (left).

years the Gold Cup, with its demanding course, has provided exciting and challenging racing, winning the hearts of jockeys, trainers, owners and gamblers alike, to become a major event in the racing calendar.

Today thousands of racing enthusiasts from all over the world descend on

Cheltenham in March, transforming the spa town's elegant streets into crowded thoroughfares. The most notable influx comes from Ireland. The Irish love of steeplechasing and the country's ability to produce first-class jockeys and horse trainers have led to repeated Irish success at Cheltenham since the very early years of the Gold Cup. Unsurprisingly, thousands of gallons of Guinness are consumed during the Festival by British and Irish alike, ensuring a good time is had by all.

VAUGHAN WILLIAMS OF DOWN AMPNEY

It is Gloucester's year for the Three Choirs Festival this August, taking its turn with Hereford and Worcester as it has since the first decade of the 18th century. The newly published programme tells us that Henry Purcell, who died just a handful of years before the three cathedral choirs first met to celebrate their music-making, is the featured composer on the 300th anniversary of his death. But, as always, there is room for major works by Ralph Vaughan Williams, whose home village of Down Ampney, in the South Cotswolds, I must visit today. Along with his approximate contemporaries Edward Elgar and Gustav Holst, fellow native sons of Three Choirs territory, he played a major part in bringing an international dimension to the festival in the early years of this century. It has never lost that status since.

ABOVE *Ralph Vaughan Williams, one of the major figures in 20th-century English music.*

In Broadheath, Worcestershire, the cottage where Elgar was born is proclaimed by the local tourist authorities as 'central to the British heritage'. In Cheltenham, the council-run museum in Holst's birthplace is a shrine to late Victorian domesticity, a favourite with school parties attracted as much by his comfortably off family's very ordinary lifestyle as by his quite extraordinary talent. Only Vaughan Williams, of the trio, remains relatively unsung in the community of his birth, apart from a little showcase in the church where his father was vicar in late Victorian times; it is Vaughan Williams Senior who is remembered in a window depicting the Resurrection in the Lady Chapel.

Ralph was born in the then-new house now known as the Old Vicarage, in the centre of the village, in 1872, and however apparently unsung he might be in his own country, in naming his most famous hymn tune after the village he ensured that never a week goes by without 'Down Ampney' being sung throughout the Christian world, most usually to the words of 'Come down, O love divine'.

Down Ampney sounds an idyllic spot, but in truth

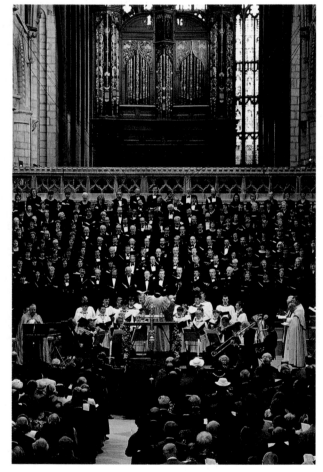

ABOVE *Magnificent Gloucester Cathedral plays host to the Three Choirs Festival every three years, alternating with Hereford and Worcester.*

it straggles along quite a busy little road that serves as a useful short cut between two major ones. That said, the country around, all meadows, is classically English pastoral, and those who live here tell you that this is a village as community-minded as any in the Cotswolds, with a post office, a primary school, a decent hall and any number of young families.

You do not hear many newcomers calling it Down Am'ney these days, any more than there is much talk of the next-door Am'ney Crucis among those who pour in from miles around to the busy Crown pub there. Perhaps the old

RIGHT *The idyllic meadows surrounding Down Ampney inspired Vaughan Williams to compose the hymn tune of the same name.*

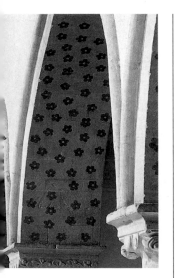

ABOVE *The cinquefoil red flowers at All Saints', Down Ampney, are popularly (though wrongly) believed to illustrate the rash that appeared on victims of the plague that struck in the 14th century.*

pronunciation lives on more healthily in Crucis's local, the Butcher's Arms, and in the less-visited villages of Ampney St Peter and Ampney St Mary. The alternative pronunciation has certainly proved more durable than 'Ciceter' for Cirencester. On the other hand, Down Ampney is now a commuter village for Swindon, drawing in young families from all over the country, who would not dream of pronouncing it in any way other than that in which it is spelled.

Ralph Vaughan Williams, then, or 'Rafe'? We shall not tread that tightrope, but simply return to his home village and enjoy the isolated beauty of the little 13th-century church the composer's father served so well. It is not entirely on its own, for next to it is Down Ampney House, built in Tudor times and made grander by Sir John Soane 200 years ago. The church, consecrated in 1265, was built by the Knights Templar, the effigy of one of whom—the Crusader Nicholas de Valers— can be found next to that of his wife Margaret in the Lady Chapel. Perhaps the church's most notable feature, however, (the Vaughan Williams connection aside) is its situation, remote from the village in a spot almost as idyllic as the image conjured up by the mellifluous hymn tune name.

It stands as testimony to the terrors of the Black Death around 1350, a disaster that led surviving villagers to abandon their settlement round the church and try again a little way to the north. Over the years, the Black Death story has also become entwined with the 13th-century cinquefoil red flowers painted on the plaster in the nave; they are a reminder of the symptoms of the disease, we are told, the rash that appeared on the skin and gave rise to the nursery rhyme 'A ring, a ring o' roses'. That little song was popular in late Victorian times, as was its Black Death explanation, and presumably two and two were put together to make six at Down Ampney around that time. Doing so ignored the fact that the flowers in the church—extremely conventional 13th-century motifs—predated the plague by perhaps a century.

At the lower end of the churchyard many modern graves bear ironic testimony to Down Ampney's role as a vital community, for without a great deal of living here there would not be nearly so much dying. The original churchyard is rich in ornate table tombs, their tablets, where they are still legible, telling at length of the virtuous glories of long-ago lives. But nothing is so moving as the single line on the gravestone of a boy who died in 1993, at the age of fifteen: *The joy of our lives*. It is apt that in the village of Vaughan Williams I rediscover how art can touch the soul by its sheer simplicity.

LAMPS AND LAMPOONS

'I see the parish lantern's bright tonight,' says my neighbour Ernie Workman, glancing up at the full moon. It is still the sole streetlight of many a Cotswold parish, though here on Chalford Hill it is supplemented spasmodically by sodium lamps on timber poles: quite how spasmodically is made plain when you look northwards across the Golden Valley from Tom Long's Post on Minchinhampton Common. Almost straight ahead, the lights of the Manor Farm estate that has

THE CRUSADING KNIGHTS

WHEN, IN 1118, the pious French knight Hugh de Payens conceived of the Poor Knights of Christ and of the Temple of Solomon—or Knights Templar—he had just eight followers. But, under the influence of the great Crusader St Bernard de Clairvaux, the Order grew to 20,000 members.

The Templars' original aim was to protect pilgrims travelling to the Holy Land, and they took monastic vows of poverty and chastity; their uniform—red crosses on white mantles—symbolised their purity. Despite the Templars' pledge of austerity, European monarchs and noblemen endowed the Order with lordships, land and castles; in the Cotswolds alone the Templars owned vast estates. Such wealth, and the Templars' exemption from all but papal law, gave the Order the means to build a formidable army to fight in the Crusades—the battles to ensure Christian control of the Holy Land.

But, as European influence declined in the East during the 13th century, the Knights Templar became redundant. In 1307, in a cynical attempt to acquire the Templar riches, the impoverished King Philip IV of France began viciously to persecute the Order. All Templars were placed under arrest, and many were tortured and forced to confess to trumped-up charges of heresy and immorality. In 1312 Pope Clement V suppressed the Order, and over the next two years several knights were executed. King Philip failed to find

ABOVE *The seal of the Knights Templar displays two knights sharing one horse, to illustrate their vow of poverty.*

RIGHT *The 14th-century* Chronicle of France *shows Templar leaders being burnt at the stake for heresy in 1314.*

the Templar wealth, though, and it remains undiscovered to this day.

In 1324 the Order secretly re-formed, but it was legitimised only in 1705 when Philip, Duke of Orleans and later Regent of France, was elected Grand Master of the Order. Today there are Knights—and Dames—Templar all over the world, part of an ecumenical and non-political organisation.

suburbanised acres of fields and woodlands around Bussage and Eastcombe paint bold bright stripes across the dark flank of the hill. Eastwards, Chalford's handful of scattered orange pinpricks tells a different story, and most of us who live here are happy to see it stay that way. Not that Ernie Workman would complain if they cut the branches and foliage down from around the posts. 'Makes 'em look like Christmas trees, and leaves us groping around in the dark,' he grumbles.

Ernie has lived all his seventy-seven years on Chalford Hill, and well recalls the day in the interwar years when electricity came to the village. It was not until the reign of the present Queen that some parts of neighbouring France Lynch set their candles and oil lamps aside for the last time, an example of how, throughout the Cotswolds, the journey into modern times has been slow and erratic, owing more to local circumstances and conditions—or simply the whims of those in power—than to any logical grand plan. If a good squire fancied the idea of this newfangled electricity, his village might have enjoyed the benefit of street lighting half a century before it came to its neighbour a mile down the road. A chance of geography set Chalford Hill close to the gasworks at Brimscombe, and there has been gas here—up the one-in-four slopes, along the twisting lanes—for all the years Ernie Workman can remember.

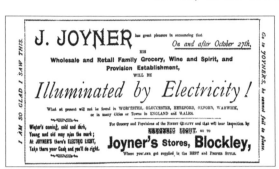

ABOVE *Electricity reached the Cotswold village of Blockley in the 1880s. This village grocer hoped to attract more custom with the new technology.*

Talk about the old days to people who remember the Cotswolds for threescore years or more, and most of them see either the internal-combustion engine or electricity as the greatest agent of change. Looking at photographs, and comparing the white dust tracks and horse-drawn carts of Edwardian days with the neat metalled roads and Austin Sevens of a generation later, those of us who did not live through those times might be inclined to put the emphasis on the transport revolution. We would be wrong to do so. Providing homes with power for lighting and heating was a less visible process, less alluring to the camera, but most who were here at its coming are certain that this was the greater breakthrough. Apart from anything else, it was an exercise in democracy that the growing availability of cars could never match.

When Ernie Workman was a lad there were only two cars in the village, one of them the Morris Cowley belonging to Dr Dill at the Corderries. It was all very well the neighbours gazing upon these gleaming triumphs of steel, glass and rubber, but they might as well have been spaceships from Mars for all the factory worker and farm hand could aspire to them.

Electricity, on the other hand, was something that could enrich every cottage. For years it had been on hand for the wealthy through little garden generators throbbing away out back, the machines you still see beside cantinas from Spain to São Paulo—the ones that, if you wipe away the dust, whisk you back to our green hills in an instant, wherever you are in the world, with their laconic plaque reading: 'Lister's, Dursley, England'. Now 'the electric' was every man's slave, and it is easy to see how it made the greater impact on people's lives. The lack of a set of wheels, after all, was no great problem for people with nowhere to go, and for those who did have to travel modest distances to work, or enjoyed an occasional outing, there was a strange, old-fashioned phenomenon known as public transport.

After he has reminisced for a while about Mr Baker charging the radio accumulators at his workshop above the Duke of York, and Mr Cook breaking the white stone down into gravel for the roads on a patch of land beside the old Congregational Sunday school, Ernie Workman tells me that if I really want to know more about Chalford he will lend me a video. Suddenly it seems a very long time indeed since the parish lantern lit the village's way to whist drives and chapel socials.

There is a tale, which I find hard to swallow, of men walking down the lane in front of the ladies, their shirt tails hanging out of their trousers to show the way— the so-called 'Dursley lanterns', though I do not suppose they called them that much beyond the South Cotswolds. This sounds to me more a way of neighbouring communities making fun of Dursley than an answer to the problem of finding your way around in the dark. Some towns and villages seem ripe for teasing, and Dursley, as an industrial town in an agricultural area, has been 'different' enough to be the butt of much dubious humour over the years.

The best-known parochial invective in the Cotswolds is probably:

> *Beggarly Bisley, Painswick proud,*
> *Mincing Hampton and strutting Stroud.*

When it comes to being made fun of, however, no community comes close to Ebrington, or 'Yubberton', near Chipping Campden, once known far and wide as a village of simpletons. There are such places all over the country, and the examples of idiocy are always the same, odd little quirks of folklore that survived for generations and spread over hundreds of miles as rural myths.

Yubberton: that was where they wanted their church tower to be as tall as Chipping Campden's, so they put manure round the bottom of it to make it grow. That was where they grew the hedges high to keep in the cuckoos. That was where they held the pig up over the wall to let it watch the parade go by. As for the cuckoos and the hedges, I have had that tale told me in the past three months, referring to a simpleton village more than 3,000 miles away across the Atlantic. All I can say about Ebrington, a village of golden stone teamed irresistibly with the thatch that we see so rarely in the Cotswolds, is that if the residents really were daft, they picked the loveliest place on earth in which to be so.

ABOVE *Ebrington is, arguably, one of the prettiest places in Britain; but in years gone by its fame rested more dubiously on the supposed stupidity of its inhabitants.*

Dark nights, of course, are not to everyone's taste. It is notable how many householders install their own security lighting to keep evil at bay. At one house, the mechanism governing the lamp is so sensitive that no cat, hedgehog, cockchafer or bobbing branch goes undetected; inside, it must be like sleeping in a violent but mercifully silent electrical storm. I shun such devices, with the result that my car was one of the first to be picked over last time the village's one-man crime wave was on the loose.

Not that he is the only villain in the business. At the moment two Strathclyde constables are at Banbury police station with something like three-quarters of a million pounds' worth of knick-knacks found in Scotland but deemed most likely to have been stolen from houses in the Cotswolds over the past couple of years. It certainly sounds like a typically eclectic Cotswold haul: naval telescopes, French clocks, a vast stamp collection, two statues of Japanese cranes, six feet tall and valued at £6,000, a pair of whale's teeth from the Falkland Islands…How could the Scottish police have cast their eyes over such loot and concluded: 'Och, aye, get it doon tae Banbury the noo'? As one of their countrymen once remarked:

O wad some Pow'r the giftie gie us
To see oursels as others see us!

FISHY STORIES

If you favour fish on Friday, then on Good Friday a trout farm is the ideal place to be, both to watch the vigorously alive ones threshing about in their ponds, and to invest in one or two of the safely dead for tea or the freezer. The farm at Bibury, beside the Coln and across from the Swan, has been a business since 1902 and a great stopping-off place for motorists for generations.

I remember Charlie Barnett, Cirencester fishmonger and swashbuckling Gloucestershire and England opening batsman of the 1930s and 1940s, telling me of a visit to the farm the day after his benefit match in Bristol. The England captain Len Hutton had journeyed down from Yorkshire for the game and had stayed overnight with Charlie at his big house on Cowcombe Hill, beside the steep road up from the Golden Valley in Chalford to the plateau of Aston Down. What the peerless Len made of a Sunday-morning drive to a fish farm is not recorded, but Barnett remembered to the end of his life a conversation he had there with the farm's then owner, a fisherman, naturalist and pillar of village life called Arthur Severn. Charlie was still seething that morning because his great teammate Walter Hammond had cried off from playing in the benefit match, pleading some pressing personal business; and his low spirits were not lifted when Arthur said, 'I had a friend of yours over, yesterday.'

'Oh, yes?' Charlie replied.

'Yes,' said Arthur. 'Wally Hammond was here.'

For the best part of fifty years after that, Charlie Barnett used to ponder on what it was that prevented Hammond from playing for him in Bristol, yet could afford him the leisure to pay his compliments to the trout at Bibury.

One answer, of course, is that one occupation is a great deal more relaxing than the other. In fact, I know of no more calming an exercise in the Cotswolds—not browsing round the antique shops of Burford, not lazing in the sun beside the Rollright Stones—than flicking food pellets made from who-knows-what into still waters and watching the surface erupt in a fury of glinting scales and threshing fins. You can, if you wish, try to anticipate the dimensions of the underwater hordes you are about to stir up: will they be tiddlers a few months old, or monsters weighing perhaps five or six pounds, with three summers behind them? Mental stress beyond this level should never play a part in the Bibury Trout Farm experience, however; nor, for me, should the dispiriting prospect of hiring a line

and catching your own fish, which you are able to do in a corner of the eight-acre grounds. Perhaps trout are not quite as daft as they look, but it strikes me, as I gaze down on them from a rustic bridge, that they are almost forming orderly queues to take the bait.

Today, few quarrel with Bibury's claim that it is Britain's best-known trout farm, possibly the biggest restocking farm in the country, but fish farms have been around a long time. You need no great knowledge of history to know of the medieval monasteries' ponds, while the first hatchery in this country was at Troutdale, in Cumberland, in 1868.

ABOVE *Founded in 1902, Bibury Trout Farm spawns up to 10 million trout a year. At the farm you can try your hand at fishing, and the plentiful stocks mean that a catch is virtually assured.*

Most of Bibury's fish are rainbow trout, though there is a small population of the traditional 'brownies'. Brown trout were the norm at Bibury until 1976, when that long, dry summer played havoc with their lifestyle. Today you are more likely to see them in the Coln, where descendants of hardy escapees and survivors do battle with the ducks for the trippers' breadcrumbs. The market, driven by the freezer trade, has decreed that eighteen-month-old fish weighing from ten to fourteen ounces are in greatest demand for the kitchen. 'The rainbow trout was introduced from North America towards the end of the last century, and its advantages over brownies are that it is better suited to enclosed water and develops more quickly,' says the farm's manager. 'It can live for up to six years, and we know of some weighing up to ten pounds here. Doubtless there are some even heavier than that lurking around somewhere.'

BELOW *Brightly coloured kingfishers can be glimpsed darting in and out of their river-bank burrows near Bibury Trout Farm.*

Beside the Coln and suspiciously close to the tanks of wriggling fry, a kingfisher can usually be seen sweeping his territory, eyes down, minding his own business; and although I have never seen herons at Bibury—in terms of big, awkward birds, I associate the village more with the loud evening rooks up on the wooded knoll beyond Arlington Row—I can believe it when locals tell me that those great, grey fish-eating machines take more than a passing interest in the fish farm's teeming, watery acres.

OPEN DAY AT WHITEWAY

The *Daily Telegraph* must have a pretty convincing tipster in these parts. Today, the Easter Saturday *Telegraph* carries a breathless 500 words on the 'artists' colony' of Whiteway 'opening its doors to the public for the first time in nearly a hundred years'. What tosh this is. There is no more obligation on residents of Whiteway to be artists than there is on Bristolians to be slave-traders, and there has been no time in its history when its doors have been closed to outsiders. What is happening is that five properties and five gardens are opening at three pounds a head, children free, with profits going to help repair the tracks down to the houses off the publicly maintained lane between Foston's Ash and Miserden. In other words, Whiteway is having a village open weekend, as communities do in the Cotswolds and throughout rural England every week from April to September.

Not that Whiteway is your average Cotswold village. It does not look like one, with its houses of wood and asbestos, corrugated iron and just plain brick, and its history is unique in England—a settlement established by middle-class Londoners in 1898, based on principles of equality, communal ownership and freedom of expression. This was all rather revolutionary then, and talk of 'free union' and tales of young men and women working in the fields wearing not very much on hot summer's days, soon had tongues wagging all over the tops from Bisley to Birdlip. So much went by the board so quickly—the free love, the barter system meant to replace money, the light Greek tunics, the belief that any community

can be self-sufficient when old folks are dying and little children fall ill. What did survive was the principle of shared ownership of land, with residents' property rights retained by the commune; and unchanging, too, was the profile of the people attracted to this remote upland spot: independent-minded, offbeat—artists, some of them, certainly, but more often people useful with their hands in other ways, whether it was baking bread, tinkering with tractors, making cheese or hammering out wrought iron.

Look around the Stroud valleys today and you will find any number of such types. They do not care what clothes they wear, so long as they are comfortable in them; swapping and sharing are part of their lifestyle, as is a sophisticated barter system. In the everyday climate of today, we are nearer to understanding what made those early colonists tick than our parents and grandparents ever were. The colony a failure? No, it was simply caught up by mainstream life.

Tramping up and down the rutted tracks on the open day, there is no denying that repair work is overdue. One of the gardens to visit, Tin Penny Cottage, is a regular opener under the National Gardens Scheme. If you live in a bleak spot and wonder what you can grow to face up to the wind and rain, this is the place for inspiration. Protheroe's Bakery is also familiar to many visitors, for it was once a thriving concern, and had carved out a sound niche in the health-food market until an explosion and fire in an oven in 1989 made Colin Price, the last baker, think long and hard about his future. Since he was past retirement age and his typical day began at half past four in the morning and finished twelve hours or more later, perhaps his decision to wind up the business was not, in the end, too hard to make.

PROTECTING OUR RARE BREEDS

Ask a child to draw a cow, and the chances are their picture will show a large black and white Friesian, complete with sizable udder. In days gone by, that same request might have generated a completely different picture—probably of a particular breed typical of the child's home region. For, as farming practices have changed in favour of large-scale production, so too have breeds of farm animals become increasingly standardised in the quest for optimum yield.

Local Cotswold sheep, known as Cotswold Lions, once grazed the area's hills in their thousands. Introduced by Roman settlers, their golden fleece of long, lustrous wool brought enormous wealth to the area in the Middle Ages, and enabled wool merchants to build great churches and manor houses. Likewise the beautiful black–brown Gloucester cow, with its distinctive white tail, once stocked the dairies of the lush Severn Vale: its milk proved ideal for cheese-making, and gave rise to the famous Double and Single Gloucester cheeses. The Gloucester Old Spot pig, too, was a vital part of the rural economy: reared and fattened on household and garden waste, its fat was much needed by a poor rural population. In the Berkeley

Vale the pigs lived in cider orchards and ate windfall apples: legend has it that the falling apples bruised the white pigs and gave them their black spots.

As farming changed, the Gloucester cow was replaced by heavier-milking breeds, and is today one of the rarest breeds of cattle in Britain; the Old Spot pig laid on too much fat for today's lean pork and bacon; and as wool and cloth production moved away from the area in the 19th century, so the Cotswold sheep disappeared from the hills. Yet thanks to the efforts of specialised rare-breeds farms, such as the Cotswold Farm Park in Guiting Power, these breeds survive—and even prosper: Cotswold sheep are once again on the increase and finding a market for their

ABOVE *Cotswold sheep are grazing the local hills once more as demand returns for their lustrous fleece.*

LEFT *Although numbers of Old Spot pigs declined in the 1950s, the breed is finding favour once more with local farmers.*

BELOW *The Gloucester cow has been a rare breed for over 100 years, despite its milk being ideal for cheese-making.*

wool at a local weaving mill, and Old Spots are starting to satisfy an increasing public demand for free-range, richer-tasting meat. And visitors to the Farm Park may still enjoy seeing a litter of marauding piglets squeeze under the gates to meet the public and have their tummies tickled.

LEFT *A young visitor to the Cotswold Farm Park makes the acquaintance of a couple of Golden Guernsey goats.*

RIGHT *Cochin chickens are among the rarities on display at the Cotswold Farm Park.*

An unoccupied house built of timber is for sale, a sign declaring it to be Dear Old Place. The room specifications are very much as one would expect of a three-bedroom detached house anywhere—Georgian-style door, Moffat oven, TV aerial point and telephone socket—and even the septic and Calor Gas tanks are no more or less than you would expect of a remote rural property. A firm of estate agents in Stroud is asking £78,950 for it freehold:

> The original idea of an independent community living in a wooded area of the Cotswolds, with a swimming pool, football field, play group and village hall of its own, is truly unusual. A community meeting is held on the first Tuesday of every month, when communal maintenance of pathways, etc. and business is discussed. We understand that there is a method of 'sale agreed' between the new purchasers and members of the community when a new purchaser wishes to buy a property on Whiteway Colony. It is understood also that conventional deeds for the property do not exist. Due to the unusual nature of the title of the property, it is believed that conventional building society funding will be very difficult...

The brave new world of the Whiteway of a century ago still cannot be tamed by the estate agent's jargon of the 1990s.

THE MODEL VILLAGE

In the King's Head at France Lynch three couples are discussing where to take the children over the spring bank-holiday weekend. A rough-and-ready top ten, in no particular order, seems to emerge as follows: the Cotswold Wildlife Park, near Burford; the Cotswold Farm Park, near Guiting Power; Bourton-on-the-Water in general; Folly Farm Waterfowl, outside Bourton-on-the-Water; Berkeley Castle; the Corinium Museum in Cirencester; Westonbirt Arboretum, near Tetbury; Slimbridge; the Oasis leisure centre at Swindon; and the various museums and sights of Gloucester Docks. This is a selection with a south-to-central slant, and doubtless in Chipping Norton and Campden similar groups of parents would have a rather different view of the world beyond the first four attractions listed here.

From my point of view, I very much admire what Joe Henson has done with rare domestic breeds at the Cotswold Farm Park, and think his lambing shed is wonderfully instructive for children; I acknowledge the Cotswold Wildlife Park as an extremely acceptable zoo and a good day out for youngsters; and I could happily spend an hour a day at Robert Opie's packaging and advertising museum at Gloucester Docks, reliving the Oxydol and Payne's Poppets years of my youth and singing along endlessly to 'Murray Mints, Murray Mints, Too Good To Hurry Mints'. Bourton-on-the-Water, however, is unique.

Generally in the Cotswolds these days it is regarded as politically incorrect to compare the hills with any other part of the world, or with the Elysian Fields themselves, for that matter. Bourton, however, is not ashamed to be known as the 'Venice of the Cotswolds' on the strength of its half-dozen low little bridges across

RIGHT *Pretty stone bridges span the River Windrush at several points as it flows through Bourton-on-the-Water, the 'Venice of the Cotswolds'. Like Venice, Bourton draws hordes of tourists.*

ABOVE *A toddler gets a giant's-eye view of the world at the Model Village in Bourton-on-the-Water. The one-ninth scale model is an exact replica of the village as it once was.*

the Windrush. It is a phrase from another age of tourism, when fewer of us knew what Venice was really like. Some observers, surveying the tearooms and gift shops and ice cream, say it is more like the 'Blackpool of the Cotswolds'.

No Cotswold community of this size has embraced tourists so whole-heartedly, or built such a large sector of its economy around them. It has developed other attributes in recent years, as a dormitory town for people who find that its charms warrant quite lengthy commuting journeys, and as the site of a busy new industrial estate. But if you do not live there, it is still hard to think of it as anything other than a place for a sunny afternoon. In Bourton and its neighbourhood there is an attraction for every day of the week.

Back in 1937, John Moore, author of *The Cotswolds*, accused Bourton of ambushing American visitors in summer and sitting out the cold months smugly on their riches till the sun brought them back with the swallows. There seem to be few Americans around the village these days, but a weekend outing here is still a high spot of summer for tens of thousands of families in the Midlands—as it is for us.

Dan enjoys the Model Village, a mini-Bourton to one-ninth scale, created, at about the time of John Moore's visit in the mid-1930s, by the landlord of the Old New Inn and his friends, one of whom had trained at Kew Gardens and knew a thing or two about miniature shrubs. I note Dan takes most interest in the two aspects of the model that would have intrigued me most as a nine-year-old: the hymns wafting from St Lawrence's Church, a recording, I am told, of the local choir; and the Old New Inn itself, which of course has a model of the model…

An hour or so later Dan is affronted when he has a sticker slapped on his chest at the Motor Museum, declaring that he has visited Brum there. Brum, it turns out, is a model car who appears on television for the edification of four-year-olds, and it is most un-hip to show any interest in him at more than twice that age. Dan sneers as we pass the little yellow sports car with his headlamps like eyes, and is much more inclined to show a manly interest in real-life Standard Flying Eights and Austin Seven Nippies among the thirty or so vehicles on show.

The museum displays very much the kind of cars you might have seen bearing comfortably-off trippers to Bourton in the interwar years, splendid convertibles and sports models. In the pioneering days of motoring for pleasure, when it was possible for ever-increasing numbers of people to aspire to sitting behind the wheel, the Cotswolds was a happy hunting-ground. Here, in real life, we see the Shell Mex and National Benzole pumps that were sprouting in even the most remote villages sixty years ago, and read the great circular signs with which the Automobile Association colonised almost every little community, put it on the map and set it in the context of a wider world: 'Marston Meysey; Fairford 3; Cricklade 3; London 84; Safety First.'

The Motor Museum, which now has an adjacent village-life exhibition, was opened by Mike Cavanagh in 1978 and has become more eccentric as time has ticked by. Its exhibits have burgeoned, and those that have been there for years seem to have become more and more a part of the old mill building. Old enamel advertising signs were in from the start, but now it is clear that the owner's magpie tendencies extend to motoring-related ceramics, garage advertising displays, mascots, tins, trophies, cards, games and indeed any collectible with a car on it. Since so much originates from the interwar years, lovers of Art Deco, for instance, could spend an absorbing hour here without so much as a glance at a real car. There are some evocative old photographs, too, and even more of them in the village-life display.

By the time we have kicked a few more elderly tyres and moved on, the tide of Bourton-on-the-Water has begun to ebb back towards the big car and coach parks. For all that outsiders shudder at the prospect of living beside the river and the green, at the thought of those endless crowds parading up and down and casting sidelong glances into your windows on a sunny day, there is still a logical pattern to life here, a tranquil start to the day and ever more peace as the sun descends. Dan and I decide that we must leave the Model Railway and Birdland for another day, and he looks worried and asks if I really mean it when I say we might just have time to look in on the Exhibition of Perfumery in Victoria Street. No, I reply, that was just a joke. 'Phew,' gasps Dan.

ABOVE The Cotswold Motor Museum is chock-a-block with vintage and classic cars, caravans and motorcycles, and an abundance of motoring paraphernalia.

CHAPTER THREE

GARDENS AND GAMES

LUNCHTIME IN A PUB IN BRISTOL, and journalists on the city's morning news-paper are huddled round a table discussing their day's work. A young woman shudders and says she has just returned from Badminton, where she has been previewing prospects for this weekend's horse trials with the organisers. 'Amazing,' she grumbles. 'They're all so horsy.' This seems somewhat akin to taking exception to the Pope being Catholic, and as the conversation meanders in other directions my colleagues lose me as my thoughts remain focused on those ducal acres just a few miles, a handful of minutes and a whole world away from the smoky Old Market Tavern.

I am back in the land of green pastures and creamy grey villages, pondering the Badminton Horse Trials, the horsy and those who return to the Duke of Beaufort's estate year after year simply to look for famous faces in the crowds and wander endlessly up and down the avenues of trade stands. That tented village of traders can keep you occupied for hours, to the extent that, if you wish, the only horses you will ever see will be in porcelain, brass or oil paint. There are those who prefer to keep it this way, for some of the eventing mounts, in the flesh, are magnificent but fearsome beasts, towering above the mere human onlooker. Once, on the road to Nether Lypiatt Manor, I had to stop my car to allow Princess Michael of Kent to squeeze through on a hunter that looked as if it had been newly burnished by valets armed with vats of Cherry Blossom boot polish. Professionally, I should have been on the lookout for details of the princess's dress that might have interested some gossip column, but all I took in was the perfectly formed toe of an immaculate boot and the fact that from my driving seat my line of vision was approximately level with her horse's knees. It is the same with the Badminton creatures. Merely to scramble aboard one would terrify me.

The Badminton Horse Trials, currently sponsored by Mitsubishi Motors, whose British Colt Car wing has long been one of Cirencester's major employers, is a three-day event which quite naturally spreads over four days of early May.

The first two are devoted to dressage, Saturday is for cross-country and huge crowds, and the Sunday finale sees the top riders battling for the title in the showjumping arena.

They say 180,000 were at last year's cross-country. The sport is certainly at its most thrilling that day, with the riders dressed like National Hunt jockeys and just as likely to end their challenge muddied and soaked. Ask spectators why the lake is their favourite obstacle, why they cram around it dozens deep, and they will explain patiently that this is the place for spectacle, the ultimate test of the mettle of both horse and rider. Translated, this means that it is here that you are most likely to see posh people famed for their horsemanship flying helplessly backside-uppermost into the murky drink—very posh people indeed, in the days when Princess Anne and Captain Mark Phillips used to compete.

That was the apex of Badminton's years as a social occasion, the Anne and Mark era, when generations of royals would honour their friend and kinsman the tenth Duke of Beaufort with their company. He was central to the horsy side of their lives, and to me it is no coincidence that the Queen's first two children made their homes in the Cotswold countryside as his neighbours. This was the duke who founded the trials, in 1949. In those days eventing was very much the sport of young cavalry officers, and it was after their poor showing in the 1948 Olympics in London that he decided a high-class annual tournament on his estate would sharpen their competitive edge and give the selectors some guide to form. Badminton, now established as the world's major event of its kind, continues to serve that latter purpose.

DUKES AND DUCHESSES

To the national press the tenth Duke, known by his intimates as 'Master', was Britain's number-one fox-hunter and an aristocrat whose funeral in 1984 brought three generations of the Queen's family to Badminton. For people all over the south Cotswolds, however, his passing, two months before his eighty-fourth birthday, marked the end of an era. He had been duke for all but sixty years, having succeeded his father late in 1924, and his involvement in a wide spectrum of local life had been total from that day on. Many an organisation celebrated its fiftieth anniversary in the late 1970s and early 1980s by inviting along the same duke and duchess who had performed the opening ceremony, but the strange sense of time warp felt by many on such occasions—usually heightened by the production of some dusty photograph or other of the earlier gathering, full of faces of people dead for generations—never seemed to affect the Beauforts themselves. They always wore their air of permanence lightly, apparently seeing no cause to marvel that their sway over this small part of the kingdom should have survived three monarchs and thirty-plus years of the reign of a fourth.

The tenth duke's duchess, the former Lady Mary Cambridge, was a niece of Queen Mary, so 'Master and Mary' were literally family to the Queen. Indeed, Queen Mary spent much of the Second World War at Badminton, busying herself by organising 'wooding parties' which saw off many a tree her hosts would have preferred to see spared. The duke was Master of the Horse for a record forty-one years, serving three monarchs—including his great friend Edward VIII, who at one time was his neighbour at Easton Grey—and his plumed helmet is prominent on grainy films of that damp and ever-receding coronation of 1953.

In common with all the dukes of Beaufort before him, the eleventh duke, David Somerset, now himself past retirement age, can trace his ancestry back to Edward III and John of Gaunt in the 14th century, but his relationship with his immediate predecessor was no closer than first cousin twice removed. His professional background was in the art

ABOVE *The tenth Duke of Beaufort (seen here on the left, in the plumed helmet) was a key member of the Royal Household and played a central role in the coronation of Elizabeth II in 1953.*

world, more specifically the Marlborough Fine Art Gallery in Mayfair; so some who do not know him are surprised to learn that in 1959 he failed by a single point—just one showjumping fence—to win the Badminton Horse Trials. It need hardly be said that his hunting credentials are sound, and since moving into Badminton he has tackled the task of bringing his properties up to scratch with vigour and no little expense. Dutiful and well loved though the tenth duke was, when he died he left a house and an estate bearing all the hallmarks of an ageing regime.

There was great sadness when the present duke's wife, the former Lady Caroline Jane Thynne, sister of the Marquess of Bath, died in April 1995. She had been a supporter of local arts and charities since long before she succeeded to the title, and prior to the health problems of her later years she had begun to nurture gardens at Badminton that were attracting admiring comment far beyond the Cotswolds, a fascinating development on an estate at which grounds, hitherto, were strictly for grazing deer or exercising horses. One of the great pleasures of a summer evening, for all too brief a spell, was to wangle your way onto one of her conducted tours of the house and grounds. Badminton is a treasure house

LEFT *Badminton is more than just horses and courses. The late duchess was a passionate and creative gardener, as the pretty south garden, pictured here, testifies.*

ABOVE *Canaletto's painting of Badminton House, which shows members of the Beaufort household enjoying the grounds, dates from the early years of the 18th century.*

of near-priceless paintings, most of them with deep family connections: two magnificent views of the house and park by Canaletto; portraits by Van Dyck, Lely, Reynolds, Kneller and Lawrence; lesser canvases and rare prints by the dozen, lining every room and corridor.

The Badminton she showed her guests was a world away from the circus of Saturday and Sunday at the horse trials. The Thursday and Friday, however, are much less busy, and these are the days when both the extremely horsy and the not-at-all-so feel most comfortable at the event. For many experts the dressage section of the three-day event, the intricate schooling and band-box grooming of both mount and rider, is the ultimate discipline; but it is no spectator sport for the uninitiated, so while the earnest can enjoy the action in comfortable near-isolation, those whose high spot of the event is to tour the trade village can equally do so in peace and at ease during the dressage days.

Saturday and Sunday are for people-lovers only—and on cross-country day for early-rising people-lovers at that. You hear much of the four-wheel-drive set cruising along the M4 with their champers and Fortnum's hampers in readiness for their picnic luncheon at Badders, but the true professionals are those who beat the mayhem of the final country-lane crawl by queuing for the gates to open at seven in the morning. By the time the overheated herd is fighting its way in they are tucking into bacon, eggs and sausages cooked on their camper stoves; for those looking in on them, the smell of breakfast has never been more infuriatingly delicious.

It used to be English roses who won Badminton, sweet but extremely hardy. Then in 1994 first, second and third were New Zealanders with the tough, laconic demeanour of professional sportsmen the world over and staccato first

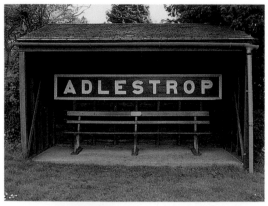

ABOVE AND TOP *Edward Thomas immortalised the railway station at Adlestrop in his poem of that name, although he never got as far as the village. In turn, his poem is now memorialised on the seat beneath the old station sign.*

names—Mark, Blyth, Vaughn. What we must remember, however, when the Kiwis are crowing over their success, is that in real life the three are Cotsallers all—our very own Blyth Tait training and schooling his horses at hilly Hazleton, Vaughn Jefferis at Dodington and Mark Todd at dear old Adlestrop.

Mark Todd, twice winner of individual Olympic gold, is leasing land on the Adlestrop estate, close by the shelter that bears witness to the little fragment of literary history that made Adlestrop famous.

The Great Western Railway sign that told Edward Thomas where he was when his train stopped 'unwontedly' in this middle-of-birdsong spot on a long-ago summer's afternoon now adorns the back of the village shelter. Beneath it is a GWR bench in the same brown and cream livery, on the back rest of which is a small plaque with the poem 'Adlestrop' in full. It need hardly be said that the railway station, immediately north of the bridge that carries the Stow–Chipping Norton road over the Worcester–Oxford line, is no more, and heavy-duty fencing isolates the tracks from its site. Only the approach down to it off the road remains, and, as in the poet's time, no one leaves and no one comes.

Edward Thomas knew 'Adlestrop—only the name', rather than the community, for the very Great Western Railway reason that the station was a mile away from the village on the main road, a more convenient location for the carriers' carts from Stow and Chipping Norton. If it had been much further away it would doubt-less have been called Adlestrop Road, in the tradition of many other stations, including Tetbury Road, which served that South Cotswold community until 1889 in spite of being some seven miles distant from it. Most veterans of GWR travel have a 'Road' tale to tell, of stepping lightly from the train expecting to be taking tea in the town square in two minutes' time, and instead finding themselves in a deserted lane discussing life with two cows and a pheasant.

Adlestrop has a reputation over and above Mark Todd and the Edward Thomas connection, for Jane Austen's uncle, Thomas Leigh, was rector here from the late 18th century, and the novelist stayed with him at the splendid old rectory, which is now Adlestrop House. It is not accessible to the public, neither are its grounds, but some of the other gardens in the village open for the National Gardens Scheme on a Sunday in June, the Edward Thomas time.

WELL-DRESSING IN BISLEY

Along with many an apparently ancient Cotswold tradition, Bisley's Ascension Day well-dressing ceremony can be traced back to an earnest Victorian clergyman rather than to Merrie England. It was first held in 1863, shortly after the Reverend Thomas Keble had tidied up and formalised, complete with Gothic knobs on, the village's main water supply in Wells Lane. Wealthy and well-connected, the younger brother of John Keble, the founder of the Anglo-Catholic Oxford Movement, he was a busy builder throughout the old Bisley parish during his long ministry, from 1827 to 1873. Oakridge, France Lynch, Chalford, Bussage and Eastcombe all have reason to be grateful for his efforts to this day, while in Bisley he provided the school and restored the church, as well as reviving the wells.

His architect for the last two projects was his curate, the Reverend W. H. Lowder, though neither man was thanked much for his efforts by the parishioners, at least as far as the church was concerned. There seems little doubt that some sort of rescue plan was needed, for in 1862 the roof had to be propped up by a pole, and the south wall, with its Roman, Saxon and Norman traces, was seen by the restorers as beyond salvation. But the villagers' gut reaction was against the wholesale rebuilding the clerics had in mind, and in the end the £4,000 bill was met largely by Keble and his circle. It is interesting to hear of such grassroots reaction against the Victorian squirearchy's craze for restoration, which swept away so much ancient craftsmanship while undoubtedly saving some buildings from terminal decay.

ABOVE AND LEFT *Pupils from the local village school are responsible for laying pretty floral wreaths at Bisley's well-dressing ceremony, which takes place every year on Ascension Day.*

The act of dressing wells with flowers has pagan origins, with its roots in the worship of the life-giving force of water. In this country it is most often associated with the Derbyshire Peak District, and there is certainly nothing remotely like it elsewhere in the Cotswolds. Neither is there any obvious connection between water and Ascension Day. Keble simply wished to mark the restoration of the wells, saw a dressing ceremony as a seemly way of doing it, and chose this time of year as a season when the meadows were ablaze with wild flowers. Perhaps, too—the well-dressing followed closely on the church work—it was also a gift from the vicar to his parish, a symbol of fresh hope and reconciliation.

What he has certainly left us is a tradition that involves large numbers of villagers and draws in spectators from miles around. The ceremony itself is relatively brief, consisting of a short service in church, a procession down to the wells and the laying of the wreaths and posies, but for the children of the Bluecoat village school the preceding days are packed with preparation and anticipation, and the flowers proclaim their message of love and beauty long after the band has packed its instruments and the visitors have dispersed. It falls to the eldest twenty-two children, about a quarter of the total, to carry the wreaths and garlands that head the procession and form the centrepiece of the ceremony. These consist of Stars of David, the letters AD and the year, letters spelling out the word 'Ascension', and five hoops.

The preparations begin at the weekend, when the children gather moss to cover the letters and symbols. That job is done on the Tuesday, and on the Wednesday the flowers are brought in. Almost all the flowers are from local gardens, and it's a great help if the lilac is in bloom. In the days of Keble, wild flowers were used. Then there was a time when the gardens of the big houses would be the main source. Today it is a general village effort, and a lot of flowers, both for the letters and for the posies carried by all the younger children, come from people with no close links with the school. Several parents help with the preparation of the flowers and with teas on the day. Bisley is a village that has attracted many newcomers, but there are still children here whose parents and grand-parents also took part in the well-dressing.

Several little ceremonies of this kind declined in the years before and after the last war, when many things Victorian were seen not as traditional but merely old-fashioned. The spirit is very different today, however, and in Bisley the will to make something memorable and relevant out of Ascension Day has never been greater. In the old days the bandsmen would stop outside the Bear and play 'God Bless the Prince of Wales', a reminder that Keble dedicated the restoration of the wells to the future Edward VII's marriage to Alexandra. Their monogram AEA can still be seen there, along with the text 'O ye wells, bless ye the Lord: praise Him and magnify Him for ever', plus a more recent proclamation that the water is now deemed unfit for drinking.

Keble's architect curate created two new spouts for the well, to bring the total to seven. The Swilly Brook, of which they are a part, springs up under the church-yard and flows down to Toadsmoor Lake and eventually the River Frome. At the same time, Curate Lowder provided three troughs for washing plus a horse pond and large cattle trough close by, and today they serve as a watery little paradise for a well-fed and contented-looking band of Aylesbury ducks. No doubt a single day a year of flowers and fanfares is a small price for them to pay for such pleasures.

BELOW *Bisley's water troughs once served local livestock. Today they are popular with the village's band of Aylesbury ducks.*

A LOVE AFFAIR WITH THE EAST

In the days before they were metalled—until well into this century in some cases—the byways of the Cotswolds were tracks of pale, compacted stone that dazzled the eye in the sunshine. Imagine the scene at this time of year, in glorious mid-May, with the white hedgerow blossom cascading over the lanes and the verges high with the cow parsley that springs up from nowhere in the early days of the month. John Betjeman wrote of the Oxford May mornings of his early manhood when he first learned country-house-weekend manners at Sezincote, just a little way out of Moreton-in-Marsh, and you can imagine him glorying in the quiet North Cotswold countryside of the interwar years, an essence of Englishness. Sezincote encapsulates a certain dotty type of Englishness, well bred and well meaning yet faintly absurd in a way to which the young poet would instantly have responded.

Sezincote is just one reminder of oriental life in the North Cotswolds, though by far the most spectacular. Its gardens' regular opening hours are Thursday and Friday afternoons, which allow you to view them much in the spirit intended, without weekend crowds encroaching on their mystic calm. Its bank-holiday openings can remind you rather too forcibly that Sezincote is closely related to Brighton.

The house as we see it today was the fantasy of Sir Charles Cockerell, who retired to it in around 1805 after growing fabulously wealthy through a career in the East India Company. There might have been a hint of nepotism in his choice of designer, his brother Samuel Pepys Cockerell, though it was a sound enough decision. Samuel too had worked for the East India Company, as its architect, and some twenty years earlier he had topped his design for Warren Hastings's house at nearby Daylesford with a discreet Islamic dome. This time, his brief to create a little part of India in the Cotswolds was aided by the appointment of surely the two finest landscape designers to be found for such a task, Humphry Repton and Thomas Daniell, the latter a painter of the Indian landscape who probably knew more about the architecture of that country than anyone else in Europe. When Repton was working on a project it did not remain secret for long, and around 1807 the Prince Regent made the long journey to the North Cotswolds to investigate stories of this potentate's palace growing out of the green English countryside. At much the same time, Repton drew up Indian designs for the Brighton Pavilion, and, though Nash finally won the contract, there is no doubt that the future George IV was greatly influenced by Charles Cockerell's country home when it came to planning his infinitely more ornate palace by the sea.

It is the great bulbous onion dome that sets the tone at Sezincote, but the theme is carried through enthusiastically to the deep oriental cornice round the roof of

RIGHT *Inspired by Eastern architecture, Sezincote House in turn inspired the Prince Regent to build Brighton Pavilion in oriental style.*

BELOW *Sir Charles Cockerell perpetuated his love affair with India at Sezincote after retiring from the East India Company.*

BELOW *Sezincote's water garden includes an Indian-style water temple and shrine. Water is a key element in Mogul garden design.*

the house, the exotic semicircular curve of the orangery and, most of all, the water garden. Brahmin bulls, elephants, deities and any number of oriental decorative devices adorn this little landscaped valley, best viewed from Daniell's Indian bridge before you drop down to investigate its strange trees, temple, fountain, pools and winding stream. They say that even the orange tint of the main block of the house owes more to India than to the golden stone of this corner of the Cotswolds, since it was apparently stained to give it that special tone characteristic of the land in which its owner prospered.

What makes Sezincote so cheering to visit is the fact that the present owners continue to lavish time and money on the garden, massing the banks of the stream with perennial plants and shrubs. This could easily be a place of faded glory and lost dreams. Instead it is a continuing delight, very odd, a place apart.

Yet while Sezincote is unique, you do not have to travel very far to walk woodland paths equally influenced by the East. About as far to the northwest of Moreton-in-Marsh as Sezincote is to the southwest—little more than a mile, in fact—is the arboretum in the grounds of another golden house, Batsford Park. It was designed and planted around a hundred years ago by Lord Redesdale, whose approach to his retirement in rural England echoed that of Sir Charles Cockerell in that he, too, wished to surround himself with reminders of his years of pomp. In his case he took Japan as his theme, since he had been British Ambassador to Tokyo, and his woodlands are dotted with arresting images, such as a mighty bronze Buddha at the top of the hill, a graceful deer and a mythical creature down by the stream.

Even more captivating is a timber rest house, modelled on those built around the mountains of Japan for the use of travellers. The fact that this one is just a couple of minutes' walk from the mansion detracts nothing from its appeal, especially in late spring, when Japanese flowering cherries add to its air of otherworldliness, as do the multi-hued maples that glow with almost unreal intensity on sunny autumn days.

In Chipping Campden, a memorial garden commemorates another great orientalist, a son of that town who was known throughout the botanical world in the early years of this century as 'Chinese Wilson'. He left Campden at sixteen, and there is no evidence that he ever gave the place another thought, but one man who saw significance in the link was the furniture designer Sir Gordon Russell, who called in a noted landscape architect in Sir Peter Shepheard to draw up designs for a fine and formally symmetrical plot, displaying a small selection of the vast number of oriental plants Ernest Wilson introduced to the Western world. Wilson first visited China, for the seedsman and nursery owner James Harry Veitch, in 1899, when he was newly out of his studies at the Royal Botanic Gardens at Kew. Veitch was seeking someone to lead his expedition to China to search for his personal 'El Dorado', the Dove Tree, fabled through the botanical world but unknown in cultivation. It was three years before Wilson returned, with

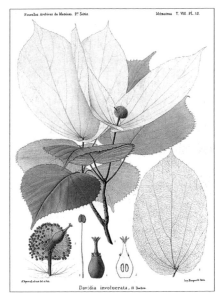

several thousand seeds, as well as tales of bubonic plague and being caught up in the Boxer Uprising and an account of trekking endlessly to the site of the only Dove Tree then known to him, only to find it had just been chopped down to help build a house. It was several weeks before he located more.

Chinese Wilson soon became the talk of the botanical and scientific world. But, most of all, he delivered the goods for those who employed him, and he brought back exotica by the thousand in three more expeditions to China and another to Japan, latterly on behalf of Harvard University's Arnold Arboretum in Massachusetts. Indeed, you will often hear transatlantic voices around his Campden memorial garden, and find they belong to Harvard men who know a great deal more about his story than do most of his fellow townsfolk. In fact the Americans' Arnold Arboretum played a prominent part in setting up the garden, and its director at that time, Peter Ashton, made it plain there were still healthy folk memories of him there. 'During the twenties Wilson gathered a considerable circle of American admirers,' he recalled at the time. 'They were spellbound by what one suspects was a carefully orchestrated air of British heart-of-oak taciturnity—punctuated,

ABOVE *This delicate botanical drawing illustrates the leaves and flowers of the fabled Dove Tree, which Ernest 'Chinese' Wilson eventually succeeded in tracking down in China. In full bloom the tree looks as though its boughs are thronged with roosting doves.*

ABOVE *Quite at odds with the lush, verdant countryside around Blockley is the minimalist Japanese dry garden,* Amai Yume Tein, *or Garden of Sweet Dreams, which is designed to induce tranquil contemplation.*

on favoured occasions, by tantalising allusions to hair-raising experiences which were never fully recounted.'

Tim Brown of Blockley is no Chinese Wilson, but for oriental authenticity you would have to travel a good many thousand miles east to equal his *Amai Yume Tein*, his Garden of Sweet Dreams. On the road to Chipping Campden, almost opposite St George's Hall and the village school—as English a prospect as you could find in the hills—his cottage hides a unique example of a Japanese dry landscape garden, without a grain of soil to be seen. Just twenty-seven yards square and bounded by bamboo fencing and a wall, it is crossed by right-angled paths of Welsh slate enclosing five rectangular beds of granite gravel, each one raked inch-perfect in precise patterns.

Six plants adorn his plot, including two black bamboos, a sinuous juniper and a cotoneaster, its red berries one of the garden's few concessions to primary colours. Tim Brown runs his own Japanese garden company from his home, and his knowledge of the traditions of the art form is thorough, since he worked for a year with experts on Shikoku Island. As for calling his plot the Garden of Sweet Dreams, he explains, 'It is there to stimulate the imagination. You sit on the ledge, and you and the garden connect together.' Increasing numbers of us are now able to do this, since he has taken to opening for the National Gardens Scheme on several summer Sundays, and will always welcome callers by appointment.

QUIET CORNERS AND ROWDY RACES

Visitors more generally in Blockley are another matter, for this is the Garbo of Cotswold villages, the one that always wants to be alone. There is nowhere more beautiful in the hills, and nowhere so different, either, with its pre-Industrial Revolution silk mills long softened into gracious homes. No wonder those who live here are happy to keep themselves to themselves, and reason is on their side when they argue that a combination of a narrow main street, lack of parking space, precipitous lanes and a dearth of teashops make the village ill-equipped to withstand a tourist invasion. I once heard a local councillor rejoicing that his village had not become 'a second Broadway or Bourton-on-the-Water', and the fate of those two communities is never far from the minds of people determined to resist the siren song of tourism. Even those who benefit most from outsiders looking in, the hotels and guesthouses, are more than satisfied with Blockley's image as the best-kept secret in the Cotswolds.

The fact that it is often referred to as such by travel writers with a readership of millions is perhaps symbolic, for the fact is that Blockley *has* been discovered by outsiders, and shaped by them for generations. By now it might have been a remote and decaying textile village if it had not just happened to be quite stunningly beautiful, and the commuters and weekenders and rich retirees had not recognised the potential of the redundant silk mills on their quiet ponds, and the golden cottages with their gardens cascading down to the streams. Dovedale, Malvern Mill, Mill Dene, the Old Silk Mill, Mill Close, Snugborough, Colebrook: wonderfully evocative names, and it is geography, more than any other factor, that has kept obtrusive commercialisation at bay.

A 19th-century Blockley figure who did become a celebrity was the prophetess Joanna Southcott, who lived in Rock Cottage in the High Street from 1804 to 1814. Her reputation was worldwide, and among those who enquired after her in the Rock Cottage years was the future George IV, then preoccupied with the North Cotswolds because of Sezincote. The last traces of the Southcottian sect survive today primarily in New Zealand, but she was a charismatic figure, and in her lifetime the Established Church was concerned about her influence. At the age of sixty-three she was reputed to have given birth to Shiloh, the holy child, though firm evidence was hard to come by. Joanna apparently died in childbirth, and the new messiah was borne up to heaven before anyone could set eyes on him. Not surprisingly, her neighbours in Blockley were somewhat spooked by all of

THE COTSWOLD SILK TRADE

ABOVE *A former silk mill in Blockley has now been transformed into a family home.*

ENGLAND ISN'T the first place that springs to mind when one thinks of silk-making. China and Thailand, of course, and India maybe, but in fact the Cotswolds played host to a thriving silk industry for the best part of two centuries. In Gloucester, imported raw silk was 'throwsted', or spun into thread, as early as 1640, and the trade duly spread through the region, becoming centred on the town of Blockley.

Silk was being throwsted in Blockley at the turn of the 18th century, and by 1824 Blockley's eight mills employed some 300 women and children (some as young as five). To these workers fell the task of twisting into workable thread the lustrous filaments of raw silk produced from the cocoon of the silkworm. From Blockley, spun thread was transported to Coventry, where a silk-manufacturing industry existed.

As the 19th century progressed, Blockley's fortunes ebbed and flowed. In 1848 there were still six operational mills, but by 1876 this figure had halved.

ABOVE *A 19th-century illustration shows the three stages of the life of the silkworm: caterpillar, silken cocoon and moth. Early attempts to farm silkworms in this country failed, so raw silk was imported.*

Indeed, local records make mention, in 1861, of a parish meeting convened to discuss ways in which to raise money to help the unemployed. Ultimately, the pressure brought to bear by the buoyant French silk trade, coupled with some fairly unkind legislation from Westminster, sounded the death knell of the silk trade in the Cotswolds. By the turn of this century, it was all but a memory.

RIGHT *Tetbury hosts the only Woolsack Races in the world. The strenuous competitions attract contestants from all over the country.*

this, and for generations—well into this century—her cottage was felt to have a jinx about it. It eventually burned down and stood for years as a ruin until comparatively recent times, when a young architect plucked up the courage to rebuild it.

The late May bank holiday dawns cloudy, but that will doubtless please contestants in this afternoon's Woolsack Races in Tetbury; you do not need the sun on a back already burdened by a sack weighing sixty pounds. The 'ancient Woolsack Races', I see the local press calls them once again, and I suppose if you are a twenty-one-year-old reporter the year 1972, when all this rigmarole began, is quite ancient enough. The fact is, of course, that our forefathers were nowhere near stupid enough to run up and down Gumstool Hill lugging the equivalent of more than half a sack of coal. But Woolsack Day, a charity fund-raiser that reminds Tetbury's neighbouring communities that there is more to the town than antiques shops, at least hints at the glory years of the wool trade, which in this case were in the 17th and 18th centuries.

The course over Gumstool Hill, which has a gradient of one in four at its steepest, lies between the Crown and Royal Oak pubs, some 280 yards apart, and there are teams of four competitors who aim to relay the sack up and down the hill in the quickest time. The men's record is just under three and a half minutes, while the best women's and youths' teams, with lighter sacks, go at around three minutes fifty seconds and three minutes twenty respectively. The town's rugby club usually fares well, but this year there is formidable opposition from the North in the form of a team of coalsack-carrying champs from near Huddersfield. Not all competitors take the challenge so seriously. A couple of years ago, a team calling themselves the Flying Elvises were not helped by the fact that their heads were encased in rubber masks of the king of rock'n'roll. Even the best teams often hide behind jokey names such as the Awesome Foursome…It is that kind of an afternoon.

Neither is it simply a time for racing. These days, the day-long programme offers a children's funfair in the Chipping (marketplace), exhibitions, morris men, Punch and Judy, street entertainers, handbell ringers and a brass band. Even Lady Godiva seems to have hijacked the celebrations with her white horse, cascading locks and very un-11th-century nylon tights.

If this is known as making your own entertainment, it is a tradition long associated with this corner of Tetbury, though not always in so innocent a form. There was certainly little clean-cut fun in bull-baiting, but as recently as a century ago the spot in the middle of the Chipping where this barbaric pastime took place was still known and pointed out. In early court-leet documents in Tetbury was the order that 'no bull shall be killed before baited': the vigorous exercise of the ordeal was apparently believed to make the meat more tender.

If there was a saving grace in old Tetburians' cruelty, it perhaps lay in the fact that they did not reserve it exclusively for dumb animals. The repair of a pillory and stocks was a recurring preoccupation of the court-leet throughout the prosperous 17th and 18th centuries, and the need to mend the whipping post is

THE STRONG ARM OF THE LAW

JUDICIAL PUNISHMENT in medieval England was usually crude and cruel—as was the test to discover guilt or innocence. Ordeal by fire, for example, required the accused to grasp a red-hot iron: if, after three days, blisters had bubbled up, he was deemed guilty. Ordeal by water was often reserved for alleged witches, who were tied up and thrown into a river or pond. If they floated, the verdict was guilty; if they sank—and sometimes drowned—they were innocent.

Although some of the more barbaric punishments were gradually phased out, some harsh and humiliating practices continued into the 19th century.

BELOW *Wrongdoers in Stow-on-the-Wold would have been locked into these stocks for a couple of days, to be jeered at by the townsfolk.*

In villages, minor offenders were locked into the pillory and stocks—which can still be seen at Stow-on-the-Wold—and had to endure volleys of jeers and rotten vegetables. 'Scolds', or nagging wives, were strapped to a ducking stool and dunked in the local pond to cool off. For capital offences, execution by hanging or beheading was the staple. Methods of extracting confessions included the grim 'Scavenger's Daughter'—an iron brace that forced the head and knees towards each other. Or there was 'pressing': the accused was stretched out on his back and a tray with weights placed on his chest and abdomen. More weights were added until his resolve—or his rib cage—caved in. Perhaps the ultimate deterrent was hanging, drawing and quartering: the guilty were first hanged until they choked, but not quite to death; then taken down and drawn, or disembowelled; and finally quartered, with their bodies wrenched into four parts.

ABOVE *The cruel practice of ducking was inflicted on sharp-tongued women, or 'scolds', to humiliate them into silence.*

noted as late as 1796. As for the ducking stool, it was in a pond at the foot of Gumstool Hill, on or close to the site now occupied by the cattle-market pens. The punishment was originally aimed at swindling traders: light measures and faulty wares were one of the banes of the town's commercial life. After a time, however, the practice turned into the institutionalised bullying of old women regarded as scolds, who would be wheeled to the middle of the pond before being tipped into its filthy depths and hauled out with ropes.

For today's woolsack racers the physical pain of the run must exceed that of a ducking a dozen times over; but at least they are cheered every step of the way, and there is a pint or two and great bonhomie at the end. Indeed, there we must leave them with their teammates, families, friends and beer glasses, before the running of the finals at five o'clock, for we must be up to Cooper's Hill for the evening's cheese-rolling. Forget about humping sacks up slopes like house roofs: what we are going to see now really is a dangerous sport.

Cooper's Hill is one of the landmarks of the Cotswold scarp, and what makes it stand out is the steep, straight swath of grassland sweeping from top to bottom of its wooded slopes. The cheese-rolling at Cooper's Hill on the evening of the last Monday in May is one of the best known of Cotswold customs, right up there with the clypping of Painswick Church or the well-dressing at Bisley. Holding hands and strewing flowers, however, this is not. Rather, it is rustic sport at its most bucolic as hordes of likely lads—and lasses, too, in a race of their own—stream and tumble down that dizzying slope in pursuit of a hefty wooden disc said to resemble a Double Gloucester cheese. Catch the cheese and you win the race; catch your foot in a divot and you break your leg. The ground rules are well understood, and there is never an ambulance too far away if it is your lot to spend the next three weeks in the Gloucestershire Royal. If we forced dumb creatures to do it, tales of our inhumanity would spread like anthrax through the civilised world. It is a spectacle that makes the shin-kicking at Dover's Games in Chipping Campden a few days later seem like a vicarage tea party, or at least what we imagined vicarage tea parties to be before the novels of Joanna Trollope shattered yet another illusion.

In a way, the rusticity is deceptive, for most of the contestants are not country swains and maids but suburban youngsters from the housing estates of Brockworth in the vale below. Some of them are so tough that their feats are more often recounted in the *Citizen*'s magistrate's court reports than on the sports pages, and one year the champ contrived to appear in both sections of the paper on the same day.

A lively night, the Cooper's Hill cheese-rolling, and one not for the faint-hearted, whether competitor or spectator. You can learn some interesting new words, too, as shoulders, knees and heads whump into the turf. But if your intent is to commune with nature, there are fine walks to be had up Cooper's Hill, through Brockworth Wood's beeches towards Cranham, and those who fear for our wild flowers should take comfort from Cranham Common, where more than 140 different varieties have been discovered in recent years.

OPPOSITE *Fearless locals risk life and limb to hurtle down Cooper's Hill in pursuit of a rolling wooden 'cheese'.*

WILD FLOWERS OF THE COTSWOLDS

LEFT *Bluebells carpet the floor of a coppiced woodland, while ransoms (wild garlic) fill the air with their rich scent.*

ABOVE *Early purple orchids in flower at Minchinhampton Common in the Cotswolds, a flower-rich area of limestone grassland.*

COTSWOLD WILD FLOWERS seem partial to deserted and derelict locations—Iron Age forts and disused gravel pits alike. Roadside verges are dotted with field scabious, meadow cranesbill and billowing bird's-foot trefoil. Abandoned quarries or railway cuttings harbour limestone fern and Cotswold penny-cress. And near ghostly mills and dyeworks once-valued plants now serve only as reminders of the region's long-lost cloth-making heyday: the prickly clothier's teasel and, valued for their precious colours, dyer's greenweed and woad.

The habitats of Cotswold wild flowers can be divided into wetland, woodland and grassland. In marshy settings, you might find such species as ragged robin, marsh marigolds and southern marsh orchids; and yellow flags thrive along river banks. As for the woodlands, covering about 6 per cent of the Cotswold countryside, they abound in common bluebells and violets, of course, as well as pungent wild garlic and deadly nightshade. But they also offer sanctuary to less familiar species such as stinking hellebore and the extremely rare alpine woundwort.

The most distinctive of the Cotswold habitats are the limestone grasslands. Each site is likely to contain at least 100 species of wild flowers and grasses; these in turn support a wealth of insect life. Thin though the soil is here, the wild flowers nurtured by it emerge somehow as glamorous showpieces: the early purple orchid, for instance (once prized as an aphrodisiac), growing on commons in the area, or the charming pasque flower, a type of anemone so rare now that it is listed as a protected species—watch in spring, when its delicate tulip-shaped buds sprout resplendent purple petals and yellow stamens.

The wild flowers' future has long been under threat. Modern intensive farming

LEFT *The pasque flower takes its name from the Old French word for Easter, which is when it blooms.*

ploughs up their foothold, and village gentrification has tended to spurn them in favour of domesticated roses and tulips. But some protection is extended by conservation agencies such as English Nature. They strive to keep the fleawort flourishing in fallow fields, saxifrage and feather-moss on dry-stone walls, celandine alongside hedgerows, and even humble poppies in the cornfields.

BELOW *The Cotswolds' wealth of wild flowers in turn supports a range of insects, including the rare chalkhill blue butterfly.*

THE COTSWOLD OLIMPICKS

Shakespeare never seems far away from Chipping Campden. The Gloucestershire County Players' open-air performance in Hidcote Manor Garden in early July can be any of the classics these days, but for years they rarely strayed far from the Bard, and never was the spectacle more moving than when some rustic shepherd or other was lolloping around under the spotlight to the wan sound of pipes and tabors while out beyond the trees and the midges the ewes were calling their young back to them on the twilit hillsides. The sheep round here in Shakespeare's day would have been the great woolly Cotswold Lions, so it is fanciful to imagine that today's sleek flocks are direct descendants of those he knew, but know these hills he most certainly did, and there are evenings when 400 years of country life seem really no time at all.

The Hidcote play is still a month away, however, and tonight, the first Friday in June, Campden townsfolk are deep in another tradition that originated in Shakespeare's time: the Cotswold Olimpicks. The man behind it all was Robert Dover, a Gloucestershire lawyer and so dedicated a traditionalist and Royalist that in 1612 he wore an old suit and plumed hat that had belonged to James I to preside over the first games on the hill that now bears his name. In his day the main attractions were cudgel-playing, pitching the bar, skittling, leaping, wrestling, cock-fighting, shin-kicking, backswords and coursing hares with hounds. Nowadays it is an offbeat evening of old sports and obstacle races and tugs of war, a mix of Merrie England and *It's a Knockout*, with the strains of morris-dance music, pipes and drums and fairground organs never far away. The boom of a cannon sets the night under way, as it did in 1612, and after the final trophy has been contested and the last skyrocket has died in the sky, a torchlit procession wends its way down the by-now dewy slope for more parading and country dancing in the floodlit town square. Tomorrow will follow the Scuttlebrook Wake, a far more recognisable and predictable town fête, with a fancy-dress parade, the crowning of the wake queen and a great deal more dancing and music.

Dover's Games have come and gone, but are now here to stay. The early days brought royal patronage as well as discarded items from the King's wardrobe, for the dashing Prince Rupert, nephew of Charles I, was an enthusiastic visitor. In 1636 some of the leading poets of the day put together a garland of verses, *Annalia Dubrensia*, to celebrate Dover and his Olimpicks, and the frontispiece of that book is an amazing fragment of history, showing Robert in the King's old clothes astride his famous white horse, the wooden castle around which the early games were played, dancing maidens, shin-kicking swains and much else besides.

BELOW *A bonfire, fireworks and torchlit procession bring the Cotswolds' very own Olimpick Games to a spectacular close.*

ABOVE *The frontispiece of* Annalia Dubrensia, *showing Robert Dover astride his horse in the foreground, and assorted competitors in his Olimpick Games.*

Eight years on, in 1644, the Puritans put a stop to the fun, and Dover died in 1652, but there must have been great rejoicing on the hill in the Restoration year of 1660.

What then followed was the usual sad story of high days and holidays in the 17th, 18th and 19th centuries. Wherever there are men pitting their strength and their racehorses against each other, there are others who will lay money on the outcome, and over the years the games became a magnet for the most feckless of Midlands society, with drunkenness, fist fights, robberies and even killings growing increasingly the norm. Rather more innocently, but still yobbishly, the lads would hoot and jeer when women raced for a smock or shift held high on a pole.

As early as 1736 a minister at Stow-on-the-Wold was voicing his concern about the games. His warning went unheeded for 100 years or more until eventually the goings-on came to be seen as intolerably out of step with Victorian tastes. The last of the old games was held in 1852, though the following day's wake, with its emphasis on more innocent entertainments for children, survived the purge. This was not the first time the Temperance and Sunday-school movements triumphed

SCHOOL ON SUNDAYS

LEFT *Thomas Herbert Maguire's (slightly damaged) painting shows Robert Raikes with pioneering Sunday-school pupils.*

EDUCATION FOR ALL is a given in Britain today, but 200 years ago working-class children spent their weekdays at work, and it was only on Sundays that some managed to attend school. Then, in 1780, Gloucestershire newspaper-owner Robert Raikes transformed Sunday schools into a widespread movement which gave hundreds of children the opportunity to escape illiteracy.

Raikes was a fervent campaigner for prison reform, and considered poverty to be conducive to vice. His aim was to provide basic literacy skills in order to reduce crime. The Sunday schools were popular with everyone: they didn't take the children away from their factory jobs, they improved their chances in life and kept them off the streets, and statistics suggest that there was, as Raikes had predicted, a reduction in the crime rate.

But with the growth of evangelism in the 19th century, many Sunday schools moved away from Raikes's original aim of educating the masses. The pupils often learned more about fire and brimstone than the alphabet; the schools' association with the puritanical Temperance movement gave them a severe image that was off-putting to the young, and membership declined.

Today, Sunday schools are run by churches for Bible study and as social groups, but as church attendance declines so fewer parents encourage their children to join in. What was once a hugely popular movement is now more often considered a relic of earlier generations.

over the dying vestiges of Merrie England which we, were we able to travel back in time, would doubtless find not very merrie at all.

It was 1951 and the Festival of Britain that saw the one-off revival of the games after ninety-nine years. A dozen years later there was another try, and this time it led to the formation in 1965 of the Robert Dover's Games Society and the coming together of a group of people with the will and enthusiasm to set the venture on a firm footing. Anyone who tries to put a stop to today's Cotswold Olimpicks can expect a kick in both shins and a backsword across the head for his pains.

STINCHCOMBE REVISITED

If it is rose time it must be Stinchcombe, for the opening of the grounds of Stancombe Park in mid-June is one of the highlights of the gardens-to-visit season. Stinchcombe, clinging to the Cotswold scarp overlooking the Vale of Berkeley, is a comfortably off village that in the past has been home to more-than-comfortably-off residents of the panache of the novelist Evelyn Waugh and Maxwell Joseph, the millionaire hotelier. Stinchcombe has a hill, one of the most prominent on the escarpment, a lonely place of beech woods and scrambly walks. The

ABOVE *In a part of the country blessed with an abundance of great gardens, Stancombe Park, with its glorious roses, is one of the finest.*

village also boasts St Cyr's Church, rebuilt in the 1850s but with a Perpendicular tower and a banquet of table tombs in its graveyard, and there are some attractive old cottages where the Cotswolds meet the vale. It is fair to say, however, that in most people's eyes it is a community of big, impressive houses and gardens—the Manor, now a nursing home, Melksham Court, Piers Court, Drakestone, the Old Vicarage—and, foremost in terms of its grounds, the mansion to which we are heading now, Stancombe Park.

Round Stinchcombe way they will tell you these gardens were laid out by Capability Brown and were the original 'Brideshead' of Evelyn Waugh's novel. Well, up to a point. The novelist was certainly living at Piers Court, just down the road, from the mid-1930s to the mid-1950s, and the scene from Stancombe's temple over the lake is described with some accuracy in *Brideshead Revisited*. As for Capability Brown, however, what can be said for certain is that the garden was created a century or so after his time. In terms of enhancing the contours of the landscape—his true speciality—Capability (Lancelot, to his friends) would anyway have been utterly redundant at Stancombe Park, for nature has worked to perfection in this tucked-away little valley at the foot of Stinchcombe Hill.

Today the names that matter Stancombe way are Gerda and the late Basil Barlow, who moved in in the early 1960s, and Kenneth Brown, gardener there for more than four decades. It was the Barlows' aim to build up a 300-acre farm and breathe new life into gardens of around twenty acres, and in the years since her arrival the Austrian-born Mrs B. has established herself as a gardener of a very high order. There are two gardens in one: an upland section with views over

a meadow valley to the pretty classical house; and then, down a winding path especially designed to stir the imagination, the romantic lakeside pleasure grounds of follies and tunnels and grottoes far below. This was Waugh's little bit of 'Brideshead'—and a little bit of paradise on earth, so it is said, for the Reverend David Edwards, a Victorian vicar of North Nibley. The story is that he married the rich but broad-of-beam owner of Stancombe and created this extraordinary love nest for his Gypsy girlfriend, who could pass through narrow alleyways and bowers to reach the parts the bulky Mrs Purnell-Edwards could not.

The garden is full of surprises and delights, and as near as most of us will come to escapism in a garden. Amid the quirky pagodas and summerhouses is an ice house entered through an arch made from the bones of a whale, a not uncommon device.

In the lake gardens the Barlows concentrated on restoration, but on the upland site they and Kenneth Brown, their very own 'Capability', swept away vestiges of fussy Victorian and Edwardian taste to create a spacious lawned area punctuated by new borders in subtle colour combinations, old roses, shrubs and a fast-maturing pleached-lime walk. In the borders, where colour schemes range from blues and

whites into lime greens and reds, the backbone of the display is a series of low yew and boxes in scrolls; in this English country garden, they reflect Mrs Barlow's admiration for her native Austrian baroque.

There are still many secrets to be revealed at Stancombe, and the frequency with which fragments of mosaic are found suggests that an eventual excavation of the Roman villa in neighbouring woods would prove fruitful.

Stinchcombe's up-market image is a world away from that of its nearest neighbour, the prettily situated but decidedly down-to-earth community of Dursley. The tweedily bohemian novelist Evelyn Waugh must have cut a quaint figure when he descended, as he occasionally did, on the town's fleapit picture house. Waugh Senior's most famous visit to the picture palace was the day he was rudely torn away from his fix of Hollywood escapism to be told that his fifteen-year-old son Auberon was to be found blind drunk and singing selections from Gilbert and Sullivan at Stroud police station after having been taken off a train, all as a result of purloining a bottle of pater's Booth's gin to fortify him on a trip to London. Next day the youth was fined ten shillings by Stroud magistrates.

This incident was one way in which the Waugh family made its mark on the South Cotswold community during its years at Stinchcombe. There were other more pleasant occasions, not least the village garden parties held in the grounds of Piers Court, at which the formidable Evelyn is most often remembered as a cheerful and considerate host. In many respects, the Gloucestershire years were not kind to him. It was in Stinchcombe that he first experienced the mental disturbances that preceded the hallucinations he suffered on a voyage to Ceylon, a harrowing incident recounted in his book *The Ordeal of Gilbert Pinfold*.

Perhaps there really is something odd in the air of that ancient hillside settlement. Not long ago I was talking to a very sane and down-to-earth chap in his later years, who had also lived in one of that cluster of Stinchcombe mansions. 'I had to get out in the end,' he explained in a genial, matter-of-fact way. 'It was the piano in the sitting room. Sometimes it would play on its own all night.'

With labour-saving and economical entertainment like this at his disposal in the village, I sometimes wonder why Evelyn Waugh ever felt the need to drive down to the pictures in Dursley for his evening's pleasures.

CHAPTER FOUR

SUMMER MADNESS

JULY AT KELMSCOT, just over the Oxfordshire border from the little Gloucestershire town of Lechlade, and could there be the spirit of a summer long past in the flicker of breeze that ripples over the water meadows? If you are of romantic bent, perhaps there could, for in this month in 1871 the relationship between Dante Gabriel Rossetti and Jane, the wife of his once-close friend William Morris, was at its passionate height.

Kelmscott Manor (with two 't's, unlike the village) was the country home of Morris—designer, writer, painter and socialist visionary—from 1871 until his death at the age of sixty-two in 1896, and it was from this 'old house by the Thames' that

RIGHT *William Morris adored his 'old house by the Thames'. Under his ownership, Kelmscott Manor became a gathering place for artists, craftsmen and intellectuals. Admirers of Morris continue to flock there today.*

he wrote his *News from Nowhere*. That the book is subtitled *An Epoch of Rest*, with a frontispiece depicting a scene of age-old tranquillity, reflects more on the family's later years there; while Rossetti was around the house at the same time as the human dynamo Morris, known to his friends as Topsy, peace and ease were in short supply.

Today, Kelmscott Manor can be visited on summer Wednesdays and some week-ends, and it is no fault of its Tudor stone and timbers, or the well-meaning people who administer it, that it tells a rather dry, worthy tale of Arts and Crafts good citizenship and rectitude. When the last surviving member of the triangle still lived there, Kelmscott was a house in which indeed all passion had been spent. Jane Morris stayed on in the manor until she died in 1914, a grey-haired widow surrounded by her dutiful daughters and nursemaids, and by the end of her life she was every inch the lady of the manor. She gave the village a group of cottages designed by Philip Webb in memory of her husband, one of them carrying a carving of the great man against a background of some of the outbuildings of his home. The village hall, built in the early 1930s, is another memorial to the Morris legacy.

But on days like this, in which the dust hangs lazily in the shafts of sunlight penetrating the manor's dim rooms, it is more alluring by far to look back on the Morrises' first three years at the manor, from 1871 to 1874, when they shared the lease of the property with Rossetti, one of the founders of the Pre-Raphaelite Brotherhood of painters. Morris was profoundly influenced by that circle, but what the two men had in common, everything else stripped aside, was love for the same woman, the Janey Burden who became Mrs Jane Morris but who is remem-bered, above all, as one of Rossetti's two most hauntingly beautiful models. Why Morris countenanced their all living together in the first place is almost beyond comprehension—although in fact it was seldom a case of living together literally, since he soon found it intolerable to stay under the same roof as his rival in love for more than the occasional weekend.

Perhaps it was a very civilised, bohemian Victorian way of squaring the eternal triangle; the alternative, when the three were in London, was a very open and undisguised affair between Janey and Gabriel, which left their circle viewing poor old Topsy Morris's private life with almost equal measures of pity and contempt. At Kelmscott Manor, all was at least out of sight of literary and artistic London—though not of the townsfolk of Lechlade, who soon caught a whiff of what was going on in the big house, and openly stopped and stared as these outlandish and fantastically dressed figures from another planet, rich enough to rent the manor at sixty pounds a year, strolled languidly along the High Street taking the air.

Rossetti had been at the heart of the Morrises' relationship from the start. In fact he had introduced Jane to William, having met her in a theatre in Oxford in 1857 and been taken instantly by that pale face, long, fine neck and thick, crinkly hair. As it happened, he was already in love with one of his models, Lizzie Siddal, whose more conventional English-rose beauty is encapsulated in such paintings as *Ophelia* and *Beata Beatrice*. But it is said that in his desperation to stay close to this new stunner, Janey Burden, the Oxford stablehand's daughter, he did all

ABOVE *William Morris, visionary creator but hapless victim of a doomed marriage.*

ABOVE *Janey Burden, whose haunting beauty stares out from so many of Rossetti's paintings.*

ABOVE *Dante Gabriel Rossetti, the third member of the infamous love triangle.*

in his power to encourage the donnish William Morris to woo and marry her. This happened in 1859, when William was twenty-five and Janey just eighteen. Rossetti married Lizzie Siddal the following year, but two years after that she committed suicide through an overdose of laudanum, a sensitive woman apparently driven to despair by being viewed as no more than a beautiful butterfly by all the clever young men around her.

Topsy Morris, too, tended to worship his new wife as a remote and romanticised icon, finding it easy to idealise her in paintings and verse as Guenevere or Iseult, but impossible to treat her in real life as the ordinary girl she was. To add to the image, she adopted in life the melancholy role in which Morris and the Pre-Raphaelites cast her in their verses and paintings. She became increasingly moody and withdrawn, suffering from any number of maladies, real or imaginary. The one beacon of hope and passion in her life was her relationship with Rossetti, and in that first year in the Cotswolds, the summer of 1871, it blossomed.

RIGHT *Kelmscott Manor's wood-panelled drawing room. The comfortable armchairs are covered with a fabric of Morris's own design.*

It is possible that when William Morris first signed the joint tenancy with Rossetti, he envisaged some kind of early time-share arrangement, the kind of agreement in which one party would be there only if the other was not. Rossetti, however, saw his part of the tenancy as a good reason to desert London for the summer, call in the builders and decorators to renovate his studio in Chelsea and take root at Kelmscott. Morris's first answer to this was to book himself on one of the fortnightly Danish mail boats that sailed to Iceland and spend the summer there pursuing his interest in the Icelandic language and the great Scandinavian sagas and legends.

A week after he left, Gabriel Rossetti moved in, beginning the first and most memorable of several long periods in which he lived under the same roof as Jane

Morris. This was the happiest time of his life, a secluded summer of bliss with the love of his life. They walked for miles in the water meadows beside the Thames, painted and posed, decorated and furnished the house, played with the two little Morris daughters on the nanny's day off, and ensured that Topsy's return would be an unhappy one by acquiring three dogs. If there was one thing William Morris detested, it was dogs around the house.

The parched floodlands of the east Cotswolds became the setting for new sonnets to be added to Gabriel's collection *The House of Life*, and some of them left little to the imagination:

> *Her arms lie open, throbbing with their throng*
> *of confluent pulses, bare and fair and strong*
> *And her deep freighted lips expect me now*
> *Amid the clustering hair that shrines the brow*
> *Five kisses broad, her neck ten kisses long.*

Gabriel and Janey awoke from their summer dream when William Morris returned home from his northern saga. Whatever chill there was in Iceland, the temperature at Kelmscott was several degrees lower, and Morris visited there briefly just twice before taking his family back to London. Rossetti stayed on until October, by which time the meadows he had wandered with his love were deep in water, and he could walk only the 'stubble fields and queer byways' around Lechlade. The clearly doomed romance was to throw Rossetti into increasingly obvious mental strife. His last Kelmscott year was 1874, when Morris took his wife away to Belgium, doubtless to put space between her and her lover. By now their circle was talking not so much about their romance as of Gabriel's ever more erratic behaviour. One day he was walking beside the Thames at Lechlade with his doctor when he believed he had been insulted by a party of local anglers. He spun round and laid into them with abuse, and before he knew it, the story was all over the little town.

Gossip had never been far beneath the surface. Now it rose to a crescendo, and Rossetti left Kelmscott for good. After that, local people had two decades in which to grow used to Mr and Mrs Morris as increasingly distinguished and dignified weekenders at the manor house, and a further eighteen years of Mrs Morris and her household, the manor by now her personal property, after that. But memories of those stormy, passionate summers of the early 1870s lived on in Lechlade until well into the first half of this century, and in folk memory for even longer than that.

JAY AND ADRIAN

A letter from Jay Stroud in Houston, Texas. His Stroudwater Scarlet jacket is ready at last. I have no idea how he got hold of a jacket length on his last visit; I have lived here the best part of twenty years and never seen a scrap of the stuff, but that is American resourcefulness for you. He is obviously thrilled with his purchase.

RIGHT *This late 18th-century depiction of Wallbridge in the Stroud valleys shows the famous Stroudwater Scarlet stretched out to dry in the fields beyond the mill.*

ABOVE *Tools of Stroud's cloth trade. The town's soft river water helps the fabric take up the vivid scarlet dye, and teasels are used to raise the nap.*

Scarlet for guardsmen's uniforms was by far the best-known product of the 150 textile mills that hummed and rattled in the Stroud valleys in the 1820s, and when you see red on the town's former coat of arms, that is what it signifies. Since then the woollen industry here has dwindled, though not to the point of extinction, and since the army is also in numerical retreat, no Scarlet is currently being made in Stroud. It is not impossible that it will be again, should the demand be there, for the teasel-based technology is still in the town and being put to good use with the production of the highest-quality green baize for billiard tables and yellow for championship tennis balls. The company best known for these exquisite napped felts, Winterbotham, Strachan and Playne of Cam and Lodgemoor Mills, has been taken over in recent times by the Americans Milliken, but the old names survive in Strachan's billiard baize and Playne's tennis-ball material. If Jay Stroud has his way, the name of Stroudwater Scarlet will also be echoing round the world again before long.

Jay and Sue Stroud, now retired after a hard-working life, are two of those rare people you meet who become passionately involved in something entirely beyond the confines of their life through some odd quirk of fate—in their case, the coincidence of their name. I first heard from them out of the blue in the early 1980s, a brief letter saying they were called Stroud, and could I tell them anything about their namesake town? In normal circumstances, I suppose I would have sent them a town guide, but the day after the letter arrived it snowed, the kind of snow that had even my neighbour John Ballinger giving up on his shovelling after ten minutes, and I put some of my unexpected day off to good use by writing to tell Jay and Sue about the scene from the window, what a funny old place Stroud was, and I cannot recall what else. The result was that they took to us, and we took to them on the two visits they have made so far.

I am less welcoming, however, to the quirky Adrian. I see him toiling up Stroud High Street and duck down the alleyway to the mellow obscurity of Mills Café. What a boon these little off-street courtyards are when people like him are around. I met him once in the Pelican, stronghold of all things Green and ruggedly individualistic for which Stroud is noted, and enjoyed his company first time around; but there are limits.

His conversational forte lies in comparing like with unlike: whether Rosemary Verey at Barnsley House is a more imaginative gardener than was old Major Lawrence Johnston at Hidcote Manor; which of Owlpen Manor or Woodchester Mansion, two large south Cotswold houses recently made more accessible to the public, is the more restful to visit; whether the monks at Prinknash do more for the public good than the pottery and bird park in their grounds; whether Catherine Parr, who lived and died at Sudeley Castle, was a more significant Tudor figure than the Bisley boy, the changeling child who was supposedly substituted for a deceased little princess and grew into a Virgin Queen who went bald, shunned marriage and claimed to have beating in her the heart of a king; and

THE LEGEND OF THE BISLEY BOY

WHEN, IN THE mid-19th century, builders were preparing the site for a new school next to Over Court Manor in Bisley, they unearthed a substantial stone coffin which was to fuel one of the most extraordinary legends of the age. Within the coffin lay the skeleton of a ten-year-old girl; her identity was a mystery.

The discovery fired the imagination of local churchman Canon Keble. Keble knew that Henry VIII's daughter, the future Queen Elizabeth I, had once visited Over Court, and he contrived to spin a fanciful yarn around her visit. Elizabeth, he claimed, succumbed to a fatal illness while staying at the manor. Her guardians so feared the King's wrath that they substituted the princess with a local child. But the only child bearing sufficient resemblance to the red-headed princess was male.

Most historians dismiss as ludicrous the idea that Elizabeth I might have been a man. But several factors make the legend of the Bisley boy seem tantalisingly plausible. It is known that

Elizabeth was possessed of immense strength of character—an attribute that her contemporaries considered markedly masculine; indeed, she even described herself as having 'the heart and stomach of a king'. In a thoroughly male-dominated world, Elizabeth enjoyed a remarkably successful reign as queen.

What is more, she refused ever to marry. And she went bald.

All of which makes it exceedingly tempting to believe in Keble's whimsical wheeze. And it has not gone unnoticed that living in Bisley today is a family whose members bear an uncanny resemblance to the 'Virgin Queen'.

ABOVE *Elizabeth I, aged about 12; her 'masculine' love of books is evident in the portrait.*

LEFT *The mysterious stone coffin found at Over Court Manor is now used as a humble flower trough.*

whether John Randle's Whittington Press, creator of exquisite hand-set books, the rarer ones of which are now much sought after by collectors, is a more interesting small business than Minola over at Filkins, who oak-smoke fish, game, poultry and a great deal more besides.

We pass on to who is number one among the Stroud valleys' best-known writers—Laurie Lee, Jilly Cooper, the Reverend Wilbert Awdry or Sue Limb? You would have to travel a very long way to stumble upon such a disparate bunch of superstar authors in and around the same small town, but any refusal to compare and contrast, say, Gordon the Big Engine with Laurie Lee's sister Doth in *Cider with Rosie* is certain to offend.

When Laurie Lee was eighty, what used to be called Fleet Street beat a path to his door. (At least, he was thought to be eighty, but apparently he had no idea of his exact date of birth.) He seemed to be feeding all the writers the same story, and you could not pick up a newspaper without reading about his sitting outside the Woolpack pub in Slad and being approached by two Americans who asked him, 'Can you show us the way to Laurie Lee's grave?'

I do not blame whoever it was for making the mistake. The world of *Cider with Rosie* seems a long time ago—indeed it *is* a long time ago. After all, the first scene of the book, the carrier's cart dropping three-year-old Loll off into the buzzing jungle of the roadside verge on his family's arrival in Slad, is set in 1917. And Americans did not expect Laurie Lee to sit, on cue, in the heart of the village he had made famous throughout the English-speaking world. You did not stumble on John Steinbeck in Salinas.

Prominent figures must sometimes wonder how they will fare at the hands of their obituarists, but there could have been no such nagging doubts for Laurie Lee. On the evidence of his birthday eulogies he knew exactly how he would be remembered, and it could scarcely have been with more affection. Yet now he has gone, that key childhood book and a handful of volumes of autobiography and collections of travel pieces have left me thirsting for more. Few writers of his brilliance and so long a career can have left quite so modest a canon of work.

ARTS AND CRAFTS

Princess Anne walks by in a baseball cap, green sweatshirt, jeans and dark glasses, a bull terrier slobbering at her heels. This is Gatcombe Park in August. It used to be Badminton where you watched the royals taking it easy in horsy company, but it was always a tweedy, country-weekend kind of relaxation, all Jaeger and Windsmoor; the late Duke of Beaufort was no great man for baseball caps and jeans. As for the princess in her funky gear, it must be said that her primary reason for decking herself out thus is to draw attention to her new line in Gatcombe Park merchandise. Somebody says her teenage children Peter and Zara are similarly

ABOVE Cider with Rosie author Laurie Lee (on the left) was often to be found enjoying a pint at his local in Slad.

OPPOSITE The village of Slad nestles in a quiet Gloucestershire valley, surrounded by the lush green fields that Laurie Lee and the 'Rosie' of his youth once walked.

BELOW *A relaxed Princess Anne proudly sports her own brand of Gatcombe Park casual clothing.*

decked out, as well as her husband Commodore Tim Laurence. Since, at one stage, the stall is so busy that the princess has to step in and help the girl at the counter, it is clear that, by hook or by crook, they have got the marketing right.

Never far from the centre of the action is Captain Mark Phillips, who still farms the estate, looking more like an off-duty royal than any of them. He and the princess launched the Gatcombe Park trials in the grounds of the home they then shared in 1983, and it has been a popular fixture ever since, growing from two days to three. There have been times when the dates have dotted around the calendar to help the British eventing team prepare for major international champion-ships, but the pulling-power of the Phillipses was strong from the start. The first winner back in 1983 was the Australian David Green; runner-up was his wife Lucinda, then the most popular British woman rider since the Cotswolds' own Pat Smythe from Miserden. Lucinda was based at Andover, some way away, but after her years of glory there was another home-grown heroine in Virginia Leng, from the south of the hills at Acton Turville, near Badminton.

The Gatcombe Park trials are still organised jointly by Captain Mark Phillips and Princess Anne, the most public manifestation of the unusual my-wife-next-door situation that has existed since their marriage broke up. It seems to work for them, however: there is plenty of space to live and let live on this glorious estate of upland meadows, hillside pastures and steep woodlands.

What frightens me more than the horses—and, as at Badminton, they scare me a great deal—is the programme of jolly japes the organisers put together to sugar

LEFT *The Princess Royal still lives at Gatcombe, while her ex-husband Captain Mark Phillips now farms the estate.*

BELOW *The hair-raising cross-country fences at Gatcombe push both horse and rider to their physical limits.*

the horse pill. There is always much tearing around in Land Rovers, a commentator burbling into a loudspeaker the while, and I have my doubts about one or two of this year's celebrity contestants. The prospect of Frankie Vaughan and Jilly Cooper parading their driving skills is enough to persuade me to seek my delights elsewhere. The last time I saw Mrs Cooper she was pussyfooting along the byways of Bisley with an L-plate on her car and a driving instructor smiling bravely but weakly by her side.

Princess Anne also has a tented exhibition at Gatcombe Park on the first bank-holiday weekend in May, dominated by craftspeople from the Midlands and North whose work we do not see too much of otherwise. It is an event worth the admission fee—bright, colourful, fun, friendly, and with goods of a very high standard. They are not, however, necessarily handmade in the Arts and Crafts tradition of the Guild of Gloucestershire Craftsmen. The Guild was founded in 1933, inspired by Ernest Gimson and Sidney and Ernest Barnsley, master archi-tects who had in turn been enthused by William Morris and John Ruskin. The organisation's standards were high then and remain so today, and their exhibition at Painswick Institute, from late July through to the end of August, presents work conforming to the highest ideals of the Arts and Crafts Movement. There are craft shows everywhere these days; the Guild itself puts its members' wares on display far more often than it used to, and this year it took a three-week spring exhibition to Great Barrington village hall, an example of how that once-dying community is regaining its foothold in Cotswold life. The output of this elite band of craftspeople, however, is just a small part of the story. Scarcely a week goes by in the most modest town without some kind of craft exhibition in a schoolroom or Sunday school hall, though exactly what nowadays constitutes a craft seems to be a movable feast.

For Guild members, craftsmanship can often be a pure, chaste thing, be it slipware pottery, a turned candlestick, a silver chalice or a patchwork quilt. To be a member of the Guild is not to every craftsman's taste, presupposing that he possessed the skills to impress the selectors in the first place. Other organisations come and go, and some of them stay, and the message they put out is always different from the Guild's. Sometimes it is a more endearing and alluring message, with works on show that appeal to larger numbers of people and a wider band of budgets; but the Arts and Crafts tradition is so deeply engrained in the fabric of the Cotswolds, a living entity, with a direct line back to Morris and Ruskin, that it is imperative that the Guild should stay central to our heritage, whatever scope there may be to stray away from its beliefs; not that it shows the slightest intention of going away, anyway.

THE ARTS AND CRAFTS MOVEMENT

THE ENTHUSIASTIC 'rediscovery' of the Cotswolds during the late 19th century, in particular their distinctive vernacular architecture, is closely connected with the Arts and Crafts Movement. This movement had its roots in the vision of a return to medieval simplicity advocated by the writer John Ruskin and artists of the Pre-Raphaelite Brotherhood, combined with a reaction against industrial mass production and materialistic Victorian ideals. Its leading spirit was the energetic designer, poet and social reformer William Morris, who in 1861 founded a design company with other Pre-Raphaelite associates.

Drawing on Gothic art and the natural world, with a strong emphasis on craftsmanship, Morris's work was highly influential, providing the cue for younger British designers and architects of the day, such as Charles Voysey; indeed, many of Morris's designs are still popular today. As a pioneering socialist, Morris was aware of the uncomfortable paradox that his firm's idealistic products were mainly serving the well-to-do urban middle classes. Nevertheless, he cherished a utopian dream of the simple, healthy, rural life sustained by pride in craftsmanship. In the 1870s he leased Kelmscott Manor near Lechlade. Despite the fact that the region had suffered severe economic decline and the depopulation of its once-thriving towns and villages, for Morris this Cotswold retreat was 'heaven on earth'.

LEFT *Ernest Gimson (seated, centre) and the Barnsley brothers, with family and friends, outside Gimson's cottage near Sapperton.*

Shout 'Is the potter here?' down any Cotswold street, and stand by for the stampede. Indeed, if the street happens to be in Nailsworth, you could well be killed in the rush; but leaving this aside, and the fact that every other one of our neighbours paints or sculpts or fashions Tibetan yurts, the communities with their roots most deeply in the Arts and Crafts Movement remain, as they have for decades, Sapperton, Chipping Campden and Winchcombe.

Gimson and the Barnsleys set the trend, moving to workshops at Pinbury Park, near Sapperton, late in the last century. At the beginning of the 1900s Lord Bathurst lent them Daneway House, close to the Sapperton Tunnel's eastern portal, to serve both as a workshop and a showroom, and their names became inextricably linked with Sapperton from that day on. As architects—and, particularly in Sidney Barnsley's case, as craftsmen—they built and fitted out half a dozen houses and cottages in the village, with all three creating homes for themselves. Gimson and the Barnsleys clung tenaciously to the creed of the finest materials combined with the skill of the hand; even their mentor Morris went on to embrace mass production, but they remained resolute. The result was that their

LEFT *A ladder-back ash chair, designed and made by Ernest Gimson in 1895, is typical of the Movement's simple style.*

RIGHT *Charles Voysey's plans for two cottages in Worcestershire, which he designed in about 1901.*

BELOW *Morris's textile design 'The Strawberry Thief' was inspired by a bird in the gardens of Kelmscott Manor.*

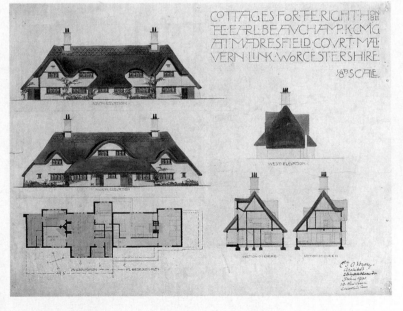

The qualities of traditional Cotswold stone buildings—a legacy of earlier prosperity—and the survival of local crafts attracted a later generation of Arts and Crafts practitioners, some of whom settled permanently. In the 1890s Ernest Gimson and the brothers Ernest and Sidney Barnsley established their workshop at Pinbury Park near Sapperton.

Like Morris, they had trained as architects but become involved in furniture design. In 1901 Charles Robert Ashbee transplanted a virtual colony of 50 craftsmen and their families from London to Chipping Campden, but the slow and expensive craft process proved uneconomic and the enterprise folded.

While social and economic changes following the First World War brought an end to Arts and Crafts idealism, the craft traditions, design principles and lifestyle nurtured by the movement live on, not least in the far more prosperous Cotswolds of the present day.

work today is to be seen almost exclusively in churches or the homes of the wealthy. Waterlane House near Bisley, Combend Manor at Elkstone and Rodmarton Manor, the last built over seventeen years by Ernest Barnsley, are three outstanding examples.

Almost as important as their output was their influence on a later generation of craftsmen woodworkers in the Cotswolds, most notably Norman Jewson and Peter Waals (more correctly van der Waals). One source of labour for them was the local wheelwrights' workshops, where they found men with all the skills necessary for their high demands. After their time, production moved to Chalford, where furniture is still made in a factory that grew from the movement. A few years ago they called in the huge former Liberal MP Cyril Smith to advertise their chairs, so they must still be doing a sound job.

There remain van der Waals in the village, too; my son Dan goes to Cubs with Patrick, great-grandson of Peter, and it is one of his dad John's great regrets that he never met his grandfather. 'He died in 1937, which was before my time,' he says. 'He came from Holland and I was born in Ireland, but my father was born locally and so were my sons, so one way and another four generations of van der Waals have lived here. People always ask us whether the family still has any of Peter's furniture, and the answer is scarcely any, apart from a couple of small pieces. Craftsmen of his talent didn't keep hold of what they produced for very long.'

In Chipping Campden, Hart's jewellery shop remains a tenuous link with the utopian arts world planned by Charles Robert Ashbee and his wife Janet when they moved into the town's Woolstapler's Hall in 1902. Ashbee had founded the Guild of Handicraft in London in 1888; when the lease ran out on his Essex House workshops and press in the East End ten years later, it was his dream to transport his fifty or so workers to Campden in the hope of reviving the crafts of woodworking, smithery, masonry, silverworking, engraving and the like. 'Cockneys in Arcadia', he called his disciples, but not all was well in paradise. By 1908 there was talk of 'commercial depression and heavy losses', and the First World War saw the end of the venture. The Ashbees left Campden in 1919, but some of the descendants of the immigrants stayed on, notably the Harts.

The Campden silversmith Robert Welch, marking the fortieth anniversary of the founding of his workshop with an exhibition in Cheltenham, is another crafts-man with his roots deep in the Cotswold Arts and Crafts tradition, and the same can be said of the potter Ray Finch, who celebrated his eightieth birthday just weeks after Laurie Lee's. He first came to Winchcombe Pottery in the early 1930s to see the work of Michael Cardew, and felt that his wildest dream had come true when he was taken on as a pupil. Producing traditional pottery— tableware, cookware, lamp bases, cider jars, bread crocks, beer mugs and the like—he and his small team, which includes his son, have also become some-thing of a tourist attraction, a relaxed counterpoint to Sudeley Castle and Winchcombe's great Perpendicular wool church, gargoyle-bedecked beneath its extravagant gilded weathercock.

ABOVE *This pop-eyed gargoyle, along with another 40 or so, adorns Winchcombe's parish church. They are said to represent unpopular monks who once lived at the local abbey, and are collectively known as the 'Winchcombe Worthies'.*

LEFT *Ice cream proves a popular refreshment on a sunny afternoon in Broadway, one of the best loved of all Cotswold villages.*

BANK HOLIDAY IN BROADWAY

There must have been a good reason for coming to Broadway on August bank-holiday Monday, but after driving around for three-quarters of an hour looking for a parking space, I confess it escapes me now. The place would be irresistible to look at, if it wasn't for the traffic in between glimpses—the Cotswold stone never more golden, the architecture never more felicitous, the whole air of the place never more comfortably off and confident. Some years ago a Dutchman brought out a book of large, glossy colour photographs of the Cotswolds, beautiful pieces of work for which he had clearly spent an entire summer setting his alarm clock to rise at five on fine mornings to capture the scene before it was spoiled by us lot, and nowhere he portrays looks more sublime than a deserted Broadway. Those who know the Cotswolds only by his book must carry round with them an image of streets of golden stone unpeopled but for a whistling paperboy here, a cheery milkman there. Using their imagination, they will realise that it is not always thus, and that occasionally the cottagers behind those wisteria-hung doorways will venture down the village street to the village shop for a joint of the roast beef of old England, or to the village inn for a pint of foaming ale. But not in their wildest nightmares will they picture in Broadway the scene before my eyes today, with apparently half the population of the Midlands and West Country parading aimlessly to and fro.

THE COTSWOLDS' COACHING DAYS

RIGHT *In a bustling scene outside the Plough Inn in Cheltenham, horses are changed before the coaches continue on their journey.*

BELOW *An 1826 advertisement for a coach service between London and Cheltenham, which took two days by wagon or one by 'fly van'.*

B EFORE THE RAILWAYS made long-distance travel easy and accessible in Britain, public stagecoaches represented the most efficient means of getting from A to B. So called because they plied fixed routes between two or more 'stages', stagecoaches were already in use by the 1640s, though their golden age came in the early 19th century, when coaches bearing names such as Defiance, Retaliator and Rapid tore, day and night, along the highways and turnpikes of Britain.

By then, an expansive network of coaching routes spanned the country, and towns straddling these routes stood to benefit. Throughout the 18th and early 19th centuries, towns like Burford and Cheltenham rang to the sounds of horns, coachmen's cries

RIGHT *Tom Long's Post, found on Minchinhampton Common, is said to mark the grave of a local highwayman.*

and racing hooves, as one coach after another thundered into town to set down and pick up passengers. In the absence of stations, inns such as the Lamb in Burford and the Plough in Cheltenham provided the focal point for coaching traffic. Even when no coach stood in their courtyards, their ostlers would be hard at work re-shoeing horses, and their innkeepers readying to feed and water the next wave of passing trade.

Passengers travelled a road of danger and uncertainty. Grim lodgings, badly kept roads and the constant threat of overturning were just the start of their worries. Until England's banking system began to develop towards the close of the 18th century, travellers were forced to carry their money with them. This left them vulnerable to the threat of highwaymen, roadside robbers who would relieve passengers of their wealth—often after a tip-off from a

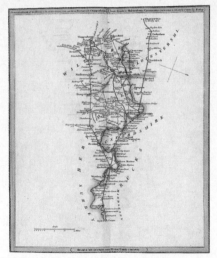

ABOVE *A map of 1806 shows stagecoach routes in orange, with asterisks marking towns where new horses were available.*

crooked inn servant—and then release or even maim their horses in order to avoid pursuit. Highwaymen stopped coaches and private carriages indiscriminately: indeed, it is said that the Lord Mayor of London himself was robbed in 1776.

Broadway has long been favoured by trippers and disfavoured by those who take a loftier view. When the motoring and charabanc revolution was cranking up in the 1920s, the green at Broadway was the ultimate place to be on a Sunday afternoon, as it still is for many nowadays. In his *Cotswold Country* of 1937, H. J. Massingham dismisses this beautiful place, with a history more interesting than most, in two curt sentences: 'If you want to go still farther north and take the lower road, you will come to Broadway. To avoid this unpleasantness, take the higher byway across the wolds from Stumps Cross at the top of Stanway Hill.' Writing in the same year, at least John Moore was more entertaining in his demolition job on the place in *The Cotswolds*: 'The place is a haven and a headquarters for all manner of arty-and-crafty people, it is the refuge of every conceivable kind of crank from the person who plays tunes on a reed-pipe at concerts to the person who wastes his time teaching nice country boys to waste *their* time dancing morrises when they'd rather be playing cricket.'

Since John Moore's years of roaming the wolds, other North Cotswold communities have caught up with Broadway in terms of commercialisation. Since his time, too, stringent planning regulations have tidied away hand-daubed wayside signs and the tatty advertising that used to sprout from gift shops and tearooms; the buildings themselves, shops and houses alike, have never been in better heart. My personal quarrel with Broadway is that, once here, I can find precious little to do. In the village centre, at least, there is no historic church to visit, no exhibition or museum in which to while away an hour, no grand public building over which to cast an appreciative glance. There are a few galleries and antique shops I should like to rummage around, but these are no places for idle browsers, which is all I should be in such top-of-the-market outlets. So I ramble along 100 yards or so either side of the Lygon Arms, glance in a pot shop here, a Scots wool shop there, take tea as you must do and wonder what to do next.

What makes me marvel is the number of shops that sell absolutely nothing at all that anyone really needs. It must take courage to set out to earn a living from peddling useless knick-knacks for six months a year. But on days like this, at least, it seems to be courage well rewarded.

In many ways it is perverse to complain about the broad way that runs through the village and the traffic it brings, since the road is what gave the community its lifeblood in the first place. There was an ancient track here down from the Cotswold heights into the Severn valley and on into Wales, and The Lygon Arms was just one of several hostelries that flourished when Broadway found itself on the coaching road on the seventeen-hour journey between Worcester and London. Broadway had thirty-three inns at its height, they say, the kind of figure that always raises a smile until you regard an inn simply as a place of refreshment or accommodation, and count up the number of hotels, guesthouses, bed and breakfasts, restaurants, cafés and tearooms within half a mile of the green today. As happened elsewhere in the Cotswolds—Burford and Northleach being prime examples—the coming of the railways brought a return to rustic poverty for communities that had catered for the stagecoaches and their passengers. Just a couple of generations before Massingham and Moore were being sniffy about the charabancs of the interwar years, houses and cottages there had been standing in near-ruin, children barefoot in the dusty cart track.

Before them, too, a short-lived economic revival, inspired by William Morris and the Arts and Crafts Movement, brought the sympathetic restoration of many of the dilapidated properties, and a lasting and satisfying source of employment in the village in Gordon Russell's furniture company and trade showrooms. Russell's family started mending and restoring antique furniture for the village inn, the Lygon Arms, in 1904, and it was after he returned to the business following the First World War that he developed it towards the design and production of superbly crafted furniture. This being the machine age, he took the conscious step from painstaking hand production to the discriminating use of machinery, a move that allowed him to turn out pieces in sufficient numbers to satisfy a wealthy market around the world. They are among the most desirable of all items of 20th-century furniture, and one could describe them as the antiques of tomorrow.

Out of town, up Fish Hill towards Campden, are Broadway Hill and its Broadway Tower. You can see thirteen counties from here on a clear day. The country-park owners should install a calculator on the viewpoint to convert that figure to account for the latest local-government shakeup. Twenty-four unitary authorities, or whatever the figure proves to be, will scarcely have the ring of thirteen stout old English and Welsh shires. Unchanging, however, both in name and contour, are the hills to be seen from here, the Malverns, seemingly so close today that you feel you could be taking the waters at the Holy Well after a brisk twenty minutes' stroll—the Wrekin, the Brecon Beacons and Whitehorse Hill in Oxfordshire more mistily remote.

Broadway Tower (originally Broadway Beacon), a fantasy of the 18th-century sixth Earl of Coventry, was built in 1798 and stands on the highest point in the Cotswolds after Cleeve Hill. Such statistics are recorded in not notably impressive metres these days. I much prefer to think of Lord Coventry's Broadway Beacon standing 1,024 feet above the Severn, and can well understand why, long before he thought of marking the spot with his fine folly, beacon fires flared out from here to bring tidings to the valley below.

The high hills, or the hills which in the Cotswolds we see as high, are ancient places in the history of man. So Crickley Hill, above the Severn plain on which Gloucester and Cheltenham now prosper, is no place to be alone at dusk. Neither are the eastern stretch of Cleeve Hill at Belas Knap, Haresfield Beacon, Cam Long Down or Nibley Knoll. I once met a woman who swore she had been sitting on the top of Cam Long Down at dusk and before her eyes the Berkeley Vale had transformed into a landscape of swamp and scrubland beside a slow, swollen Severn—the scene, indeed, as it might have been a thousand years ago.

On Broadway Hill there is even better reason to cast your eyes anxiously around you as night falls, for this was the scene of as macabre a miscarriage of justice as any in rural England's history. In 1660 William Harrison, the trusty steward to Juliana, Lady Campden, set out from Chipping Campden to collect rents in Charingworth,

just two miles from his home. Aged seventy, he had served the Noel family for fifty years, so when he did not return that night they became anxious for his safety. John Perry, Harrison's servant, was sent out to look for him, and when he, too, failed to come back, the elderly man's son, Edward, rode out the next morning to investigate. He met Perry near Ebrington, and though Perry at first denied having seen his master, he confessed to killing him after William's bloodstained hat, neckband and comb had been found. In doing so, he implicated his brother Richard and his mother Joan, though between his first statement to the magistrates, and their hanging on Broadway Hill, he changed his story so many times as to cast doubt on his sanity. None of this could save him or his family, and his mother's local reputation as a witch doubtless hastened their journey to the gallows. The fact that no body had ever been found apparently caused the authorities no qualms.

So the file was closed, and the odd little rustic tragedy was fast being forgotten when, two years later, home walked William Harrison saying he had been set upon by three horsemen late on the night of his disappearance, robbed of his £23 in rents and shipped off to Smyrna in Turkey to be sold as a slave. When his owner died he had managed to sail the length of the Mediterranean to Lisbon, where he had met a wealthy Englishman who had put him on a ship back to Dover. Mrs Harrison, whom one might have expected to have been pleased at this turn of events, instead saw his return as a cue to commit suicide.

ABOVE *Broadway Tower, a folly built in the late 18th century, today houses regular exhibitions. The 65-foot tower commands panoramic views across to Oxfordshire in the east and Wales in the west.*

Nobody ever fathomed the reasons behind William Harrison's disappearance, but the 'kidnapped by Turks' tale seems rather too glib for most commentators' tastes. For centuries, the fear of being captured by pirates from the Levant was as hackneyed and outrageously unlikely as, say, being whisked away in a flying saucer by little green men would be seen to be today.

SOUTH TO SNOWSHILL

The road to Snowshill, south of Broadway, passes St Eadburgha's Church, a place of worship for almost 1,000 years and a wonderfully peaceful haven after the rigours of the great broad way. Entombed here in even more peace is Sir Thomas Phillipps, who lived across the road at Middle Hill, until his mania for collecting books forced him to expand to a second mansion in Cheltenham. He lived from 1792 to 1872, and in those eighty years he put together the largest collection of manuscripts ever accumulated by one man, and an almost equally vast library of printed books. I believe he told us everything we need to know about his obsession when he declared: 'I wish to have one copy of every book in the world.' Books and his compulsion to acquire them left his life in utter chaos. The unsurprising statistic that he spent a quarter of a million pounds on them goes no way towards painting an adequate picture of the ruin that his one-track mind brought to his relationships with his family, his friends, the tradesmen who served him and almost everyone he knew.

He fought constant battles against booksellers, against public officials who were unable to come up with records on cue, and against his son-in-law, the Shakespearean scholar James Halliwell, whose growing reputation as an academic caused Phillipps considerable grief. He believed Halliwell had committed the most grievous offence possible in his eyes—stealing manuscripts, in this case from Trinity College—and in the late 1850s he strove in vain to prove this as the younger man climbed the ladder of success.

In 1863 Phillipps, the illegitimate son of a rich Birmingham manufacturer, spread his collection to Thirlestaine House, now a part of Cheltenham College. It is in a tucked-away corner of town, but those who are familiar with it will tell you that it is a vast place—which is of course why he was attracted to it in the first instance. Even then, he soon discovered that space would be tight. 'I much doubt whether I shall be able to get my library into the house without intrenching upon the gallery,' he wrote to a friend. 'I have sent five hundred box shelves, and they seem to half fill the rooms and there are a thousand more to come, besides I know not how many more packing cases, of which a hundred have already arrived.'

At first Phillipps was a tenant at his Cheltenham home, but in 1867 he bought Thirlestaine for £12,000 from Lord Northwick. Inevitably, he soon fell out with the nobleman, replying to a letter of congratulation from him on the purchase of the house with a characteristic little note: 'If anybody is to be congratulated, it is yourself in having apparently got rid of an ill arranged and inconvenient house. The kitchen and offices being on the other side of the road, the dinner is cold before it is set on table. And it is difficult to get servants to answer the bells, these being on one side of the road and the servants on the other.'

ABOVE *Sir Thomas Phillipps, photographed c.1865: his life was governed by a quasi-fanatical obsession with books.*

LEFT *Sir Thomas bought Thirlestaine House for its vast size— the previous owner had added room after room to house a substantial art collection, seen here—but it still barely accommodated his book collection.*

As for poor Lady Phillipps, all she could do was bewail the fact that she was 'booked out of one wing and ratted out of the other'.

All those books and documents: did Sir Thomas Phillipps ever read them? Not according to his friend Sir Frederic Madden. Though Oxford-educated, Phillipps was no great intellectual, and Madden flared up in anger when he was described as such in the *Athenaeum* journal after his death. The article's description of him as a fine scholar and one of the most learned men of the age was the height of absurdity, Madden grumbled; his real interest in manuscripts was confined to picking out their names in his registers and records, and 'nor did I ever see him read a book, or ever look into one'. It is a characteristic of the human magpie, of course, to be obsessed with being the possessor of the desired object, for the thrill of the chase to be the be-all and end-all of collecting. The sad sequel to Phillipps's life was that after he himself had been filed away at St Eadburgha's, his fanatically amassed collection was scattered to the winds over years of famous auction sales, lasting well into this century, with the world's great libraries vying for his choicest possessions.

South of St Eadburgha's, in Snowshill, the residents are grumbling that these days the village should be twinned with Disneyland in Paris. When I first visited the National Trust's Snowshill Manor here some twenty years ago, the car park was little more than a lay-by. This season, to coincide with its centenary, the Trust has opened a full-blown visitor centre with space for 100 cars, a restaurant, shop and toilets.

This being the North Cotswolds and this being the National Trust, it need hardly be said that all is pristine stone, expensive glass and rural tastefulness. But the locals are riled by the National Trust's declaration that the facilities 'would make life easier in a popular village'. Who made life difficult here in the first place?

'It was the Trust that brought 60,000 visitors a year to this village of 130 residents,' one opponent to the centre argues. 'The Trust has bought workers' cottages and turned them into expensive holiday lets. It knows as well as any tourism developer that if you create attractions and facilities, the hordes will follow.'

Many Cotswold countryside issues are at stake here—commercialisation, holiday cottages versus workers' cottages, the generally accepted economic desirability of tourism but dispute about its scale. The Trust argues that since demand for visiting Snowshill Manor is already well established, it should be handled in the most efficient way possible, one that takes parked cars off the streets and gives visitors all the facilities they need under one roof. When the village used to be clogged by traffic on busy days everyone said 'something must be done'; lo and behold, something has now been done.

I believe the National Trust deserves the benefit of the doubt. Short of turning back the clock a very long time indeed—to the years when the manor was privately owned and the majority of the villagers earned their living from the land—we are never going to return to a Snowshill 'unspoilt' in the true sense of the word. Indeed, there are next to no 'unspoilt' villages in the Cotswolds, though there are a great many more isolated than Snowshill. Those workers' cottages, for instance: are we truly to believe that had they not been turned into holiday homes they would today be occupied by toilers in the field with their flagons of cider and cheese-and-pickle sandwiches wrapped up in red spotted handkerchiefs? In Snowshill? A couple of miles down the road from Broadway? The fact is, the National Trust has been in this village for

LEFT *This Javanese theatre mask, one of a collection, is typical of Snowshill Manor's eclectic paraphernalia.*

BELOW *These suits of Samurai armour are thought to constitute the finest collection outside Japan.*

RIGHT *The manor's curiously asymmetric façade sets the tone for the eccentric contents housed behind it.*

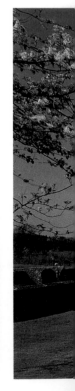

a long time—longer, one would surmise, than most of those 130 residents—and if I had been seeking true rural tranquillity, I should not have bought a house in Snowshill even before recent developments. Every tenpenny guide to the Cotswolds tells you that Snowshill Manor is one of our major tourist attractions, and that has been the case for decades.

I do not blame visitors for being attracted to this Tudor house, dating from around 1500, with its 17th- and 18th-century alterations. Not that many are drawn to it for its architectural merits, but to gaze upon the extraordinary collection of—well, you name it, put together by its architect owner Charles Paget Wade between 1919 and 1951. That was when, five years before his death, he donated the property to the National Trust. It was Wade who restored a very run-down house and stuffed it with clocks, musical instruments, nautical curios, oriental furniture, veteran bicycles, dolls' houses, shadow puppets, wind toys, model carriages and a terrifying detachment of dummies dressed in Japanese Samurai armour. He shunned electricity and lived his life in, at best, a mellow half-light, both in the house and in the cluttered outhouse where he spent his last days. It is hard to imagine the state the place was in when the National Trust took it over; it must have been chaotic, and even as it is presented today it is still a glorious amalgam of images, a jumble sale from heaven or hell, depending on your tastes and sensibilities. After all this, a few minutes' silent contemplation in St Barnabas's Church, rebuilt in 1864 with walls so stout that no demons could hope to pierce them, might be the answer for some troubled visitors. The walk takes you through the exquisite heart of the village, but tread softly lest you disturb the residents.

ABOVE *As rewarding in their own way as the interior are Snowshill's pretty gardens.*

AUTUMNAL
TINTS

TWIN VILLAGES ABOUND in the Cotswolds, but, as twins go, they are
rarely identical. The Barringtons and Swells are cases in point, while Upper
and Lower Slaughter vary quite considerably in character, the one a well-
tended showpiece with its water wheel, stone river banks and footbridges, the
other a more pragmatic farming village which is nevertheless a place of great

beauty. Perverse as people are, you often hear those who know the Cotswolds, or pretend that they do, declaring that they prefer unspoilt Upper Slaughter, but for my part I can see exactly why the tourists are drawn to its sister village; besides, I do not see Lower as 'spoilt' in any way. It was built pretty, it remains pretty, and commercialisation is just about as discreet and minimal as it can be. There would certainly be some long faces if there was nowhere to buy a pint of beer or a pot of tea. Admittedly, I should not want to live in those lovely cottages around the green on the north side of the Slaughter Brook. There are infinitely worse fates in life than doing so, but I can well imagine that there are more secluded and unfrequented places to live in Upper Slaughter, and indeed elsewhere in Lower, where you are closer to the fields and the lambs and the hedgerows.

Stanton and Stanway, too, are seen as twin villages. Each in its way is sublime: Stanton for its lovely village street, and Stanway, which is little more than a hamlet, for a grouping of church, manor house, gatehouse and tithe barn as satisfying as any in rural England and more golden than the rest put together. We have already reflected upon Sir Charles Cockerell and his designers deepening the honey-coloured hue of Sezincote to ape the Indian tradition. If they had had access to the stone available to the builders of Stanway, they would have had to go the other way and tone down the glow with limewash.

In Stanton, most of the houses in the street were built fifty years either side of 1600, and there is not a finer period of Cotswold building than that. The estate was

LEFT *As the leaves turn to shades of russet and gold, the farming village of Upper Slaughter will be preparing for winter, while its pretty twin, Lower Slaughter (in the middle distance to the right), will be recovering from a hectic holiday season.*

BELOW *Lord Neidpath stands before his magnificent ancestral home, which is now open to public view.*

RIGHT *The ornate styling of Stanway's gatehouse is accentuated by the rather more plain church beside it.*

bought in 1906 by a North Country architect from Oldham, Sir Philip Stott, who moved into the Jacobean Stanton Court and proceeded to restore a tired village in the thirty years he spent there until his death. He went even further, laying a cricket pitch, installing electric lighting in old-fashioned lanterns and bringing water to the village in a way that even allowed for a tucked-away swimming pool for residents. He is also to be thanked for the village cross, with its 17th-century sundial and globe on a medieval base and stem. It is a happy focal point for an almost entirely residential street.

Stanton lies below the foothills of the Cotswolds, which at this point are green and gentle slopes swathed in woodland and dotted with sheep, a very different proposition from the steeper, loftier escarpment further south. At the far end of its street, up a sharp pitch, is the Mount pub, with a terrace looking out on village gardens and orchards, the Vale of Evesham, the Malverns and Bredon Hill. It is a largely non-Cotswold scene, in fact—apart from the plump outliers of Dumbleton and Alderton Hills—but a sweeping vista of rural Middle England, all the same. Food and drink are to be had at the Mount, and people drive in from miles around to have it. As a consequence, the atmosphere is surprisingly suburban, and if you expect of Stanton an olde village inne at one with the olde village street you will perhaps be disappointed.

Stanway House, built in Elizabethan and Stuart times but with 18th- and 19th-century additions and alterations, was begun by the Tracy family in the 1500s and has descended from them to the Scottish Earl of Wemyss. It is occupied by his son and heir, Lord Neidpath, who runs the 5,000-acre estate with great care and enterprise, and has taken to opening his house and grounds in summer. Many families make their way to this corner of the Cotswolds these days to ride

ABOVE *Like all bats,
lesser horseshoes have a
penchant for quiet, dark
places; in Stanway's attic
they have found a very
up-market home.*

the Gloucestershire and Warwickshire Railway steam trains along the pretty Honeybourne Line from Toddington, and a stately-home visit can round off a happy afternoon.

Inside the house, visitors tend to be most impressed by the light, lofty and airy Tudor hall with its great bay window, while among Lord Neidpath's outside projects has been the restoration of an eye-catching hillside water feature to the east of the house, a cascade dropping steeply from a pyramid dating from 1750.

Presumably when Lord Neidpath succeeds to his earldom he will be seen less in these parts, which will be a sad loss for the Cotswolds. Behind the bow ties, wing collars and slightly distracted air he is a caring landlord, conservationist and wildlife enthusiast. He is pleased to think of hundreds of badgers roaming his estates, and while not everyone would happily boast of a colony of lesser horseshoe bats in the attic, he takes a keen interest in these dubious house guests. His tenants know his *bêtes noires* include caravans, up-and-over garage doors and television aerials on chimneys, and he is very careful about the siting of satellite dishes.

To the bypasser's eye, the cog around which the hamlet of Stanway revolves is not so much the manor house as its ornate three-storey gatehouse, dating from around 1630. By this time the Tudor fad for greeting guests through a gate of a grandeur disproportionate to that of the house beyond was fast losing favour, but this late manifestation of the whim pulled out all the stops—extravagant coats of arms, plinths, pediments, scallop shells, all in several rows. Tradition has it that Inigo Jones was the author of this fantasy, but maybe it was simply the work of a master craftsman of the Cotswolds. One with the yeoman name of Timothy Strong was the hunch of the late architectural historian David Verey.

St Peter's Church dates from the 12th century but was over-thoroughly restored in 1896. This was the year in which William Morris died, and though one of his myriad campaigns was against the scraping of medieval plasterwork from church walls, his advice fell on deaf ears at Stanway. A more comely sight in some visitors' eyes is the great tithe barn built for a 14th-century abbot of Tewkesbury at a time when the monasteries were at the heart of wheeling and dealing. Secure under a mighty stone roof supported by stout crucks, the barn was repaired in the 1920s and has been well kept up since, serving a number of community uses as a meeting place and theatre. The rustic cricket pavilion, standing on staddle stones, is a far more flimsy structure, but it has nonetheless stood the test of time; and clearly set to stand as long as there's an England is the village's outstanding roadside war memorial. The sculptor of the arresting bronze *St George and the Dragon* was Alexander Fisher, while for the lettering the sponsors went to the greatest in the land in Eric Gill. The two also combined to produce the memorial in the church porch, a piece of work that still glows in mellow September light.

THE TITHE: GOD'S PORTION

ABOVE *The vast tithe barn at Great Coxwell dates from the 14th century, when it was owned by Cistercian monks.*

DESCRIBING A VIRTUOUS ploughman in the *Canterbury Tales*, Chaucer says that 'his tythes payde he ful faire and wel'. Paying a tithe 'ful faire and wel' meant giving a tenth of your produce from farming or cultivation—or its monetary equivalent—to the parish priest for the benefit of the local church and the poor.

In England, King Offa made tithes obligatory in Mercia in AD 794; and, by 1000, the system had spread to all parts of the country. Tithes were classified as produce of the ground, such as grain; produce of labour, such as milling; or a mixture of them both, such as milk. Over the centuries, however, money was often used as a substitute—a practice that was eventually regularised in 1836 by an Act of Parliament. This situation continued until 1936, when the government abolished tithe charges altogether and granted the former beneficiaries equivalent annual payments until 1996.

Although this relic of medieval taxation has now disappeared, the world of tithes lingers on through the great, cavernous tithe barns that still dominate a few English villages, including Great Coxwell and Stanway in the Cotswolds. These huge storehouses of local tithes were typically built of buttressed stone walls with stone-tiled roofs supported by a network of sturdy timbers. Some were more than 180 feet long and provided not just the sustenance but also the focus of a village. No wonder the Victorian architect Sir Gilbert Scott remarked that 'the tithe barns of an English village are as admirable and as appropriate as the minster in Rheims.'

ABOVE *A coin dating from the reign of King Offa, who first made tithes compulsory in AD 794 in the kingdom of Mercia.*

FEASTING ON TRADITION

It is grey and misty for the clypping at Painswick—not ideal weather for a quite lengthy open-air service—but they perform the old ritual with great joy. Clypping is nothing to do with trimming the yew trees of the churchyard—ninety-nine of them if you believe the yarn about the devil never allowing the hundredth to grow.

Clypping is embracing the church and the faith it stands for, circling it with an unbroken chain of hands and worshipping the Lord with a simple and cheerful little song. The service is held on Feast Sunday—September 19 or the first Sunday after it. This is the formal birth date of the Blessed Virgin Mary, the church's patron saint, or it was until September 1752, when eleven days were lost with the introduction of the Gregorian calendar. Elsewhere, September 8 is Mary's day, but Painswick remains true to the old date.

In Merrie England, the day was marked by the Painswick Feast, a time of roistering that had little to do with religious observance. Painswick was not alone in this; holidays, after all, are simply holy days with the 'holy' taken out. Where Painswick differed from many places was in its early realisation that institutionalised

ABOVE *Each September parishioners gather in Painswick churchyard for the unusual clypping ceremony, an old Saxon tradition of 'embracing' the church.*

boozing and brawling had no place in well-ordered community life. In 1786 Gloucester's pioneer of the national Sunday-school movement, Robert Raikes, declared that recent Painswick Feasts had been marred by scenes that 'would have disgraced the most heathen nation'. It was through him that the service became the focal point of the weekend.

H. J. Massingham, in his *Cotswold Country* of 1937, described the clypping as 'a pedantic perpetuation of the old rite'. In fact, he found very little good generally in the town of sixty years ago: 'Painswick is a matronly body to all appearance, but the cancer of decay is within.' He was presumably alluding to the community's transition from a town in which people lived and worked into one in which most simply lived, but why so gloomy? Threescore years on, it is hard to imagine that many residents would wish Painswick to be in the industrial front line, whatever that might mean these days. And as for that 'pedantic perpetuation of the old rite', St Mary's has not for generations been more temperamentally attuned to the clypping service. It is one of those churches that has embraced whole-heartedly the idea of cheerful family worship, and as the children and their mums and dads dance around the building, surging in and billowing out in what can only be described as a holy hokey-cokey, there is nothing remotely faint-hearted or wan about their efforts. The Avening Silver Band lays down a jaunty beat, and the tune is catchy, even though the chorus is strictly Sunday-school traditional:

O, that I had wings of angels,
Here to spread and heavenward fly
I would seek the gates of Sion
Far beyond the starry sky.

Some of the little girls look as if they should indeed be sprouting wings of angels, since they boast everything else the well-dressed cherub should be wearing—white satin dresses, sashes, posies, socks just so. But most of the little ones have simply come along as they are. One little bruiser in an Aston Villa shirt is putting severe strain on the line, almost dragging his neighbours into the moat beside the church as he rushes in to embrace the old walls. But he is singing about his wings of angels as heartily as anyone, and no doubt they will be measuring him up for a pair in around the year 2075.

After the final hymn, little knots of people drift away through the yews and the table tombs, parents and aunts and grannies taking the children home to tea, as they have for generations. Many of the adults are carrying white wands. 'I'm a sidesman,' one explains to me. 'I'm a welcomer,' says another.

A welcomer: what would Massingham have made of that? What he would recognise in present-day Painswick church are many of the traditional points of interest: the iron spectacle stocks just over the wall; the lych gate of 1901, built with old timbers from the belfry and with the musical setting for the hymn 'Rejoice in the Lord' inscribed in its plasterwork; and vestiges of Civil War damage from 1644, when the building was occupied by the Roundheads and fired on by the Royalists. Even the Victorians' great tidy-up of St Mary's towards the end of the last century could not sweep away the last traces of those acts of human folly.

BLISS AT CHIPPING NORTON

I have always admired the Bliss Mill at Chipping Norton. Factory chimneys are few and far between in the Cotswolds, but the one towering from the classical dome here could scarcely be more imposing. Another much-photographed Cotswold building is the mill on the Slaughter Brook at Lower Slaughter, where a weathered old red-brick chimney adds as much to the scene as the silent water wheel.

Elsewhere, factories' smokestacks and reminders of them are less welcome in this part of the world. Here in our village a company from Kent has been advertising a set of six porcelain plates showing 'cherished scenes singled out from the Chalford of the olden days', and for some reason it has latched on to three images of mills and two other more general scenes in which smokestacks are also prominent. No sign, here, of the bread donkey the old-timers remember, the Roundhouse, Chalford Place, our maze of lanes, our grey walls, our rushing wells. 'Makes us look like blooming Wigan,' a neighbour grumbles in Paul Dutton's butcher's shop while Tony slices the ham. She has obviously never been to Wigan, but I take her point.

Chipping Norton's Bliss Mill is not quite the industrial North either, but there are pictures of it in the 1880s, smokestack belching, that make it look dark and satanic enough. It dates from 1872, put up to replace a building destroyed by fire the previous year, and such was the sophistication of its machinery that it employed few more than a hundred people at its peak.

The first Bliss in Chipping Norton, Thomas, arrived in 1756, from one of those smoky Chalford mills, in fact, to sell cloth for his clothier father. He married the daughter of the landlord of the Swan Inn; his new father-in-law set him up in business in a small way, and so evolved a family firm that survived through four generations. The Victorian William Bliss was one of those paternalistic employers-cum-civic-and-religious leaders who shaped the lives of their workers and their families almost from the cradle to the grave, housing them, getting them out hoeing their allotments and illuminating their leisure hours with social events, sports days and outings. He even organised the coming of the railway to the town, to bring in coal and take away his products, in the relatively early year of 1855. It is not fashionable to admire such types today, but it is easy to imagine that, for many, life in the Chipping Norton of Victorian times would not have been nearly so tolerable without him. It was also impossible to envisage, at the height of his powers, that the town would ever be anything other than a part of the Blisses' extended family.

Times were changing, however, and when he died in 1884 his son, another William, inherited a business in which power swiftly slipped out of the hands of the family. The last Blisses moved out in the 1890s. There were several changes of ownership after that as Britain's textile trade ebbed away. If our friends in Wigan and their neighbours could not cling to their belief in Britain's bread hanging by Lancashire's thread, what hope was there for Bliss Mill out there in the sticks? Nevertheless, few of the older residents of Chipping Norton could ever have believed that they would hear the great monument of a factory described as a 'hassle-free weekend retreat'—but that is what is being said about it now.

Bliss Mill ceased production in 1980 and stood worryingly idle through the years of prosperity in that decade, only to be taken on as a residential development project when the recession came to bite. Now five years of financial ups and downs have seen the restoration at last completed, the stonework cleaned to its former glory and the chimney made safe and sound. There are thirty-five apartments and eleven cottages on the site, and those who live in them have use of a leisure centre complete with a gym, squash court, tennis courts and an indoor swimming pool. 'It's a great base for people working in London,' says the sales manager, from which it is but one small step to talk of a 'hassle-free weekend retreat'.

WM BLISS & SON.
ESTD 120 YEARS. CHIPPING NORTON, ENGLAND.

ABOVE *Bliss Tweed Mill temporarily transformed rural Chipping Norton into an industrial centre in the 19th century.*

ABOVE *William Bliss, a paternalistic employer who provided his workers with good living and working conditions, an education and holidays.*

RIGHT *A full house at The Theatre in Chipping Norton. This popular venue is a converted Salvation Army citadel.*

Changing times, changing social moods, but the stone and mortar are still intact, and indeed have never been in better heart. For native Chipping Norton townsfolk who see the medieval woollen merchants' St Mary's Church, the classical early Victorian Town Hall and Bliss Mill as a blessed trinity of landmarks, at least there is the comfort of knowing that all three are safe for posterity.

So, too, it is cheering to see The Theatre at Chipping Norton serving the community so imaginatively with a diet of films, live shows and exhibitions, at a time when theatre in the regions is under intense pressure—the Everyman at Cheltenham, while beautifully restored in recent years, is deep in a cost-cutting exercise, and the future appears even more bleak for the Roses in Tewkesbury. Every night, all over the country, small and dedicated touring companies are keeping theatre alive in towns like Chipping Norton, and some of the very ablest are looking in here over the next few months—Bath Theatre Royal, Yorkshire Theatre, Bunbury Touring, Red Shift, the Gate. They are around the little venues of the Southwest so often that we can be inclined to think of them as our own, and when they pile sleepily into their transit vans at the end of the evening it can be a surprise to hear that they will be in Lincoln tomorrow, Scarborough the day after that.

INVITING VILLAGES

Whenever I am in the Chipping Norton area I try to visit neighbouring villages, such as Chastleton. Chastleton House, with its ancient topiary work and Jacobean structure so classically correct that it might have come from a textbook of early 17th-century architecture, was sold by Robert Catesby to pay fines for non-attendance at Protestant church services; now it is in the hands of the National Trust.

The gardens and the silent little village are places of great calm, in particular the church with its monuments and brasses. On one of my more recent visits I realised I was there on the 400th anniversary of the death of Katherine

Throckmorton—a Tudor name steeped in history. Four hundred years; it would be misguided to believe that nothing in that small church had changed since her family and friends had gathered to bury her there that day, but glancing around me I could see that a great deal had certainly not.

I feel a compulsion, too, to visit Great and Little Tew, to the north of Chipping Norton. When I was a child in the early 1950s, my uncle was a great buyer of the illustrated magazines, and one day he showed me an article entitled 'The Most Beautiful Village In England'. Living in the mill town conurbation north of Manchester, I knew of villages only from fairy stories. Gazing at those sepia images of the stage-set thatch and stone of Great Tew, I was ready to swallow the headline word for word, which made my sense of shock all the more acute when I at last sought out the village in the late 1970s, and found only a scene of desolation and ruin. Private ownership of villages and its consequences, for good or ill, are one of those facts of Cotswold life the outsider finds hard to comprehend. Happily, the situation has improved immeasurably and at great expense in both Great Tew and Great Barrington, the other problem community of a couple of

THE THROCKMORTONS

THE THROCKMORTON FAMILY's long— and frequently ill-fated—association with the Tudor monarchy began in 1494, when Robert Throckmorton was knighted by Henry VII and made a member of the Privy Council. Robert's son George came into conflict with the next king, Henry VIII, over his divorce from Catherine of Aragon and was imprisoned for a time in the Tower, but soon regained Henry's favour. Ironically, George's son Nicholas was a fervent Protestant who got into trouble with the Catholic Queen Mary, objecting to her marriage to Philip of Spain. He survived to become influential in the court of Elizabeth I, and his daughter Bess was one of Elizabeth's ladies-in-waiting—until her secret marriage to Sir Walter Raleigh, without the Queen's permission, landed her, too, in the Tower.

The family later suffered for their Catholic faith under Elizabethan law, and the family home, Coughton Court, was regularly searched for priest-holes and secret chapels. George's daughter-in-law Elizabeth left her estate at Chastleton to her grandson Robert Catesby, but he was forced to sell it after incurring fines for refusing to attend Protestant services. He was later executed as the ringleader of the Gunpowder Plot. George's grandson Francis had also been executed, for his

involvement in the so-called Throckmorton Plot to put Mary, Queen of Scots on the English throne. The cloak she wore on the scaffold still hangs in the house, a poignant reminder of the persecution and suffering that plagued the family.

ABOVE *The coat of arms of the Throckmorton family, in the Tower Room—used for secret Mass—at Coughton Court.*

RIGHT *Sir Nicholas, one of a long line of Throckmortons who suffered for their faith—in his case Protestantism.*

decades ago. Salperton seems to change hands with some frequency but to no apparent detriment of the residents, and the dawning of democracy in Guiting Power was another example of the old order changing, if not before time.

Other Chipping Norton villages on my tour include Chadlington and Great Rollright, with their scary church gargoyles, the former being a must to visit at around noon, if only for the luscious Tite Inn. Cornwell, restored by the Portmeirion visionary Clough Williams-Ellis, is an exquisite little spot with its Norman church beyond a park. Finally, I cannot be in that corner of the world without paying my respects to the Rollright Stones, though in truth I always walk away wondering why. The sense of anticlimax is reminiscent of visiting the Four Shire Stone, just east of Moreton-in-Marsh, an 18th-century lollipop topped by a sundial and ball and marking, before boundary changes and perhaps some time again in the future, the meeting of the shires of Gloucester, Oxford, Warwick and Worcester. Edward Thomas wrote of no one leaving and no one coming at Adlestrop Station, but he painted a picture of animation compared with an average day at the Four Shire Stone. Monuments seem meaningless if they skulk in obscurity. The statue of Neptune that used to lounge in a field by the railway line at Thames Head, one of the Cotswolds' two alleged sources of that river, is much happier now he has been moved beside St John's Lock at Lechlade, where he can watch the boats and the river rolling along to the mighty sea. Incidentally, I see the latest Ordnance Survey map is quite sure of itself in marking Thames Head, off the Cirencester to Tetbury road near Kemble, as the source of the Thames, with ne'er a mention for Seven Springs, a couple of miles east of the Air Balloon pub at Birdlip. Local rivalries being as they are, I cannot but feel there must have been ructions when the map was published.

The Rollright Stones should not leave me cold, but more often than not they do, perhaps because the winds always seem to be rolling across the high wolds when I am there. The stones stand tall enough, and the folklore surrounding them is vivid. There are two groups of them: the Whispering Knights and the King's Men, with the King's Stone standing at a distance from them on the far side of the lane. There are some seventy King's Men in a Bronze Age circle some 100 feet across, while almost a quarter of a mile to the east, the five Whispering Knights are all that is left of a Bronze Age burial chamber, the remains of the insides of a long barrow. Four of them stand upright and the other lurches in a way that suggests tippling more than whispering.

Sir Arthur Evans, the archaeologist who made his name at Knossos, the site on Crete bound up in the legend of the Minotaur, visited the Rollright Stones in 1890 and became intrigued by the folklore surrounding them. The favourite story is

ABOVE *Legend has it that the ceremonial circle and burial chamber making up the Rollright Stones are the petrified remains of a bewitched invading king and his army.*

OPPOSITE *Chocolate-box-pretty thatched cottages have been carefully restored in Great Tew.*

that a regional king, intent on further conquests, was stopped in his tracks by a witch and turned to stone along with his circle of men. The Whispering Knights were lagging some way behind; they were plotting to overthrow their leader when they, too, met the fate of their loyal colleagues. The witch herself became an elder tree. 'Come on, Dad, get a life,' my daughter Rose groaned when I told her this little gem. In this rare case I fear that the cynicism of the young is not misplaced.

ROMANY FAIRS

Walk into Tayler and Fletcher's, the auctioneers in the Market Square at Stow-on-the-Wold, and enquire about horse fairs, and you will be given a handbill listing three Cotswold Horse and Pony Sales at Andoversford on Thursdays in May, July and October. Hunters, hacks, cobs, ponies and youngstock are on offer, as are horseboxes, trailers, four-wheel drives, tractors, agricultural implements, saddlery, harness, tack and horse-drawn vehicles; and on top of all that we are promised more than fifty stalls which *cognoscenti* know will be selling everything from

THE WAY OF THE GYPSIES

TWICE A YEAR, the horse fair at Stow-on-the-Wold draws Gypsies from all over the country, and among the reunions of families and friends some serious horse-dealing takes place. In times past the Gypsies would have gone back on the road when the fair was over, but many now return to permanent caravan sites or even to houses as the traditional nomadic way of life disappears.

The first Gypsies arrived in Britain in the early 16th century. Their descendants had set out from Asia as early as the 11th century, and gradually made their way across Europe; nomadism thereafter became a hallmark of Gypsy life. Many people believed, erroneously, that these wandering folk were Egyptians ('Gypsy' is an abbreviation of Egyptian), but linguistic evidence—Romany is derived from Sanskrit—traces their origins to India.

The Gypsy way of life is based on freedom and independence, and duly dictates what trades a Gypsy practises—horse-dealing, scrap-metal collecting and hawking goods are customary, as they require little or no equipment, land or

TOP *The logo of the Gypsy Council, an organisation that protects Gypsy rights.*

LEFT *A traditional Gypsy family sets up a roadside camp near Bourton-on-the-Water.*

Barbours to buckets. They sound quite some events, these sales at Andoversford, but as residents of Stow will be quick to tell you, there is another story that finds no place on the auctioneers' leaflet.

The charter fairs in Stow, in May and October, are beacons in the year of Britain's travelling Romanies. They descend in their hundreds, as they have apparently been doing since Edward IV first authorised the fairs in 1476. The upheaval this causes to a town far more at ease with the prospect of attracting the top end of the tourist market can be well imagined.

The position of the Gypsies became considerably more isolated a few years ago when Tayler and Fletcher's pulled out of their side of the trading and took their horse sales and accompanying non-Romany stallholders a few miles down the road to Andoversford. With a respectable local business interest no longer part of the equation, calls for an end to the Gypsies' revels have grown in intensity. Seventy traders have demanded an end to it all, claiming that the shenanigans cost them £45,000 worth of business last year, though against that some 400 local people have signed a petition for the tradition to continue.

LEFT *Stow-on-the-Wold fair gives old friends the opportunity to dress up and catch up.*

BELOW *In this now rare ritual, photographed in 1947, a dead Gypsy's caravan is burned.*

staff. The original Gypsies would have slept in makeshift tents, their famous colourful caravans becoming popular only in the Victorian era. According to tradition, a Gypsy's few possessions were burned after their owner's death, although the spectacular funeral ritual of burning the caravan is a rare sight today.

These unusual ways have led to Gypsies being treated with suspicion and fear, and they have been persecuted throughout their history. In 1596 there was a mass execution of Gypsies at York; and in the Second World War large numbers of Gypsies were, like Jews, murdered by the Nazis in the Holocaust. Today they are still victims of ignorance and prejudice: many people take offence

ABOVE *Piebald ponies—a firm favourite among Gypsies—change hands at Stow.*

at their often messy roadside caravan parks (Gypsies are, in fact, fastidiously clean within their homes), and they are readily accused of petty crimes wherever they appear. Increasing government regulations, along with the general public's opposition to events like Stow-on-the-Wold charter fair, threaten to destroy traditions that the Gypsies have tried to maintain for centuries.

A swarthy Irishman named Spike, leading a mare so piebald that it might be a grey stippled with Indian ink, says his people's real fear is that their opponents will pull out all the stops to thwart them through the government's Criminal Justice Act, part of which has been framed to keep New Age travellers moving on.

'Lots of us are wondering whether this will be the last time,' he says. 'Then again, we've been saying that for years, and ask any of us if we plan to be back here next year, and the answer will be yes. We're family people, and Stow is one of the few times in the year when we meet up with many of our relatives. I don't see how anyone has the right to deny us that. It's important for business too. I'm looking for £1,000 for this animal, and there are not many times a year when enough people are gathered together to give me the chance of a price like that. We Romanies don't have many possessions, no more than we can carry around or lead along, and because of that our customs and birthrights are important to us. As far as we're concerned, buying and selling horses at Stow is a birthright, one going back 500 years. Of course we'll all be back next year, and I'd like to see anybody stop us.'

Laws of the land are undoubtedly broken at the Gypsies' fairs. Some of the parking needs to be seen to be believed, not to mention bald tyres, windscreens unburdened by tax discs and defective rear lights. As rolls of twenties and fifties change hands over a £900 Shetland and buggy or a £5,000 stallion, it could even be that not every last penny of profit from this grassroots capitalism will come to the notice of Her Majesty's Inland Revenue. Talk of cockfighting has been rife for years, and there is certainly never any shortage of prime young cockerels around the campsites. Young men brawl quite openly with their bare knuckles for hours on end, if they see fit, and a mere outsider has no way of knowing whether this is simply a settling of scores or big-money gambling. I hear a sum of £10,000 mentioned for the winning fighter alone, which would suggest that his canny backers would stand to make a great deal more; then again, outsiders love to fantasise about the Gypsy life, and my informant is decidedly more Reliant Robin than horse-drawn caravan.

Since the conventional traders moved out, Stow's May and October fairs are not the draws for visitors they once were. Many shops now close for the day, and 'residents only' signs appear on hotel doors. But the thought of the Criminal Justice Act bringing scores of extra police to the fields and lanes around Stow is scarcely enticing to the Gloucestershire council-tax payer, in light of the county force's deep commitment to safeguarding its three royal residences, and its high-profile activity in the South Cotswolds almost every summer solstice when New Age travellers, a very different group of people from the Romanies, head for Inglestone Common, near Chipping Sodbury. Bearing these financial burdens in mind, Cotswold dwellers from outside Stow are perhaps content to see their neighbours there put up with this extraordinary influx twice a year, while themselves steering well clear of the proceedings. True, it is still a wonderful place for people-watchers and glimpsers of another culture—the tanned faces and trilbies, hand-slaps and blarney, lace curtains and crystal windows—but since we no

longer have the excuse of going there to buy at the market, Stow on the Romanies' days is fast becoming a saturnalia in which members of conventional society are the outsiders for a brief, eccentric spell, and the world belongs to the shadowy travelling folk. Living many miles to the south, I find it easy to applaud the 400 or so townspeople who are happy to accept that state of affairs. If it were in my own back yard, who is to say?

BIBURY REVIEWED

'Bibury really deserves all that has been written about it,' Massingham noted in *Cotswold Country* in 1937. 'Only the Jacobean Court, a kind of genteel barracks of a place, has been overpraised.' Life moves on. And as for the village deserving all that has been written about it, if Massingham had in mind William Morris's description of it as the most beautiful village in England, as he doubtless did, then I wonder. This is a delightful place to be, that is certain, and one can well imagine it in Morris's time: nestling by its trout stream in the still of a remote Cotswold valley, its old church and cottages a poem in stone, rooks circling its treetops as dusk descends, wood smoke rising lazily from a dozen hearths and the cries of children playing their last games for the evening on its old dusty track before the chill of the night drives them in.

And there's the rub: the old dusty track is now the A433 between Cirencester and Burford, a road that carries thousands through the village every day, and bears hundreds to it if the weather is anything like fine. Today, what you notice first about Bibury on a fair day is not the architectural splendour of the 17th-century Arlington Row or Mill but the glinting of sunlight on car roofs, mobile and stationary, alongside the River Coln.

Nowadays, the really fortunate Cotswold communities, from the aesthetic point of view, are the ones upon which motor transport has made the least impact, those happy enough to be on no road to anywhere in particular. We all know isolated upland or valley hamlets to which this applies. Some of the more spectacularly beautiful villages include Castle Combe, the Slaughters, Stanton and Stanway, Blockley, the Duntisbournes, the Colns. Bibury has not been blessed in this respect, and what William Morris would make of it now, who is to say? It is debatable whether ice-cream vans, toddlers wobbling along the riverside parapet clinging to nan's hand and older children chasing ducks along the footpath would please his eye were he to return today. Like many another socialist intellectual, he tended to be more charitably inclined and understanding towards his fellow men *en masse* in theory rather than in practice.

Another of time's tricks has been to split Bibury into two communities, the very visible roadside village and the less visited little corner around St Mary's Church.

ABOVE *New Age travellers were regular visitors to Inglestone Common until the local authorities clamped down on their annual gathering to celebrate the summer solstice.*

In the pre-motor age, when the main road through was simply a track among tracks, this would have been far less apparent. Now the A433 is cambered and waymarked in such a way as to sweep you past the church and its neighbours and out towards Aldsworth before you know it—doubtless a delight for those fortunate few who live down there and are happy to be left in peace.

By accident or design, Bibury has hit upon a mix of tourist attractions that appeals to a wide number of people. The trout farm, Arlington Mill with its museum of local history, two up-market hotels, the odd tearoom and souvenir shop, the National Trust's gem of a terrace of cottages in Arlington Row: it is a dignified little portfolio for a village that has been admired by outsiders for a long time.

Alexander Pope, born nearly 150 years before William Morris, spoke of Bibury's 'pleasant prospect'; and immeasurably more influential in putting it on the map, in late Victorian times, was J. Arthur Gibbs, whose impact on our world-weary towns and cities was immediate and far-reaching when his book *A Cotswold Village* was published in 1898.

Gibbs, educated at Eton and Oxford, is best remembered today as a complex man, a huntin', shootin' and fishin' member of the squirearchy who combined his vigorous pursuit of the outdoor life with bookishness, a deep interest in natural history and a religious spirit bordering on pantheism—the recognition

RIGHT *The picturesque workers' cottages that make up Arlington Row are now highly prized homes for tenants of the National Trust.*

of God through nature and the universe. He is also described in the preface of the third edition as a kind and sympathetic squire to the villagers of Bibury's near neighbour Ablington, 'ever ready to give what is of greater value than money, personal trouble and time in finding out their wants and in relieving them'. Indeed, much of our present-day perception of him is based on the character reference of that preface, and what we must bear in mind is that it was written by a member of his sorrowing family within a very short time of his death, at the age of thirty-one, in 1899.

If we now revise our views of him in the light of opinions he expressed in the book, we find very much a man of his times. Thus, while his liberal contemporaries might have praised his opposition to absentee landlords, or his view that 'there is too great a gulf fixed between all classes', we today can only shudder at the complacency of such sentiments as: 'A kind word, a shake of the hand, the occasional distribution of game throughout the village, and a hundred other small kindnesses do more to win the heart of the labouring man than much talk at election times of small holdings, parish councils or free education. A tea given two or three times a year to the whole village… does much to lighten the dullness of their existence and to cheer the monotonous round of daily toil…'

ABOVE *An idyllic scene of rural life at the turn of the century that would have heartened J. Arthur Gibbs, but which belies the reality of long days of hard toil.*

The last years of the 19th century were a time of desperate poverty in this and most other country areas, and there is little of the caring, sharing squire in Gibbs's joyous 'Time passes quickly for the sportsman who has the good fortune to dwell in the merry Cotswolds'. He admits that there are those in the village for whom time does not pass so quickly: 'But what part of this earth is there…that is not dull to those who live there, unless we drive out dull care and *ennui* by that glorious antidote to gloom and despondency, a fully occupied mind?' Countrymen who really feel discontented with their lot, he concludes, should visit the Black Country, or the foggy streets of Birmingham, or the engine room of an ocean liner, and realise how lucky they are.

Large parts of the book might have been written a century before 1898, and whether this is an indication of the gulf between country and urban life at that time, or merely a reflection of the writer's conservative outlook, for all his liberal pretensions, is difficult to say. The Birmingham Gibbs so scorned was a world away from Bibury, where lives were still ruled by the rising and setting of the sun and the changing of the seasons. Gibbs could not have been unaware of what was going on in our cities, but in turning a deaf ear to the outside world he produced a sublime piece of escapism acclaimed by readers who knew nothing of the country way of life, and drew succour from the belief that here was a little corner of England where the old order was changing not and would never do so.

THE HOLY BLOOD OF HAILES

Chilly dusk at Hailes Abbey, and though it is gone five, it is cheering to see the light blazing through the gloom at the little museum there. In a few days' time, in November, the site will be staffed at weekends only, not daily as it is now. English Heritage does well to keep a significant presence here all year through, and even when the exhibition is closed you can still imagine the scene here when the abbey pulled in pilgrims, the devout and, doubtless, the merely curious, from far and wide. Chaucer knew what was going on here. 'By the blode of Christ that is in Hayles', we read in the *Pardoner's Tale*, and that was quite a relic upon which to swear an oath.

The Holy Blood of Hailes: nothing more than duck's gore, one former monk claimed, while at the time of the Dissolution of the Monasteries in 1539 it was written off as a mere concoction of clear honey coloured by saffron. Maybe it was, for at the time the Holy Blood was brought to Hailes, in the mid 13th century, the bones, robes and personal possessions of saints and members of the Holy Family were changing hands rather as Elvis's shirt and John Lennon's boots do at auction today, with just as much scope for misattribution and deceit. What we do know is that the blood performed little less than a miracle of its own by transforming a remote and obscure religious community into a pilgrimage centre talked of with awe throughout the land.

Hailes Abbey was founded by Cistercians from Beaulieu in 1246, four years after Richard, Earl of Cornwall, the younger brother of Henry III, had been all but wrecked off the Scilly Isles while returning from a Crusade to the Holy Land. He praised God for his good fortune in escaping with his life and vowed to build a religious house as a token of thanks. The King was at the heart of the venture from the start, granting Richard the manor of Hailes and bringing Queen Eleanor to join his brother, a clutch of nobles and thirteen bishops for a magnificent dedication ceremony in 1251.

After that, the order apparently led a quiet, contemplative and basic existence until 1270, when Richard's second son Edmund presented the abbey with the holy relic of the Blood of Christ. It had been bought from the Count of Flanders some three years earlier and authenticated by the Patriarch of Jerusalem, who was later to become Pope Urban IV. Pomp and ceremony returned to Hailes when the blood was placed in an elaborate shrine there, a holy of holies that called for the entire rebuilding of the abbey's east end. But after the last of the dignitaries had ridden away this second time, the monks were not left to their devotions and solitude: in poured the pilgrims, and so did the donations.

One story that emerged was that the godly would be able to view the blood more clearly than the sinners, though even they might grow to see the light if they atoned in their hearts and with their purses. The disillusioned monk who told the tale of the duck's blood reckoned that the phial in which the relic was kept had a thick, opaque side and a finer, transparent one, and the better-off the pilgrim seemed, the more likely he would be to be peering initially through a glass darkly.

ABOVE *This medieval tile depicting a mythical beast—half bird, half boar—is thought to be from Hailes Abbey.*

LEFT *Majestic cloister arches span the atmospheric ruins of Hailes Abbey, and hark back to its days of glory.*

Most notable among the remains today are some seventeen cloister arches, remnants of a building upon which had been lavished a very high standard of workmanship. Beautiful roof bosses from the chapter house, now in the museum, tell a similar story of high masonic achievement, while floor tiles with heraldic designs are to be found here, in the British Museum and nearby at the little church of Hailes, which was built before the abbey but eventually possessed by it and used as a chapel of ease for visitors. The spectacular rebuilding of the abbey's east end, from 1271 to 1277, was modelled on that of Westminster Abbey: the ground plan of its five radiating chapels can still be traced clearly. After the Reformation, much of the abbey was quickly pillaged for building material, mostly by the Seymours of Sudeley Castle, and in St Nicholas's Church, not far away at Teddington, the tower arch and west window are simply parts of Hailes borne away and re-erected in 1567.

After excavations in the early years of this century, the footings of the abbey were re-covered and trees were planted to mark its dimensions. These, together with the raggedy, ruinous cloister arches, made for an eerie and romantic spot. Today, amid its manicured lawns, what is left of Hailes Abbey stands safe, very much your conservation site of the late 20th century, with the full might of English Heritage and the National Trust behind it.

Is not this, though, the place where Richard of Cornwall, son of King John and the abbey's benefactor, was buried by solemn, chanting monks beside his wife Sanchia of Provence in 1272, and where in turn his son Edmund was laid to rest in 1301 in the presence of his cousin, the great, grizzled, ageing Edward I? On an evening such as this, with easterlies sweeping in off the wolds and howling around the cloister arches, it takes more than mown grass and cleared scrubland to strip Hailes of its aura of mystery and antiquity.

CHAPTER SIX

WINTER WONDERLAND

T HE BONFIRE TRADITION blazes as brightly as ever in our Cotswold villages. On Chalford Hill, flames leap from the school fire on the Pleasure Grounds. The backdrop to the fireworks is the dark flank of Aston Down: that and an inky sky, not one of your sodium-tinged suburban glows but the perfect black canvas on which skyrockets can paint their pictures. Good old November the Fifth. And was not Guy Fawkes a good Stroud boy? No, he probably was not, but there is a Fawkes Place in town, and I have heard stories that link his family to Lypiatt Court, near Bisley. They have yet to convince me. We know a fellow plotter came from Chastleton, up near Chipping Norton, but that is no reason for the Cotswolds to take responsibility for the whole motley crew.

I am on my way to Nailsworth. Driving over Minchinhampton Common these dark nights you are apt to glimpse on the grassland, when your headlamp beam swings away from the road at a bend, a disembodied yellow slash in the night sky, hovering some feet above the ground like the smile of the Cheshire Cat. I am used to seeing the golden eyes of foxes in such circumstances, flitting across the common like fireflies, but what are these new horrors? When I glimpse not a disembodied grin but one with a great white face above it the answer becomes clear: luminous collars for cows. Safe, see; until you have just got used to seeing them and another herd without them starts using the common, and you are back where you started. I shall go via Stroud and the Bath road in future, and blow the five-mile detour.

ABOVE *A blazing bonfire and a burning guy light up the countryside every November the Fifth.*

In his house near Nailsworth, Kit Williams is holding his main studio show of the year. Like Kit Williams himself, the old place has been transformed by the success of *Masquerade*. This was the elaborate puzzle book that seemingly had the whole of Britain scrambling around with metal detectors in search of a jewel-studded golden hare back in 1979, and briefly made a media personality of this private, otherworldly man. That side of celebrity has ebbed away, but to remind him of the *Masquerade* phenomenon and its financial rewards, his cottage is now a substantial house, with a studio annexe built on in the finest Cotswold craft tradition.

Masquerade also set the seal on Kit Williams's reputation as one of Britain's most collectible contemporary painters, one whose major works consistently command five-figure sums in his favoured London gallery. For much of the 1970s this quirky former seaman had built up a reputation for staggering craftsmanship in a variety of fields: not only painting but cabinet-making, marquetry, sculpture and jewellery. The best-selling book told the rest of the world what his admirers had known for some years, and the revelation was reflected in the market value of his works. At this exhibition on his home turf the price tags on his paintings range from £450 to £11,000, but when I call in towards the end of the final day, red spots to denote a sale are not to be seen on anything valued at more than £2,750. The studio show is the place to pick up a Kit Williams bargain, but it is clear that he still needs a London outlet to be sure of regular trade in the £10,000-plus range.

MASQUERADE: THE THRILL OF THE CHASE

PUBLISHED IN 1979, Kit Williams's treasure-hunt book *Masquerade* became an international phenomenon. The book's intricately detailed paintings held clues to a riddle whose solution would point to the whereabouts of a valuable golden hare, studded with rubies and turquoise, made by Williams and buried somewhere in Britain.

Thousands of treasure seekers began an obsessive hunt for the hare, and the chase soon spread around the globe as the book was translated into eleven languages. One American company even began selling Masquerade Treasure Tours: the price included a flight to Britain, hotel, car hire—and a shovel. Finally, in 1982, a man calling himself Ken Thomas traced the hare to a Bedfordshire park. The hunt was over.

But that wasn't quite the end of the story. It was later revealed that Thomas—real name Dugald Thompson—had a business partner who lived with a woman who had been Williams's girlfriend when he wrote *Masquerade*. She knew of the hare's approximate whereabouts, and pointed the men to the park, which they successfully searched with metal detectors. When the truth emerged, Williams was shocked and angry on behalf of genuine hunters. Although the proceeds from the book's success made him a wealthy man, he swore that, after being inundated with 30,000 letters and having people turning up at his door in the quiet Cotswold valley where he lives, he would never write another riddle.

ABOVE *Masquerade's intricate pages hid clues to the whereabouts of the golden hare.*

RIGHT *Kit Williams with another of his creations: a giant wooden fish now displayed in Cheltenham.*

ABOVE *The jewel-studded golden hare that Williams buried in a Bedfordshire park.*

One of Kit Williams's painting preoccupations of recent years has been with life-sized full-frontal nudes of both sexes, rendered with such *trompe l'oeil* accuracy that when they are reproduced in print they simply look like very graphic photographs of naked people. The focal point as you enter the studio is the £11,000 *Anatomy Lesson*. 'Golly, that's different,' gasps a woman of middle years as she turns in through the door, and it is likely that this is not the first time the painter has heard such squeaks of surprise over the past few days.

The picture shows a naked youth with a girl in her mid teens painting his internal organs—heart, lungs, arteries and so on—textbook style, on his body. The way she is seated before him, the most interesting part of his anatomy to a girl of her age, or indeed to girls many years her senior, is just inches in front of her face. It is a Williams classic, combining sexuality with a visual pun, the girl painting crudely on what, because of his virtuoso talent, you have to pinch yourself to remember is itself a painting.

I am less at one with *The Fisherman's Wife's Dream*, in which a naked woman is seen in a boat embracing a gigantic plaice that looks anything but a cold fish. I find myself admiring the technical skill involved in re-creating the creature's speckled skin, until I reflect that this line of criticism echoes the country sports magazine of 1959 that reviewed *Lady Chatterley's Lover* solely from the point of view of its treatment of the gamekeeper's craft.

'This one has undertones of *The Scapegoat,*' barks a young man not far away. There's a sharp intake of breath by Kit Williams, and I imagine I detect a momentary glazing over of his one good eye, but he responds cheerfully and patiently enough. Perhaps, after all, there are worse masters than Holman Hunt with whom to be compared. *The Scapegoat* is famous as a symbol of the Pre-Raphaelites' fad for authenticity; Hunt bought a poor old goat and tethered it beside the torrid Dead Sea for days on end until it obliged him with the desperate expression of defeat and exhaustion that haunts the painting. One has yet to see Kit Williams chasing goats over the hillsides of Horsley, but in terms of meticulous detail he yields to no painter and to no artistic school. The truth is, he would have made a splendid Pre-Raphaelite; indeed, with the prodigious talent at his fingertips, he could have been just about any kind of painter he wanted to be.

WRITERS PAST AND PRESENT

I scarcely recognise the Williamses' Nailsworth neighbour David Goodland. The last time we met was at the BBC studios in Bristol when he was a reader in a Radio 4 adaptation of a Cotswold Christmas anthology I had put together.

That afternoon David Goodland had struck me as an Identikit actor: good eyes, firm chin, cropped hair, slightly greying, the kind of face onto which could be painted anything the role demanded, from suburban librarian with a guilty secret to Hamlet, Prince of Denmark. Today, with white hair straggling over his collar, he is treading not the boards but the lonely, demanding—and for him, right now, harrowing—path of the playwright.

He has been writing these past few years, for TV and for the regional stage, and much of his work has been inspired by Gloucestershire people and places—deft tributes to Ivor Gurney and John Moore, as well as the more complex *Anzacs Over England*, telling touching, humorous and tragic tales about the Aussies and Kiwis based at South Gloucestershire aerodromes during the First World War.

He brightens when I ask him what it is that drew him to Nailsworth, that arty, crafty but above all unpretentious valley community on the Bath side of Stroud. 'I moved here fifteen years ago, after I had been acting for the previous fifteen years and got a bit of money together,' he says. 'I was renting in London and looking for somewhere to buy in the country, and my first view of the Stroud valleys was as my pal and I were driving over the tops from Aston Down, down into Chalford where you live, and seeing the lights coming on in the little cottages up the hill. We had been on holiday in the Dordogne, and it immediately stirred memories of there. I love this cottage dearly, and I love Nailsworth. It's not the *bijou* Cotswolds, and it's a peculiar place in many ways, but it's the people who make it what it is.'

It is hard to believe that it was not the same combination of unfussy living, glorious valley scenery and that intangible something that appeals to the artistic temperament that worked its spell on W. H. Davies when he came to Nailsworth in the early 1930s. He enjoyed contrasting claims to fame—as the author of *The Autobiography of a Super Tramp* and the poet who posed a question that grows in pertinence as the years roll by:

> *What is this life if, full of care,*
> *We have no time to stand and stare?*

ABOVE *The poet W. H. Davies made his home in the quiet town of Nailsworth, after experiencing the highs and lows of London and America.*

As a poverty-stricken Welshman living in a London dosshouse when his first book of poems was published, Davies became famous overnight as a result of *Super Tramp* in 1907. *Super Tramp* was a restless, anarchic road novel that anticipated the American beat generation by half a century. George Bernard Shaw wrote the introduction to the book, and gave it its 'Super' title as a direct reference to his recent stage success *Man and Superman*. It was the private poet Edward Thomas, however, rather than the public playwright Shaw, who offered the raw Welshman the practical help he needed to bring the book to publication, from preparing the manuscript to filling his belly with food. Davies stayed with the Thomases in Kent, and his shy and secretive nature became a family byword. Davies had a wooden leg, having mangled a limb while jumping a freight train in Canada, and when he needed a new one he was very anxious the villagers should not know about it. Edward Thomas made a sketch of the appliance and took the order along to the local wheelwright. In due course the new leg was delivered, along with an invoice for five shillings for a 'curiosity cricket bat'.

Davies was aged about sixty when he settled in Nailsworth, while his pretty young wife was not much more than thirty. They lived a quiet life in various houses in the town—there is a plaque on their last one, Glendower, on Watledge. By this time, his artistic output had reverted to verse, but the seventh decade of life is rarely the most fruitful one for a lyric poet, and so it was for the Super Tramp.

When he moved to Gloucestershire, Davies was not without friends in the county. One of them was John Haines, a literary Gloucester solicitor; another was the painter William Rothenstein, who lived in considerable splendour on the tops above Stroud's Golden Valley at Iles Green, Far Oakridge. What the Davieses' neighbours did not know, however, were the extraordinary circumstances of the couple's meeting shortly after the First World War—and it was only after Mrs Davies's death in 1980 that the remarkable story of their meeting and early marriage emerged in the posthumous publication of Davies's book *Young Emma*.

Davies was in his early fifties by this stage, the girl he called Young Emma in her twenties, and, as he explained in the book that told her story, he simply went out onto the streets of London and picked her out of the crowd to be his wife. An odd mixture between the conventional and the bohemian, the bold and the shy, the ageing Davies had decided, after a string of failed relationships, that almost the only criterion for a wife was a woman who did not drink; after that it was simply a case of hanging around the streets until such a paragon came into view.

That is how Davies met the good-natured, hard-working country girl who brought him love and companionship for the rest of his life. In the short term she also brought him a dose of venereal disease and the pain of having her in his care when she suffered a horrific miscarriage: unbeknown to either of them at the time, she was pregnant when they met. In terms of years, it was not long between London in the early 1920s and Nailsworth in the early 1930s, but the Davieses knew their part in small-town Cotswold society, and as far as their new neighbours were concerned, they were simply the distinguished literary lion and his attentive wife.

THE LAST LINKS IN THE COTSWOLD WAY

From atop the November-misty Cotswold scarp that gives the town its name, Wotton-under-Edge shows all the signs, for better or worse, of a country community that has not been left behind by the 20th century. Its situation within commuting reach of Bristol and its history as a town in which to work, as well as to relax and sleep, have both played their part in moulding the townscape we look down on today, with new housing lapping up against the foothills and utilitarian factory blocks contrasting with the lichened tiles of the old central streets. By the time we have abandoned the uplands and made our way into the heart of the town, however, it becomes clear that on balance, modern generations have treated the environment by no means harshly. Long Street and its neighbours still bear the hallmarks of an 18th-century weaving town, but here, as in so many Cotswold centres, the handsome town houses and public buildings are sounder now than they have been for centuries. Not that a lick of paint would do some of them any harm. Back in 1975 the regeneration of Market Street scooped a major architectural award, but it would not win many gongs the way it looks at present.

At the lower end of Long Street, the Hugh Perry Almshouses in Church Street, dated 1638 and impressive with their six steep

BELOW *These 17th-century almshouses, with their distinctive gables, were a gift to Wotton-under-Edge from Hugh Perry, an alderman of London.*

BELOW *In 1627 local wool merchant Sir Baptist Hicks gave Chipping Campden its Market Hall, which now marks the start of the Cotswold Way.*

RIGHT *This milestone provides either a challenge or a sense of achievement, depending on whether you are starting or finishing the 100-mile walk.*

gables and cupola, have also benefited from thorough renovation. The Chinese and Indian takeaways nearby are a reminder that this is a town that has always been happiest working for its inhabitants rather than being mollycoddled as a museum piece, a lack of self-consciousness that perhaps lies in the fact that before the age of the car Wotton was a very remote community indeed, rarely visited by outsiders.

A cupola even more easily recognised than the almshouses' is to be found on the Tolsey House, a timbered 17th-century building hiding its light under a plain brick façade of a later date. Not that it is passed unnoticed. Its Diamond Jubilee clock, topped by a respectful portrait of Victoria, is a focal point throughout the aptly named Long Street, and plays a part in local timekeeping. What a pleasure, too, to see a high street with all the old-fashioned shops you could wish for—butchers and bakers, tailors and jewellers, hardware stores and newsagents—interspersed with up-market gift, fashion and interior-design outlets. There is even a cinema, the Town, bucking the trend and now so successful that the company running it has expanded to other Cotswold centres. These days Wotton is one of the links in the Cotswold Way path chain, and for this and other reasons it now boasts a purpose-designed tourist-information point in the heritage centre beside the old Chipping marketplace.

Here the Gloucestershire Ramblers' useful little guide to the Cotswold Way says, 'Time should be allowed to explore the historic city of Bath.' I am happy

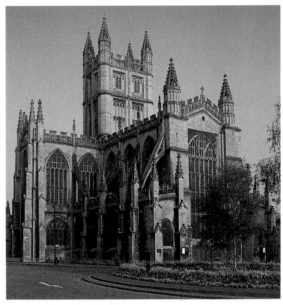

LEFT *The long-distance Cotswold Way offers extensive views across some of the most beautiful countryside in western England.*

ABOVE *Start the walk at Chipping Campden and you will be rewarded at the other end with magnificent Bath Abbey. Built on the ruins of a Norman abbey, the present building was the vision of Oliver King, Bishop of Bath and Wells at the turn of the 16th century.*

to heed it, even if it means stashing away the boots and woolly hat and changing into something a little more befitting one of the most elegant little cities of Europe: the teashops of Bath are not bedecked with signs reading 'HIKERS WELCOME'.

The planners of the Cotswold Way did well to begin and end it with a flourish—the sublime Market Hall in Chipping Campden in the north, and Bath Abbey to the south. Beautiful Campden, as Cotswold as they come, could never be disputed as the start of the trail, but if the purists had had their way, the route would have ended somewhere high up on Lansdown, with the spa city tantalisingly distant below. Instead, Bath Abbey is the goal, so the long walk begins with a temple to Mammon, albeit an antiquated one, and snakes its 100 miles south to a temple of God. It also carries us from the region of golden stone to the palest oolite of England's limestone country.

They say that when Bath was new, its terraces dazzled the eye with their brightness. By the middle of this century, after 200 years deep in its damp, smoke-hung valley, it hid its glories behind a patina of grime so murky that visitors whose appetite for the city had been whetted by Jane Austen's *Northanger Abbey* felt like actors who had prinked themselves up for a pretty period piece, only to land on the set of a kitchen-sink drama. They had but to raise their eyes to roof level and the ranks of black chimney pots to see the reason, but it did not make the truth any more palatable.

JANE AUSTEN AND BATH

THE CITY OF BATH in the 18th century was the most fashionable watering hole in Britain, boasting all that London had—shops, balls, parties, concerts, theatre—but with the additional blessing of health-giving waters.

One of the most famous 18th-century visitors to the city was the novelist Jane Austen. In her early twenties she twice visited relatives in Bath, and these sojourns in the fashionable spa city provided material for her light-hearted romance *Northanger Abbey*. Her heroine, Catherine Morland, derives much innocent pleasure from the society and novelty of the city, and exclaims, 'Oh! who can ever be tired of Bath?'

The wealthy came to the city for the sake of their health—to drink, and immerse themselves in, the

LEFT *A watercolour of Jane Austen, painted by her sister Cassandra c. 1801.*

LEFT *A scene from BBC TV's adaptation of* Northanger Abbey, *in which bathing beauties take the waters.*

water—but also to see and be seen. The city's society life was dictated by 'Beau' Nash, Master of Ceremonies, who controlled codes of social conduct and even dress.

But, surprisingly perhaps, in 1801, Austen fainted with horror when her parents announced that they were to leave the Hampshire rectory where she had lived all her life, and move to Bath. From the evidence of her letters, though, it seems that her time there was not unhappy. She, like her heroines, would

have visited the Pump Room to take the waters, and the Assembly Rooms to play cards and attend balls and concerts. Austen despised the more shallow elements of Bath society, however, and did not write any novels in the five years she spent there. In 1806 she left the city with 'happy feelings of escape'.

Ten years later Austen used Bath as the backdrop to her final novel, *Persuasion*. Her portrayal of the city has none of the naive excitement of the earlier book— rather, she paints a picture of a hectic, bustling place, full of shallow followers of fashion. The streets are crowded, noisy and oppressive, and her heroine has a 'disinclination for Bath'.

Today's visitors show no such disinclination for the city: Bath is one of the most popular tourist attractions in Britain. Architecturally, little has changed since Austen's day: there is nowhere better to experience 18th-century England, and those who visit can still walk around the streets in Jane Austen's footsteps.

BELOW *The magnificent ballroom at the Assembly Rooms in Bath has witnessed dances and banquets since the 1700s.*

ABOVE *Drinking fountains provide glasses of the soapy-tasting spa water in the Pump Room at Bath.*

LEFT *Bath's Royal Crescent, built between 1767 and 1774, is one of the most beautiful streets in Britain.*

Today, three decades of cleaning and restoration have left the city looking more splendid than at any time in its history, and as high-profile as it was in the days when Master of Ceremonies Richard 'Beau' Nash set the social tone in the early 18th century. There have been times since then—the Victorian years, and right on into the latter half of this century—when Bath has been content to be low-key and as anonymous as it could possibly be, given its history. The fact that Victoria never once visited the city as Queen is a sign of the way in which it had been pleased to sink back into the pack, knowing that raffishness and seediness had never been too far removed from its age of gold. If that was the price to be paid, then the Victorian burghers wanted nothing to do with it; far better the straight and narrow way of anonymity.

That is not how Bath does things today. Tourists and shoppers by their millions are vital to its economy, and the image the city presents is vibrant, cosmopolitan, very, very European—and not so much prosperous as rolling in wealth. I need no reminding that today, as at the time of the Beau, there is want and poverty in Bath, and that in between the extremes of those who inhabit the hostels for the homeless and the Royal Crescent and Bath Spa hotels there are tens of thousands for whom the focal point of the city is the mundane 'high street' trading centre of Stall Street and Southgate Street. There is even a modicum of grime with us still: Walcot Street, of the areas most often seen by visitors, keeps alive just a hint of that down-at-heel air of the past, mingled these days with the offbeat manifestations of the city's deep-rooted alternative society.

There is no doubt that Bath is built of the stone that fashioned the Cotswolds, and that South Cotswold people see it as a city that offers them everything they need, plus a great deal more of which they would never have dreamed. To be able to show visiting friends and relatives such world-ranking treasures as the Roman Baths and Pump Room, the Assembly Rooms and Costume Museum, the Royal Crescent and Circus, Pulteney Bridge and Milsom Street, the Theatre Royal and the antique shops, is a pleasure to be savoured. That said, the user-friendly vernacular architecture of the Cotswolds, the gables and mullions and dripstones, could not have been further from the mind of John Wood the Elder, the architect of so much that is fine in Bath and the inspiration of most of those who followed him.

The son of a builder, he was a dreamer rather than a plodder of the country byways in search of ideas. He had it firmly in his mind that there had been a glorious pre-Roman Bath built by Bladud, the mythical British founder of the city. The story is that the young prince contracted leprosy and was cast out to find work as a swineherd in Keynsham. He lost no time in passing on his illness to his pigs, but they found a miraculous cure by wallowing in swamps of steaming mud nearby, and before long he, too, was cured. His return to court was followed by time in Greece, and this was his spur, when he became king, to build a classical city worthy of the land of the Parthenon.

As a historian, John Wood was an excellent architect, but he genuinely saw himself as the Restorer of Bath, the re-creator of its former glories, rather than as a mere speculative developer. We should be grateful that he did, for there is inspiration of a very high order indeed, something far transcending small-town English planning, in his Royal Crescent and Circus. Had he had his way, he would have joined the city end of Great Pulteney Street with North Parade on the one hand and Cleveland Bridge on the other, and one can imagine a long, graceful sweep of boulevard that would vie with the great set pieces of Paris. On the other hand, if he and his fellow developers had had their way, the city would not have been blessed with nearly so many green spaces. Bath Rugby Club would not be playing on the Rec, either, and that would never do.

HATS AND HIS ROYAL HIGHNESS

The newspapers recently were full of the television adaptation of *The Rector's Wife*, written by the Cotswold-based novelist Joanna Trollope and filmed rather prettily in these parts. The actress in the title role specialises in playing superficially drab women with a certain subtle allure, but Rosemary Hawthorne, the vicar's wife across the aisle from me in Tetbury parish church this afternoon, is sheer up-front glamour and animation. Not for the first time she is staging a fashion show in St Mary's, this one devoted to hats through the ages.

ABOVE *Rosemary Hawthorne, wife of the vicar of Tetbury, models stylish headgear for one of her fashion shows in St Mary's Church.*

She is an avid collector of antique and vintage costume, and one of our most lively lecturers and writers on the subject. Trouper that she is, she often gives her audiences what they want by banging on about knickers and brassieres, but her interests cover far more of the body than this, and many of the hats on show are from her own collection. Others are from famous hatters and some of the old county families, and by the time she has set them off with complementary pins, plumes, ribbons, silk flowers, handbags and purses, they catch the eye in spectacular fashion. Some are 200 years old and more. Others are straight out of some of this year's most avant-garde shows, while a former Bishop of Leicester has weighed in with a mitre, in honeycomb and cable stitching. Bearing him in mind, and the mothers of brides beyond counting over the centuries, fancy hats and church go well together.

Apart from anything else, the newly refurbished Tetbury church cries out to be seen and enjoyed by more than its regular attenders, numerous enough though they are, for it has never looked more splendid in its theatrical way. Tetbury is many people's classic Cotswold town, but this is not a classic Cotswold church in the medieval wool tradition. Tetbury did indeed once have one of those, but by the second half of the 18th century it had fallen into such disrepair that its vicar, the Reverend John Wight, launched a determined campaign to have it replaced.

Wight and his supporters dug deep in their pockets and hit upon various other means of raising funds, including a society in which members paid two shillings and sixpence if they attended its quarterly meetings—and three shillings if they did not. More than £535 was collected by this means alone, and by 1777 work was under way, with only the tower and spire of the earlier building surviving. Wight did not live to see the opening in October 1781, but by the time of his death the design and building of the church were firmly in the hands of Francis Hiorn of Warwick. His efforts produced a striking early example of neo-Gothic architecture, a lofty, light and airy place of slender columns and clear glass, and, in contrast, dark and bulky box pews. A curious feature was his insistence on ambulatory corridors on three sides, with doors leading to the side aisles. 'More like the Opera House at Covent Garden than anything else,' ruminated the architectural writer David Verey, a man who surely knew more about churches in the Cotswolds than anyone.

Verey was not overcritical of the Victorianisation of the church in 1900, but it must be said that many others were, not least of them a succession of vicars. In 1971 the Reverend Michael Sherwood compiled a church guide based on the work of his predecessor, the Venerable W. S. Llewellyn, and it pulled no punches: 'The proper place for the organ is obviously in the gallery in the west end. The recess in the wall was evidently made to house the organ. It was moved to its present position, where it blocks the light from the chancel, in 1900, at the same time as the platform was erected on which the choir stalls now stand. This was done in the pious imitation of the layout of a cathedral, which has done so much damage to our parish churches. It was musically, aesthetically and liturgically unfortunate.'

This was the background to the major work carried out in the church in the early 1990s, culminating in its re-dedication by the former Archbishop of Canterbury Lord Coggan in the presence of Prince Charles in July 1993. A mighty undertaking costing £600,000, it saw the organ restored to the gallery and the choir seated up there too, the removal of the raised chancel and chancel screen of 1917 and the church redecorated throughout in white. The great stained-glass east window is now revealed in all its glory. Like some other

ABOVE *The magnificent stained-glass window in St Mary's, Tetbury, would look equally at home in the grandest cathedral.*

LEFT *The 186-foot spire of St Mary's dominates the Tetbury countryside and ensures the church is visible from afar.*

replacement windows of the Victorian era it is not to Hiorn's original plan, but thankfully there was no move to include it in the purge. One imagines that what has been done—cruciform votive candle stand, plate-metal pulpit et al.— has been quite enough to last some of the more traditionalist members of the congregation a lifetime.

The year 1993 also marked the centenary of the church tower and steeple. The 15th-century originals had been spared in the rebuilding of 1777, but a note in an old prayer book tells us that within a dozen years 'great thunder and lightning happened by which the parish church, and particularly the steeple, became greatly damaged'. In fact the steeple lasted the best part of a further hundred years, but by late Victorian times it was a curiosity of the South Cotswolds, leaning eight inches to the east and four feet six inches to the south. Folks came from miles around to view this oddity, and could not believe there was a more spectacular lean to be seen in Chesterfield or Pisa.

ABOVE AND RIGHT
Prince Charles honours Tetbury, his local town, by turning on the Christmas lights while members of the church choir herald the festive season with carols.

Tetbury has gone one better than its neighbours this year by enlisting Prince Charles to turn on the Christmas lights. Watching lights come on is now a popular evening out in our Cotswold towns in early December. It is commercial, of course—the traders' association, with its late-night shopping, is invariably at the heart of the venture—but then again, few of us would recognise as Christmas a season in which spending money was not a part of the proceedings, and what cannot be denied is that old Cotswold stone and a starry winter sky form the perfect backdrop to coloured lights, Christmas trees and cheerful, excited crowds. There have been times in recent years when some of the younger Stroud revellers have found the event rather too exciting, and have taken to dashing around the central pedestrianised streets squirting aerosol gunge at all in their path, but by and large it is not only shopkeepers who look forward to the evening with a warm glow.

Two thousand townsfolk turn out to see Prince Charles, and he rubs shoulders with them with scant regard for security, and overstays his schedule by well over half an hour. He shows up in a brown tweed overcoat that makes him look every inch the local squire, and warm to boot. In contrast, the chamber of commerce chairman on the rostrum is the most underdressed man in town in his best suit, but he looks delighted at his organisation's coup, and is scarcely likely to be feeling the cold with the adrenalin pumping his blood around at 1,000 miles an hour.

The prince looks in on half a dozen or more shops, not all of them scheduled stops. The long-established Phillips Bakery is a nod to tradition, but he stresses his offbeat, mystical credentials by calling in on an Aladdin's cave of a courtyard and shop in Long Street that specialises in oriental carpets, furniture and carvings. He delights Karen and Belinda in the catering shop in the modern Chipping shopping mall by telling them he has called in simply because their food smelled nice, and everywhere he is on the top of his royal-visit form, showing a bright and questioning interest in everything from cheese to old oak to bicycle wheels, and all the time leaving in his wake, but still within earshot, squeals of 'He touched me!', 'He shook my hand!!', 'He said those look good!!!' What a life! No wonder, when it is at last time to stoop into the car and head back to Highgrove, that an expression of blank-eyed release sweeps over his face before he musters another smile and wave for the little town that takes very seriously and loyally its role as his nearest neighbour.

COTSWOLD CHRISTMASTIDE

Christmas Eve. The rector at my childhood church would have taken a dim view of some of the music at the Tabernacle's Christmas show this evening. In his view the sin of making light of the Word Made Flesh was compounded by cloying sentimentality. 'Little Donkey', 'Mary's Boy Child', 'The Little Drummer Boy': my rector was not alone among Church people of his time in his misgivings about these songs, but hearing them sung by the Tabernacle players tonight, and welcomed with murmurings of warm recognition of the kind that would have greeted a favourite First World War music-hall song in my childhood, I'm reminded again of how familiarity can breed not so much contempt as content. Now, among believers who praise the Lord with far greater joy and up-front sincerity than he ever did, they are as much a means of spreading the Christmas message as 'Good King Wenceslas' and 'Away in a Manger'.

In the interval we spill out through the night to the downstairs room where coffee and mince pies are being served. 'See those railings?' says Mike Mills. 'They used to be round the old post office halfway down Marle Hill. I can show you a photo of them. As for this room we're going to, it's where the minister used to stable his horse. They've done it up a bit since then, mind you...'

Now in his early sixties, Mike has taken to helping Stan Gardiner with his slide shows of the village's past since the death of Lionel Padin, and as always I am in awe of his nodding acquaintance with almost every other stick and stone of this old place. On the other hand, though I am far closer to Mike in years than to his son Andrew, I feel I am much more in tune with what the young man is going through at present. Only this afternoon he has returned home from university, and here he is back among his old friends of the church's youth fellowship, catching up with who's in, who's out, who's up, who's down—and, most important of all, whether he counts for anything in these parts any more. Though thirty winters have passed, I can remember more clearly than many an incident of the past year that first homecoming after ten whole weeks away: the new allegiances and groupings that had formed among my friends in my absence, the people who let me down by being distressingly distant and others who knocked me off my feet and delighted me with the unforeseen warmth of their welcome.

Last night, if you could spot him among the dirty dishes and the socks hanging over the radiator, Andrew Mills was part of the ever-shifting scenery of a shared

DEATH AND REBIRTH: THE MUMMERS' PLAYS

LEFT *Marshfield's troop of mummers dress up in paper costumes each year on Boxing Day to perform an age-old ritual.*

TAKE A CAST of zany characters in paper costumes, a simple but surreal plot and a dialogue delivered in thumping rhyming verse, and you have the makings of a mummers' play.

These traditional plays were—and in some parts of the Cotswolds, such as Marshfield, still are—a comical interlude in midsummer and, especially, Christmas celebrations. Although the plays were written down they were transmitted orally, so variations on a theme inevitably occured. But the basic plot involved a hero, such as St George, fighting a dragon or an evil villain known as the Turkish Knight or Bold Slasher—or even a contemporary bogeyman such as Napoleon. The fight would end in injury or death and signal the entrance of the Noble Doctor, who could 'cure the itch, the stitch, paralysis, palsy and the gout'. It was his task to bring the dead to life with a magic pill, an action symbolising the rebirth of the new year. The names of other cast members read like characters from a children's comic: Bungler, Happy Jack, Beelzebub, and even Father Christmas, who introduced the play.

The origins of mummers' plays are uncertain. In late medieval and Tudor times, the name 'mummers' referred to masked actors who performed in revels at court; most of the evidence for the plays themselves dates only to the 18th and 19th centuries. Yet their theme of death and resurrection suggests they were part of an older folk tradition and were perhaps originally staged to mark the new year's conquest of the old, and light's victory over darkness.

student house in Southampton; now, where his dad remembers the old minister stabling his horse, he munches mince pies among friends he has known all his life in a village that has been his family's home for generations. And in five years' time, where will he be? Will his future lie here in the Cotswolds?

Christmas Day. The turkey is in the oven, and no sooner is it beginning to sizzle than Rose is off to help at a crisis centre for homeless people in Grosvenor Street, Cheltenham.

It takes up much of her Christmas Day, but once back home she says she felt it had all been made worthwhile when a petrol-station attendant had unwittingly rewarded her for her efforts. As she was paying for her fill-up he asked her whether she believed in Father Christmas. Of course she did, she replied, and he gave her a chocolate bar on the strength of it.

They had seen about a dozen homeless people at the centre, by no means all of those who do not have a permanent roof over their head in Cheltenham tonight. There had been a ban on alcohol with the Christmas meal, but no attempt had been made to deprive those given refuge of the drugs upon which so many of them relied. Rose had spent much of her time there with an addict named Dave, who kept his heroin and needle in a bum bag emblazoned with Mickey Mouse's vacuous, innocent smile.

BOXING DAY

Purists will tell you there is nothing more pagan than our midwinter mumming plays, when characters such as Beelzebub, Dr Phoenix, Saucy Jack—and these days, good old Father Christmas, too—tell a tangled tale of the death of winter and the rebirth of a new age. Parallels with ancient fertility cults are irresistible, according to scholars, but this does not explain why Cotswold people are out in their thousands on the streets of Gloucester, Cheltenham, Marshfield and elsewhere this Boxing Day morning, or why the mummers and their rum goings-on are as much a part of Christmas for many folks as the equally pagan delights of yule logs, mistletoe, plum puddings and holly.

There is a well-established pattern to the City of Gloucester Mummers' festivities with the Gloucestershire Morris Men this morning, starting at Imperial Gardens in Cheltenham and moving on to the Gloucester Cathedral precincts by noon. This is certainly the place to see them in Gloucester; their last port of call in the city, the medieval New Inn courtyard off Northgate Street, can be unbearably crowded.

We, however, are a long way south of there in Marshfield, where the 'paper boys' are again going through the ritual of putting on the town's unique mumming play. Who knows when it was first performed? Only its 20th-century revival is documented, for it was in 1930 that the parson here heard his gardener muttering some strange mumbo jumbo and was inspired to piece together the community's gone but not-quite-forgotten mumming ritual. The players are 'paper boys' simply because, their funereally dressed bellman apart, they are swathed in smocks and hoods of paper from their heads almost down to their ankles.

ABOVE *The tradition of hanging mistletoe at Christmas time has diverse origins: according to Norse legend, the plant will protect the love between those who kiss beneath it; when hung in a doorway, it is also supposed to protect a house from witches.*

A black sack is tumbling along and sullying the pristine High Street, Tesco bags and juice cartons scurrying in its wake. This seems most un-Marshfield-like, for it has always struck me as a town well in control of its destiny, give or take its identity crisis of a postal address. You write to it near Chippenham, Wiltshire, though it is traditionally a community in Gloucestershire's South Cotswolds, and found itself putting up with being in Avon for a couple of decades after the short-lived local government reorganisation of 1974. Wherever it is, since it ceased being a stopping place for travelling riffraff on the old Bristol to London road, it is not the kind of town where you expect to find sacks of rubbish bowling down the street, and I am pleased to see a young woman giving chase to the worst of the offending items, bringing a plastic bottle under control with a right foot clad in a slipper fashioned to look like Snoopy. 'You should be playing for Bristol Rovers,' I comment. 'Swindon!' she hisses vehemently. It is not always easy to pick up on the nuances of local allegiance out in the sticks.

On Boxing Day evening we frighten ourselves with ghost stories, tales of stagecoaches plying the highways of the Cotswolds for all eternity, for those with eyes to see them. A workmate of mine, Peter Beard of Woodmancote, near Cheltenham, was forever spotting spooks. He saw the headless horseman of Cleeve Hill and lived to tell the tale. As if Prestbury were not already shoulder-to-shoulder with spectres, he discovered another, a man dressed in an old fawn raincoat riding a prewar bike, and when his account of it was published, people wrote to him with full details of the cyclist's identity and the tragic circumstances in which he had died on that stretch of road. Tonight we recall the stagecoach Peter saw, complete with horses and passengers, floating eerily from the wall of the Farmer's Arms on the Cheltenham to Evesham road beyond Bishop's Cleeve. When he went back to investigate the next day, there was a bricked-up archway at the very point where he saw the apparition.

ABOVE *The Cotswolds has its fair share of ghost stories: perhaps the presence there of so many old buildings helps to keep them alive in the popular imagination.*

Scary stagecoaches: there are strong traditions around Burford, with so many inns catering for travellers on and around its steep and strikingly attractive main street in the old days—the Lamb, the Ramping Cat, the Bird in Hand, the Bird's Nest, the Roebuck…Then there was the tale that tireless ghost-hunter Wilfred Cox used to tell of a Cheltenham delivery-van driver heading home along Ermine Street at early dusk one evening in 1972. He had passed the big Highwayman road-house, formerly the Mason's Arms, and had reached the approaches to the Syde turning when he was astonished to see a white coach drawn by four white horses cross the road obliquely some fifteen yards ahead of him. It was so close he was forced to brake hard. Wilfred Cox knew all about this spot. It was where a minor road used to meet Ermin Street at an angle at what was called Smith's Crossing, before heading towards Elkstone; and it was here that the Gifford family of Brimpsfield waylaid a treasure train belonging to Edward II, an act of treason that brought about the fall of their castle…

POST-CHRISTMAS AUCTIONS

Philip Taubenheim is nursing a beer at the White Horse in Buckover in the Berkeley Vale, looking back on a job well done. His Wotton Auction Rooms, based in the old Tabernacle at Wotton-under-Edge, have started the pleasing practice of holding a sale between Christmas and New Year, and this year's has again been a success. Not that all who cram into the saleroom are potential bidders. 'After days at home looking at the relatives, people just want to get out,' he muses. 'We're one of the few things open, so in they come.' But there are plenty of dealers and keen collectors too, who welcome a little action in the quietest week of the year.

Auctioneers in the Cotswolds know there is a rich source in every town and village of the good 'fresh stock' they crave, so long as the housing market keeps ticking over well enough to release the effects of deceased estates. Furniture and other valuable household goods can otherwise lie under wraps in unoccupied houses, a state of affairs many executors are happy to see continue until the property is sold: a house viewed at its best with beautiful furniture is more easy to sell than an old place with all its uneven floorboards and wall stains exposed to the world.

Wealthy retirees who bring a lifetime's amassed possessions into the area are clearly important potential vendors, but Philip Taubenheim often finds that landed and farming families who have been here for generations can be at least as fruitful. 'It's the nature of farming people, as much as anything,' he says. 'They never like to throw anything away; they will maintain and recycle, rather than buy new, if they have the choice. You will see what I mean in their farmyards and in the corners of fields: old Ferguson tractors, ancient bits of equipment, everything

LEFT *Farming folk, according to the Wotton auctioneer, are notorious hoarders. It is certainly true that old farm machinery tends to end its days rusting away in forgotten corners.*

down to scraps of twine and worn-out tyres. In the house, you can find that successive generations have bought furniture from time to time, but rather than throw the old away, they have moved it up a flight of stairs. By the time you have climbed up to the attic in some of these old houses, you know you are getting somewhere.'

Stripped pine, painted furniture, longcase clocks and old oak still abound in unpretentious farmhouses, and the area's reputation for oak in particular pulls in traders from throughout the country, both to buy and to sell. 'Many dealers bring country furniture, oak and fruit wood, to Cotswold auction rooms,' says Philip. 'People expect to see it for sale round here, wherever it might originate from, and it just keeps on coming in. The fact is, with competition from three sale-rooms in Cirencester alone, we put from a thousand to twelve hundred lots under the hammer every four weeks, with occasional specialist sales in between. That shows you how productive this area can be. I leave it to the sociologists to decide whether the Cotswolds are a community of old people; but what I do know for certain is that they are stuffed full of antiques.'

THE YEAR CLOSES

Rose's friend James is over from Chandler's Ford in Hampshire, and they decide that Egypt Mill at Nailsworth is to be where they see in the New Year. The only trouble is, how do they get there, and how do they get back, student grants, or the absence of them, being what they are? I am not an admirer of men who drive around in cars labelled Dad's Taxi, but it is plain that it is going to be one of those nights, which restricts my festive evening's alcohol intake to a small sherry on the stroke of midnight. James is spooked by Minchinhampton Common, and by the time we are slaloming down the Nailsworth zigzag of road that they call the 'W', he is moved to remark that this doesn't look at all like Chandler's Ford. Towards the bottom of the hill I point out the astonishing sight of the Britannia pub in Cossack Square, dressed up like two dozen Christmas trees with hundreds of red and gold lights between which you could scarcely put a pin, or indeed a pine needle. We drive up for a closer look before we double back for Egypt Mill, and James glances behind at the Britannia one last time and says that doesn't look like Chandler's Ford either.

Having driven back to Nailsworth to collect them in the first hour of the new year, I take them home via Stroud. 'It gets pretty lively outside the Sub Rooms and around the clock,' I say, but when we approach via London Road we can see through to the clock, which is now showing 12.40am, and apart from the two police officers at the roundabout, not a soul is to be seen. The proverbial gun could be fired without risking damage to life and limb, apart from possibly to the tough little foxes, more streetwise than traditionally sly, that take over Stroud after the last of the humans has turned out the light and left for the night.

Back home, Rose and James hurry in to put the kettle on. I tramp down the drive to close the gate. Above, the stars are out in their thousands, that swath of Milky Way, the amber one I swear must be Mars, the Red Planet, and all those

LEFT *Spectacular firework displays celebrate the dawning of a new year—a time for nostalgia as well as future plans, and, for the author, the end of a year of contemplation.*

constellations the names of which I am determined to learn some day. I already recognise the Plough, and in the past twelve months I have learned to identify Orion with his belt. That is a constellation for every twenty-four years of my life, so I should be good for another one or two before my time is through. The new year is now more than an hour old, and most of Chalford Hill seems to have seen enough of it for the moment. Time enough in the morning, and 364 mornings after that, to discover what prizes and heartaches it has in store for us. The gate latch clicks against the world; the cat hears it and is on the wall in an instant, and by the time I am up to the house he is clawing impatiently at the door. An owl calls in the woods below Abnash. After that, all is still—until across the valley, somewhere towards Minchinhampton, some bright spark has discovered that he can wish the whole neighbourhood a Happy New Year by setting off fireworks so loud that they sound like nautical maroons. ■

HIGHLIGHTS

The best that the Cotswolds have to offer

BELOW *The Whispering Knights are the remains of a Bronze Age burial chamber (see page 163).*

ABOVE *The bronze statues at Batsford Park (see page 158) were brought back from Japan by Lord Redesdale.*

BELOW *Morning light in the historic town of Burford shows off the Cotswold stone buildings at their best.*

ABOVE *A hobbyhorse joins in the morris dancing at Scuttlebrook Wake (see page 169).*

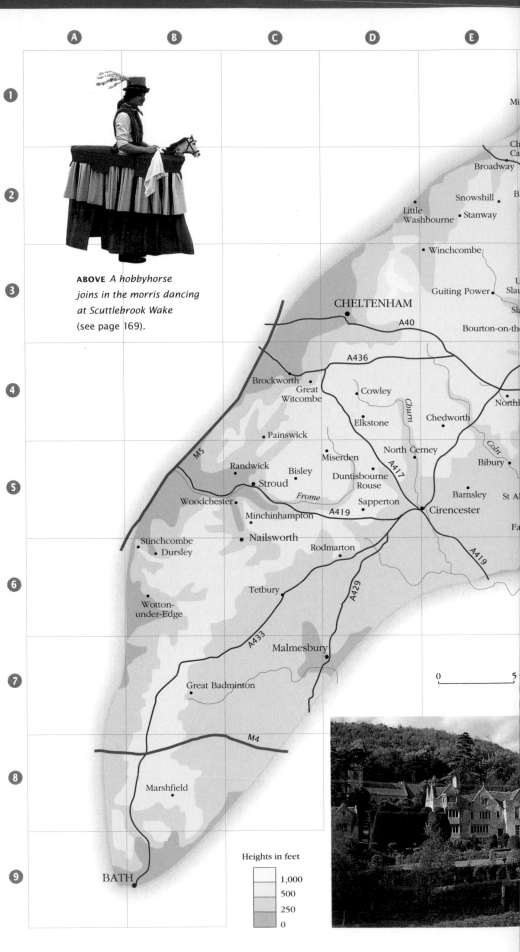

Broadway

Snowshill

Little Washbourne • Stanway

• Winchcombe

Guiting Power

CHELTENHAM

A40

Bourton-on-the

A436

Brockworth
Great Witcombe

Cowley

Chedworth

Elkstone

Painswick

North Cerney

Bibury

Randwick

Miserden

Bisley

Duntisbourne Rouse

Stroud

Barnsley

St Al

Woodchester

Frome

Sapperton

Cirencester

Minchinhampton

A419

A417

Nailsworth

Rodmarton

Stinchcombe
Dursley

A419

Tetbury

A429

Wotton-under-Edge

A433

Malmesbury

Great Badminton

M4

0   5

Marshfield

Heights in feet

1,000
500
250
0

BATH

G   H   I

RIGHT *A fantasy clock by Kit Williams hangs in Cheltenham's Regent Arcade (see page 154).*

eton-in-Marsh

astleton

Adlestrop

Great Tew

Chipping Norton

A44

Evenlode

issington

Woodstock

Barrington

Burford   Minster Lovell

A40

Kelmscot

mes or Isis

Faringdon

HT *Westonbirt*
oretum (see page
) is seen to its best
antage in the
umn, when it is
aze with the dramatic
and yellow foliage of
rs and larches.

T *Owlpen Manor*
page 160), mostly
ing from the 15th
tury, and the Victorian
rch that stands
ind it are tucked
ay at the bottom of
eep, wooded slope.

RIGHT *The late Laurie Lee's local pub, the Woolpack, indicates the importance of wool to the Cotswolds.*

CONTENTS

FREE HOUSE

THE WOOLPACK

ABOUT THIS SECTION

THROUGH THE PRECEDING PAGES author John Hudson has guided you on his personal tour of the Cotswolds. Now it is your turn. Whether your taste is for exploring villages, viewing gardens or just watching the world go by from the comfort of a country pub, you can use the selection of places in 'Highlights' to arrange your perfect Cotswold trip.

If you plan an overnight stay, the 'Historic Inns and Hotels' section on page 168 suggests some interesting places. Go in May and you can witness the daredevil cheese-rolling down Cooper's Hill, while September in Painswick sees the altogether more genteel 'clypping' ceremony round the village church. 'The Fame of the Cotswolds' from page 165 introduces you to the likes of Laurie Lee, the Mitford sisters and local hero Eddie 'The Eagle' Edwards. On page 169 are details of local tourist offices, which can provide additional information about opening times, entry fees, disabled access, etc.

Places listed in the 'Highlights' are followed by grid references that relate to the map on this page.

TOWNS AND VILLAGES

(but not open to the public), and Arlington Mill, now a museum of local history (*inset*). Views extend across the water meadow known as Rack Isle, which is a haven for wildlife (*see feature opposite*). Rococo tombstones are dotted around the churchyard of St Mary's Church, which has Saxon origins and many features dating from the 12th to 15th centuries.

Bisley C5

The distinguishing feature of this hilltop village is its set of wells which form a semicircle beneath the church. Thomas Keble, a 19th-century vicar, added gabled waterspouts and instigated the tradition of well-dressing on Ascension Day (*see pictures on page 69*). Bisley also retains its two-cell lock-up which dates from 1824.

Blockley F2

The village prospered in the 17th to 19th centuries when the textile industry was at its height. The mills, powered by Blockley Brook, supplied silk to the ribbon-weavers of Coventry, and the village was busy with small factories and foundries. Today, huddles of artisans' cottages in the valley and imposing merchants' houses in the High Street are reminders of those industrious times. In 1887 Blockley became England's first electrically lit village, with electricity generated in a converted mill.

Bourton-on-the-Water F3

Tiny stone bridges cross the clear, shallow waters of the Windrush as it glides through the central green, edged by 17th- and 18th-century cottages and presided over by the 1784 lead cupola of St Lawrence's Church. Numerous attractions cater for visitors, including the Cotswold Motor Museum and Toy Collection, the Model Railway and a meticulously created one-ninth-scale Model Village (of Bourton) built in the 1930s of Cotswold stone. Just outside the village are two bird collections: Birdland, with rare and exotic birds including penguins, and Folly Farm Waterfowl, a conservation centre for rare breeds.

Adlestrop G3

'Yes. I remember Adlestrop,' mused Edward Thomas in his evocative poem which reminisces about the time his express train made an unscheduled stop there on a hot June day, and 'no one left and no one came on the bare platform'. The station no longer exists, but the old sign is now in the village bus shelter. An earlier visitor was Jane Austen, who, in the early 1800s, stayed with her uncle, the Reverend Thomas Leigh, at Adlestrop House (formerly the vicarage); this may have been the model for the abbey in *Northanger Abbey*.

The Barringtons F4

On opposite sides of the tranquil Windrush valley stand Great and Little Barrington, the former an estate village built beside Barrington Park, the latter with a sloping green flanked by groups of attractive cottages. Local quarries supplied the materials for a distinguished array of buildings, including the original medieval St Paul's Cathedral in London, as well as the crypt of Sir Christopher Wren's later replacement, and a number of City of London churches and various Oxford colleges.

Bath B9

Although peripheral to the Cotswolds, Bath is one of the great sights of the region. The Romans began the spa tradition, and the city's popularity was revived in the 18th century when Bath was developed with classical terraces, fine squares and the magnificent Royal Crescent and Circus. Much of the city was designed by John Wood the Elder and his son John Wood the Younger, and built in locally quarried Bath stone. 'Beau' Nash was Master of Ceremonies, responsible for ensuring the city's status as the most fashionable place to take the waters. Even today, the Pump Room is a focal point, where visitors sip tea to the strains of chamber music; close by are Bath Abbey and the magnificently preserved Roman Baths. An impressive range of museums includes the Assembly Rooms, housing a fine costume collection, the Roman Baths Museum and the Postal Museum. Robert Adam's Pulteney Bridge, designed with shops along it, is the starting point for cruises on the River Avon. (*see also feature on page 136*).

Bibury E5

The 19th-century designer, pioneering socialist and writer William Morris thought Bibury the most beautiful village in England, and little has changed architecturally since his day, thanks in part to his conservation efforts. Bridges span the duck-populated River Coln, and beneath a beech wood stands Arlington Row, a picturesque group of 17th-century tenanted cottages now owned by the National Trust

WATER MEADOWS: A WILDLIFE HAVEN

TRUE WATER MEADOWS are a curious artificial creation—fields deliberately flooded by means of sluices and channels from an adjoining river or lake, in order not just to soak the land thoroughly but to fertilise it with a coating of silt. From the late 16th century to the early 20th, farmers in southern England carefully maintained such fields to grow lush pasture for livestock, especially the vital grass in early spring that would feed lambs and ewes.

Two of the Cotswolds' best-known former water meadows are now in National Trust hands: Rack Isle, beside the Coln in Bibury, and the Sherborne Meadows, along the Windrush. Rack Isle, now raised and moated since its early pasture-land days, takes its name from the drying racks on which the weavers' wool used to be hung after washing. Today it is a home for ducks and a refuge for nesting birds, voles and other wildlife—all apparently unperturbed by the tourist bustle surrounding them.

The Sherborne Meadows site, 140 acres in extent, was restored in the 1990s, and is steadily resuming the life of a fully

BELOW *Water voles are in decline and are now on a protected-species list. Rack Isle offers them a valuable haven.*

mature water meadow. Varied grasses and wild flowers underlie an entire mini-ecosystem: beetles and bees, flies and butterflies, dragonflies haunting the ditches; voles and mice scuttling about—and attracting barn owls in turn; snipe, lapwings and redshanks feeding in the muddy soil. As with the water meadows of old, it is a heartening case of human meddling that enhances rather than spoils the landscape, and assists rather than obstructs the welfare work of nature.

LEFT *Rack Isle water meadow is a home for birds and other wildlife despite the tourists visiting scenic Arlington Row behind it.*

Broadway E2

At the foot of Broadway Hill, beneath the Cotswold escarpment, the village of Broadway stands on the threshold of the Vale of Evesham but is entirely Cotswold in character, with its honey-coloured stone. The busy A44 that runs through it was originally the 'broad way'. The village has kept a distinguished range of Tudor, Stuart and Georgian houses, farm-labourers' cottages, inns and shops. At the top of the hill stands Broadway Tower, built as a folly in 1798 by the sixth Earl of Coventry, and with views that extend as far as the Malverns, Warwick, Worcester and the Welsh borders. It is now within a privately run country park.

Burford G4

The High Street of this handsome former coaching and wool town slopes steeply down to a bridge over the River Windrush. Remodelled in the 15th century, the vast parish church contains two notable monuments: one to Sir Lawrence Tanfield (1628), with effigies of himself and his family beneath a macabre skeleton; the other commemorates Edmund Harman, barber to Henry VIII, and is carved with four Amazonian Indians—probably the first depiction of these people in Britain. Numerous wool merchants are buried in the churchyard, their tombs carved in the form of bales of wool (*right*). In 1649, during the time of Oliver Cromwell,

mutinous Roundheads were imprisoned in the church for three nights, and one prisoner's graffiti can still be seen. At the nearby Cotswold Wildlife Park, rare Asiatic lions and other exotic animals are kept in the grounds of a 19th-century manor house.

TOWNS AND VILLAGES (CONTINUED)

Cheltenham D3

The discovery of a spring here in 1716 turned Cheltenham into a major spa resort. During Regency times the town was at the height of fashion, and many elegant terraces and crescents survive from the period, some fancifully adorned with iron verandahs and canopies. Visitors can still sample the salty, alkaline waters at the Greek Revival-style Pitville Pump Room, and stroll in the meticulously tended ornamental gardens and along the tree-lined Promenade. The Regent Arcade, a two-storey shopping arcade built in the 1980s, houses a fantasy clock made by local artist Kit Williams, which blows bubbles on the hour and half hour. Cheltenham has a busy arts scene, with music and literature festivals, and is Britain's major steeplechase venue: the National Hunt Festival in March attracts spectators from afar, and features the Gold Cup and Champion Hurdle (*see feature on page 50*). The Art Gallery and Museum has a collection of Arts and Crafts silver and furniture, with designs by Charles Voysey and Ernest Gimson. The terraced Regency house in Clarence Road where Gustav Holst, composer of *The Planets*, was born in 1874 is now a museum dedicated to his

life. The town also boasts two famous public schools.

Chipping Campden F1

Perhaps more than anywhere else in the Cotswolds, Chipping Campden gives a clear idea of how a wool town would have looked in its heyday. Wool money helped build the church, where a monument commemorates Sir Baptist Hicks, who lavished part of his fortune on the cobbled, open-sided Market Hall of 1627 and the nearby almshouses; two lodges by the church were all that remained of his estate after the mansion was burned down during the Civil War. The broad main street is lined with honey-coloured buildings, including the 14th-century home of another wool merchant, William Grevel, and, dating from the same period, the Woolstapler's Hall, built as a meeting place for fleece merchants and now a privately owned house.

Chipping Norton G3

This pretty hilltop town has hosted markets in its triangular marketplace since the 13th century. The early 16th-century guildhall today houses the Tourist Information Centre. On the town's west

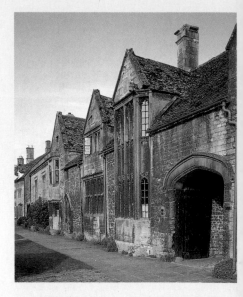

ABOVE *The handsome house built in Chipping Campden's high street in c.1380 for wealthy wool merchant William Grevel is an architectural jewel in a golden-hued terrace of houses.*

side is the Bliss Tweed Mill of 1872, a magnificent industrial relic with an impressively tall chimney. The mansion-like mill has now been converted into flats.

Cirencester E5

Known to the Romans as Corinium, Cirencester was Britain's largest town after Londinium (London), but its Roman remains were virtually obliterated by Saxon settlers in the 6th century. Prosperity returned in the Middle Ages as the wool trade boomed. Trade is still a mainstay: there is a twice-weekly market, and there are craft stalls in the Corn Hall and in a former brewery now known as Brewery Arts. In the marketplace stands the greatest of the Cotswold 'wool churches', St John Baptist, mostly dating from 1350 to 1530, with a 15th-century tower supported by flying buttresses. Its three-tiered south porch was added in 1500, designed specially as an office in which to conduct secular business, and later used as a town hall. The streets reveal a wealth of 17th-century and Georgian architecture, and there are pleasant strolls to be had in the Abbey Grounds—the former abbey site that is now a public park—and in landscaped Cirencester Park, which extends for five miles behind the town. The Corinium Museum, closed to the public until Spring 2004, has a major Roman collection, with full-scale reconstructions of a kitchen, dining room

BELOW *The well-preserved Regency buildings in Montpellier Walk, Cheltenham, are supported with caryatids—columns sculpted in the form of female figures in classical dress.*

and butcher's shop. South of the town, the Cotswold Water Park is an area of over 100 lakes, created by filling in disused gravel pits; it encompasses Keynes Country Park which offers swimming, walks, water sports and birdwatching.

Elkstone D4

No other village in the Cotswolds boasts a more rewarding Norman church than this. The south porch is decorated with rich carvings featuring an array of men and beasts, with a tympanum over the door depicting Christ in Majesty, the symbols of the Evangelists and the Hand of God. A central Norman tower was replaced by a Perpendicular one at the western end, but the position of the original is marked by the arches that separate the nave from the tiny choir; this is lit by modern yellow glass, giving a golden hue to the east end. A spiral staircase climbs behind the pulpit to a dovecote.

Fairford F6

Straddling the River Coln, the town has an appealing blend of timber-framed and stone houses and inns on its marketplace, but is best known for its parish church. This is unique in Britain in having a complete set of pre-Reformation stained-glass windows, depicting the Bible story from the Creation to the Crucifixion. The church was rebuilt between 1490 and 1500 by John Tame and his son Sir Edmund Tame, both wealthy wool merchants, who employed the great glazier Barnard Flower and the best masons and sculptors money could buy. Tiddles, the long-serving church cat, is commemorated in the churchyard by a tombstone (*above*) bearing a carved likeness.

Great Tew H3

Thatched roofs and ironstone walls set the tone for this epitome of the old English village. It is not, however, all that old, having been built during the development of the manorial estate in the 19th century. An avenue leads to St Michael and All Angels' Church, which contains genuinely old medieval wall paintings.

Guiting Power E3

One of a series of timeless villages tucked into the folds of the western slopes of the

ABOVE *St John's Lock, Lechlade, with the statue of Old Father Thames to the left. In summer the river is busy with pleasure boats, presenting a lively scene to walkers on the tow path.*

Cotswolds, Guiting Power, with its cottages and two village greens, was restored by a village trust established in 1958. Near its sister village of Temple Guiting, where the River Windrush formerly powered cloth mills, is the Cotswold Farm Park, home to an array of rare farm breeds (*see feature on page 60*).

Lechlade F6

The rivers Cole, Coln and Leach join the Thames (also known in its upper reaches as the Isis) here at its westernmost navigable point; in earlier times barges were loaded up with building stone, bound for Oxford and London. Near St John's Lock is a Neptune-like statue known as Old Father Thames, which was sculpted in the 1850s and originally exhibited at the Crystal Palace. The spire of 15th-century St Lawrence's Church soars over the village. When the poet Percy Bysshe Shelley visited the town in 1815, he was inspired to write the poem 'A Summer Evening Churchyard, Lechlade'.

Malmesbury D7

A small market town on the borders of Wiltshire, Malmesbury is dominated by its ruined abbey (*see feature overleaf*), facing a green at the heart of the town. In the

TOWNS AND VILLAGES (CONTINUED)

MALMESBURY'S MEDIEVAL MYSTERY

DOMINATING the small market town of Malmesbury are the imposing ruins of its Benedictine abbey, founded some 1,300 years ago. In the former abbey grounds stands a grey stone house: with ivy and wisteria growing up the walls and an idyllic rose garden, Abbey House is a picture of tranquillity. But in 1997 its peace was disturbed when the gardener's spade hit a stone coffin—over seven feet long and exhibiting some fine stonemasonry—during a routine gardening session.

English Heritage, which owns the site, excavated the coffin, and inside it a complete skeleton was discovered. The coffin's location and high-quality stonework were the first clues to identifying its occupant: it must have been somebody of importance within the abbey. Next, the skeleton was dismantled and the bones taken to a laboratory for

LEFT An aerial view of Malmesbury shows the abbey and, to its right, Abbey House, where the medieval stone coffin was found.

forensic work, which revealed the skeleton to be male. Tall by medieval standards at five feet ten inches, he was in his fifties when he died. During his life he would have suffered from severe toothache and had a limp. Examination of his stomach contents showed that fish had been a staple in his diet, indicating that he had been a monk, for whom meat was taboo.

The final step was to establish what the monk had looked like. Gaps in his skull were filled with wax and the contours scanned into a computer. Using 3-D imagery, some 'average' men's features were then combined and wrapped round the skull image, with the result that the monk's face, hollow-cheeked and with a broken nose, eerily appeared on the computer screen, just as it may have looked seven centuries ago as he went about his daily life and prayers in Malmesbury.

LEFT An archaeological illustrator's reconstructive drawing of the monk shows him black-habited and tonsured.

11th century, a monk made himself wings and, in an attempt at flight, jumped from the tower—he covered a short distance before crashing and breaking both legs. The Old Bell Inn, St John's Almshouses and the 16th-century market cross are among the town's other ancient buildings.

Moreton-in-Marsh F2
By the Market Hall in the wide, grass-verged main street stands the Curfew Tower, possibly 16th century, whose bell was rung daily until 1860. Moreton is the largest town in the northeast Cotswolds and its location on the Fosse Way meant that for many centuries it was an important staging post. Despite this, Moreton was less successful as a wool centre than many

other towns in the area. Today, however, it has the largest open-air market in the Cotswolds. Close by, the Cotswold Falconry Centre runs conservation and breeding programmes for falcons, hawks and owls.

Northleach E4
After the London-to-Gloucester turnpike opened in 1746, many houses in the High Street gained new façades. Today the town is bypassed, but it draws in visitors to two absorbing museums. Housed in the former House of Correction, the Cotswold Countryside Collection offers a glimpse of yesteryear, with a collection of old agricultural vehicles as well as a restored cell block and courtroom. Meanwhile, Keith Harding's World of Mechanical

Music displays working musical boxes and a range of automata (*below*). Known as the 'cathedral of the Cotswolds', the 15th-century Church of St Peter and St Paul has superb memorial brasses, and a corbel shows a cat playing the fiddle to an audience of three rats.

Painswick C4

Graced with silver-grey building stone, the small town slopes down to Painswick Brook, with its former cloth mills. In 1792 the churchyard was planted with 99 yews, now trimmed into bulbous shapes; some are joined together to form arches. Among them stand some remarkably diverse tombs—oblong, hexagonal, triangular or pepperpot in shape, and adorned with carved features such as scrolls, foliage and shells. Just to the east of Painswick lies the countryside around Slad, immortalised in Laurie Lee's childhood autobiography *Cider with Rosie*, while to the north 20th-century Prinknash Abbey is a Benedictine monastery with a celebrated pottery on view to the public.

The Slaughters F3

Situated on the banks of the River Eye, Upper Slaughter boasts one of the finest Elizabethan manor houses in the Cotswolds (not open to the public), a small square surrounded by cottages and a Norman church, restored in Victorian times. Its neighbour Lower Slaughter attracts more visitors. Here, the Eye flows past a water mill with a large water wheel.

Stanway E2

The Cotswold escarpment shelters this immaculately preserved village, with its manor house, tithe barn and gatehouse. While staying there, J. M. Barrie is thought to have gained the inspiration for Tinkerbell, the fairy in *Peter Pan*, when moonlight, reflected off the church weather vane, shimmered on his bedroom wall. Barrie was a keen cricketer and

designed the thatched cricket pavilion (*above*). A short walk away are the villages of Stanton, restored by the architect Sir Philip Stott after he purchased Stanton Court in 1906, and Buckland, where the church displays magnificent furnishings,

including 15th-century pews and a late 17th-century gallery.

Stow-on-the-Wold F3

Eight roads meet here at a high point on the Cotswold plateau. The town was originally known as Edwardstow, possibly after St Edward. After a Civil War battle some 1,000 Royalists were captured and held in the church, which was by then in ruins; it was restored in the 1680s. The spacious market square, where the town stocks still stand, hosted major sheep sales, and farmers drove their flocks here in great numbers. Today the numerous antique shops and hotels indicate the town's role as a popular centre for exploring the Cotswolds. The nearby village of Broadwell has a particularly attractive green, cut by a small stream.

Stroud C5

Sited at the confluence of five valleys and at the junction of the Thames and Severn Canal and the Stroudwater Canal, Stroud was a busy centre for cloth production until the 19th century. Many of its mills can still be seen, although most are now converted to other uses.

Tetbury C6

In medieval times the town grew as a market centre, attracting traders in dairy produce from the Vale of Berkeley and Wiltshire, and wool merchants from the Cotswolds. The Chipping Steps, an early medieval cobbled street, leads from the market. The Market House of 1655 is built on sturdy stone pillars and topped with a cupola and weather vane in the form of two dolphins. Tetbury acquired some striking buildings in the 18th century, among them St Mary's Church, an elegantly proportioned example of Georgian Gothic Revival style, with two fine brass chandeliers and high-backed pews. Cells inside the old courthouse are now home to the Police Bygones Museum.

Winchcombe E3

Beautifully placed, deep in the Isbourne valley, this small town was once capital of the Saxon shire of Mercia. Its old town hall houses a Folk and Police Museum with police uniforms from all over the world. Steam and diesel locomotives haul carriages on the Gloucestershire–Warwickshire Railway to Toddington, passing close to the ruins of Hailes Abbey,

ABOVE *The houses on Vineyard Street in Winchcombe put on a bright display in summer.*

a Cistercian house founded in 1246 by Richard, Earl of Cornwall. In 1539 it became one of the last monasteries to be closed during the Dissolution; the cloisters and stone outlines of the floor plan are all that remain. The nearby parish church of St Peter contains floor tiles from the abbey.

Woodstock I4

This prosperous town on the edge of the Cotswolds is best known for Blenheim Palace (*see entry on page 158*), which lies immediately to the southwest, but is rewarding enough in its own right. In the past Woodstock was a centre of glove-making, and the triangle of streets around its town hall of 1766 has much Georgian character. Within a fine town house near the stocks, the County Museum recalls the archaeology and industries of Oxfordshire.

Wotton-under-Edge B6

Despite being burnt to the ground in the 13th century by mercenaries of King John, Wotton-under-Edge went on to become a prosperous town during the heyday of the cloth industry in the 17th century. Buildings dating from this period are the Tolsey House and an attractive group of almshouses. The 14th- and 15th-century Berkeley family memorial brasses are outstanding features of the church.

HOUSES AND GARDENS

Barnsley House Garden
near Cirencester **E5**

Gardener Rosemary Verey transformed the gardens of Barnsley House after moving there in 1951 with her husband, the architectural writer David Verey. Key features of the four-acre garden are statues, a fountain, a lime and laburnum walk and two 18th-century summerhouses. A meticulously planned vegetable garden in the form of a decorative potager based on 16th- and 17th-century designs has a chequerboard of paths around goblet-shaped fruit trees.

Batsford Park Arboretum
Moreton-in-Marsh **F2**

In the 1880s the 1st Lord Redesdale returned from a diplomatic posting in Tokyo and established a wild garden of bamboos, specimen trees and exotic shrubs on a hilly, watery site overlooking the Evenlode valley. Today this arboretum is said to be one of the largest private tree collections in the country. It presents magnificent seasonal colours: notable times are spring, when cherry and magnolia are in bloom, and the ground is carpeted with daffodils and narcissi; and autumn, when the vivid reds and oranges of the Japanese maples are quite stunning.

Blenheim Palace Woodstock **I4**

Britain's finest example of Baroque civic architecture, Blenheim stands on a former royal estate given to the first Duke of Marlborough, John Churchill, after his part in the defeat of the French at the Battle of Blenheim on the River Danube in 1704. Designed by Sir John Vanbrugh and built between 1705 and 1730, the palace has carvings by Grinling Gibbons, a chapel and doorways by Sir Nicholas Hawksmoor and a painted ceiling by Sir James Thornhill depicting the first duke in Roman costume presenting the plan of the Battle of Blenheim to Britannia. Some rooms are dedicated to the memory of Sir Winston Churchill, who was born here and is buried in the churchyard at Bladon nearby. There are formal Italian and French gardens and a huge park, laid out by Capability Brown (*see feature on page 34*) some 50 years after the palace was completed. The park features a lake spanned by a 390-foot bridge, a maze and the Column of Victory—a 134-foot-high stone column erected to the memory of the first duke by his widow.

Buscot Park near Faringdon **G6**

Built by James Darley between 1779 and 1783, the plain grey 18th-century house is set in a large park. As well as its water garden, designed between 1904 and 1912 by Harold Peto, and such features in the grounds as an Egyptian avenue guarded by sculptural sphinxes, Buscot Park is memorable for collections amassed by two former owners—Alexander Henderson, Lord Faringdon, and his grandson the second Lord Faringdon. These include paintings by European masters, including Rembrandt and Rubens, and some fine Pre-Raphaelite works, notably a portrait by Rossetti of Jane Morris as Pandora and a series on the legend of the Briar Rose (the *Sleeping Beauty* tale) by Burne-Jones. There are also examples of Chinese porcelain.

Cerney House Gardens North Cerney **D5**

Sited above the Churn valley, the gardens have an air of informality, with a meadow bright with wild flowers and woodland flecked with snowdrops and bluebells. The scented walled garden contains herbaceous borders, old rose varieties and a sweet-smelling herb garden.

ABOVE *Designed as a picture gallery, the Long Library at Blenheim Palace houses over 10,000 volumes and is one of the longest rooms in England, extending for 183 feet.*

CROQUET: THE ORIGINS OF A GENTEEL SPORT

LEFT *Chastleton House, home in the mid 19th century to Walter Jones Whitmore, who drafted the definitive rules of croquet.*

ABOVE *The World Croquet final is played on the lawns of the Hurlingham Club, London, in 1990.*

RIGHT *The essential tools of croquet: balls and mallets, first manufactured in the mid 1800s.*

CROQUET, THAT GENTEEL GAME played on the lawns of timeless country houses, seems quintessentially English—yet it is probably not English at all. Time's passing has obscured the origins of the game, but historians claim to have traced it back to India, China, even to Ancient Greece.

Whatever its provenance, by 1860 croquet was de rigueur at every English garden party. By then, John Jacques and Son of London were making sets of equipment. Those were formative days for the game, and no single set of rules achieved general circulation. That croquet graduated from a frivolous distraction for the landed classes into a legitimate sport is thanks largely to Walter Jones Whitmore, who was born at Chastleton House.

Whitmore was a man of impulse and enthusiasm, and a dreary stint in the civil service spurred him to try living off his wits. Sadly, these were found lacking. A board game he invented proved a failure. Attempts at writing poetry and novels were similarly ill-starred, and by the mid-1860s, his bills were mounting.

Whitmore was, however, destined to make his mark on the world. He first played croquet around 1860. Soon he was hooked, and had two lawns laid at Chastleton. Realising there were no formal rules, he set about drafting a set himself, with customary gusto. These appeared in the countryman's magazine *The Field* in 1866. Though Whitmore died in debt in 1872, the sport he helped popularise never looked back, and croquet is increasingly being played at all levels from family games in the garden to international club matches.

Chastleton House Moreton-in-Marsh F2
The estate was once owned by Catholic Gunpowder Plot conspirator Robert Catesby, who sold it to Walter Jones in 1602 to pay debts incurred for his part in an uprising the previous year. Jones built the current house, and since then his descendants have been in continuous occupation. After acquiring it in 1991 the National Trust conserved the Jacobean manor as found, rather than restoring it to its original state. Most of the contents have survived virtually intact—rare tapestries, Civil War relics and period furniture, as well as more commonplace objects of yesteryear. Walter Jones's coat of arms sits on the chimneypiece in the Great Chamber, beneath a pendant-embellished plaster ceiling. In the gardens, which include topiary, is a lawn where the modern rules of croquet were codified in 1865 (*see feature above*).

Chavenage near Tetbury C6
This E-shaped Elizabethan manor dates from 1576. Its interior—lit by two Perpendicular windows with medieval glass possibly originally installed in Horsley church—contains furniture, tapestries and Civil War memorabilia.

Cirencester Park E5
This huge estate was laid out in the grand manner, with long avenues and rides,

HOUSES AND GARDENS (CONTINUED)

by the first Earl of Bathurst in the early 18th century. He erected eye-catching features such as Alfred's Hall folly and Queen Anne's Monument—a column topped by a statue of the Queen. There is free access to the 3000 acres of parkland, but the house is not open to the public.

Hidcote Manor Mickleton F1
So much at the forefront of horticultural innovation has this garden been that it has given its name to numerous plant varieties. Created in the early 20th century by Major Lawrence Johnston, it is sheltered from its exposed site by hedges and topiary which enclose it into a series of outdoor rooms and corridors. These in turn provide an exciting series of contrasts and vistas, mixing light with shade and the formal with the informal. The garden was

given to the National Trust in 1948; the manor itself is not open to the public.

Kelmscott Manor Kelmscot G6
In 1871 the poet, pioneer socialist and craftsman William Morris leased this Grade I listed 16th-century manor house made of local limestone. It was to become his 'heaven on earth' until his death 25 years later. The travellers described in his utopian tale *News from Nowhere* end their voyage here. For the first three years he shared the house with the artist Dante Gabriel Rossetti, but their relationship was soured by Rossetti's affair with Morris's wife Jane, the subject of many of his paintings. Fabrics, wallpapers and tapestries by Morris, along with Pre-Raphaelite paintings, are on display.

Kiftsgate Court Gardens Mickleton F1
Three generations of female gardeners have made Kiftsgate what it is today. After the First World War Heather Muir created a garden whose hallmarks are a richness of colour and an informal setting, around a late Victorian house surrounded by steep banks. Her daughter continued the work, and her granddaughter owns it today. June and July see a profusion of rose varieties, including the rambling white Kiftsgate rose. There is a sunken garden with bulbs that create a colourful display in spring.

Minster Lovell Hall G4
By the Windrush at the edge of the attractive village of Minster Lovell stand the eerie ruins of this 15th-century hall, the former seat of the Lovell family. Ranged around a quadrangle, they include a great hall and kitchen, as well as a fine dovecote. In 1457 Francis Lovell was involved in the ill-fated scheme of the pretender Lambert Simnel to secure the Crown; after the failure of the rising he hid in a locked room in the hall, where he eventually starved to death after the servant who looked after him passed away. During building work in 1708, a room was discovered containing the skeleton of a man, said to have been sitting at a table, with the skeleton of a dog at his feet.

Misarden Park Gardens Miserden D5
Graced with the backdrop of the Golden Valley, these quintessentially English gardens were partly designed by Edwin Lutyens, who rebuilt a wing of the 17th-century manor house (not open to the public) in 1920, and added yew topiary and some other garden features. Grass steps lead to the south lawn, and beyond two fine herbaceous borders is a rose garden. Blossoms and bulbs give a bright spring show.

Newark Park near Wotton-under-Edge B6
This four-square castellated house was a 1790 'Gothick' remodelling by James Wyatt of a Tudor hunting lodge. The original structure was built of stones and timber taken from nearby Kingswood Abbey, which was demolished in 1540. Standing on the edge of a 40ft cliff, the flat roof was designed to offer spectacular views of the surrounding panorama.

Owlpen Manor near Dursley B6
Dating from the 15th to 17th centuries, this fine Tudor manor underwent some remodelling in the early 18th century but was uninhabited from 1850 and fell into neglect. It was rediscovered by Norman Jewson, an adherent of Arts and Crafts principles of conservation and design, who in 1926 began a sensitive restoration. The interiors reveal an intriguing mixture of the centuries, with 17th-century painted cloth wallhangings in the Great Chamber, and Arts and Crafts items. The house stands in a typical old English manor hillside garden, with roses and box parterres, at the foot of a wooded valley.

Painswick House Rococo Garden C4
The renaissance of this unique 18th-century garden has been made possible as a result of a painting produced by Thomas Robins in 1748, showing an aerial view of the site with the house as a centrepiece, and hedges, pavilions, orchards and trees all part of the garden layout. Much of the restoration has now been carried out, making for an enticing blend of the geometric and the naturalistic. Snowdrops give a magnificent display in early spring.

Rodmarton Manor Gardens D6
Surrounding an early 20th-century house built by Arts and Crafts architect Ernest Barnsley, the garden retains much of its original design. It was planned as a series of outdoor rooms with a distinct character. Clipped hedges of yew, holly, beech and box compartmentalise much of the site, and there are splendid borders in addition to wild areas and kitchen gardens.

Sezincote near Moreton-in-Marsh F2
Sezincote is a startling feature in the Gloucestershire countryside—an Indian fantasy resplendent with a Mogul-inspired onion dome and a semicircular orangery. It was an early 19th-century collaboration between the architect Samuel Pepys Cockerell, who had worked as an architect for the East India Company, and the topographical artist Thomas Daniell, who had also travelled to India. Its interior is purely classical, while the grounds include a bridge decorated with Brahmin bulls, an Indian shrine and a water garden backed by parkland. In 1806 the Prince Regent visited the house and determined to build his Royal Pavilion in Brighton as a similar Indian extravaganza.

SUDELEY CASTLE, ROYAL RESIDENCE

ABOVE *Sir Thomas Seymour, husband of Catherine Parr, was made Lord of Sudeley by his nephew and her stepson, the child-king Edward VI.*

LEFT *Sudeley Castle lures visitors with its beautiful gardens, priceless treasures and enthralling stories of the lives of past inhabitants.*

WITH ITS honey-coloured walls, medieval ruins and fragrant gardens, Sudeley Castle is a rare jewel in a setting of parkland and wooded hills near historic Winchcombe. Sudeley has been associated with kings, queens and nobility for more than a millennium.

Although its origins go back to Saxon times, the castle was rebuilt in 1441 by Ralph Boteler, Lord Admiral of the English fleet. During the Wars of the Roses, Sudeley became the home of the future Richard III; and in Tudor times it was the residence of Catherine Parr, the widow of Henry VIII, and her husband Sir Thomas Seymour. Catherine died soon after childbirth in 1548 and was buried in the castle chapel; a year later her husband paid for his court intrigues with his head. The next owner was Sir John Brydges, Lord Chandos, and it was one

of his descendants who entertained Elizabeth I in 1592; during the three-day feast, local shepherds presented the lucky Queen with 'the Cotswolds' best fruit'— an unwashed fleece.

In the Civil War Sudeley was a stronghold for the staunch Royalist Chandos; but, after King Charles's defeat, it was 'slighted'—deliberately ruined—on Cromwell's orders. Left to the elements, Sudeley was given new life only in 1837, when it was bought by the Worcester glovemakers John and William Dent. They began to restore the castle, and, after their deaths, the work was continued by their nephew John Dent and, most notably, his energetic wife Emma Brocklehurst. Emma died in 1900, having laid the basis for the restored rooms, artistic collections and magnificent gardens that can be seen today.

Snowshill Manor E2

This Tudor manor was transformed by Charles Paget Wade after the First World War. He filled the rooms with collections paying homage to the craftsmanship and design aesthetic of the Arts and Crafts Movement, in addition to musical instruments, tools, clocks, toys, bicycles and even Japanese samurai armour. Carved on an outside wall of the manor is a 1922 statue of St George and the Dragon (*right*).

Stanway Baroque Water Gardens E2

Formerly a holding of Tewkesbury Abbey, the manor house was purchased by Richard Tracy at the time of the Dissolution. He and his successors remodelled the house, which is largely Jacobean in character, and around 1750 the garden was adorned with a pyramidal folly, the centrepiece of a cascade which has now been restored.

Sudeley Castle near Winchcombe E3

(see feature, left)

Westonbirt Arboretum near Tetbury C6

In 1829 Robert Holford began planting groups of Wellingtonias, Douglas firs, redwoods and other North American species in the grounds of his mansion, Westonbirt House. With more than 18,000 trees and shrubs from all parts of the globe, the arboretum is today one of the largest temperate collections in the world. It is ablaze with colour in all seasons, particularly in spring, with magnolia blooms and carpets of bluebells, and in autumn, when its glades are bright with the dramatic foliage of Japanese maples.

Woodchester Mansion C5

This unfinished Victorian house is, in effect, a 19th-century building site caught in a time warp. The house was commissioned by William Leigh, who employed a local man, Benjamin Bucknall, as his architect. Work started in 1850, but the project was abandoned 20 years later; lack of funds, the illness of Leigh and the deaths of two of his children may have contributed. The house is now being restored (to its incomplete state) by the Woodchester Mansion Trust, and is interesting as a testament to the high skills of stonemasons at the time.

PREHISTORIC AND ROMAN SITES

HUNTER-GATHERERS *first appeared in the Cotswolds—then an area of forest—around 5000 or 6000 BC, and lived off wild fruits and game. During the Middle Stone Age, Mesolithic tribes began to clear the trees and hunt wild cattle and deer. They left behind arrowheads and animal-bone tools as evidence of their occupation.*

During a warmer and drier period around 3500 BC, settlers arrived from the Mediterranean and farmed the land. They buried their dead in long barrows and stone cairns, of which some 85 have been discovered. In the Bronze Age, burial mounds took the form of round barrows; over 350 of these have been identified.

Even more evidence survives of the next stages of settlement. A series of strategically sited Iron Age forts lines the lofty western escarpment; many, such as Haresfield Beacon (west of Painswick), are magnificent viewpoints, and the ramparts of others are visible. The Roman town of Corinium (now Cirencester) stood at the meeting of long, straight, cross-country military roads— Akeman Street, Ermine Street and the Fosse Way, which linked Exeter with Lincoln and is followed in part by modern main roads. An impressive legacy of Roman villa sites recalls the numerous country estates established in those times.

Bath B9

For over 2,000 years, the natural hot springs of Bath have drawn visitors to the area. In the 1st century AD the Romans built a bath complex here, and a temple dedicated to Sulis-Minerva, a goddess combining the attributes of the Roman goddess of the arts, Minerva, and the Celtic water goddess Sul. The Romans named their spa town *Aquae Sulis*—'the waters of Sul'. The baths fell into decline after the departure of the Romans in the 5th century, but at the Roman Baths Museum today's visitors can stroll around the Great Bath, and see the remains of the hypocaust (underfloor heating) systems. The museum contains various finds dating from the time of the Roman occupation and displays a gilded bronze head of Sulis-Minerva (*above*), discovered on the site of the temple in 1727. The bathing complex is one of Britain's most popular tourist attractions, and one of the country's most outstanding monuments to the Roman era.

ABOVE *Belas Knap, situated at a high point just outside Winchcombe, is one of the finest Stone Age burial mounds in the country and has been restored by English Heritage.*

Belas Knap near Winchcombe E3

This impressive 4,000-year-old long barrow, complete with dry-stone walling, contains four burial chambers and a false entrance on the northern side.

Chedworth Roman Villa E4

Occupying a sheltered valley, this was a notably grand villa for its day. It boasted underfloor heating, mosaic-floored baths and a nymphaeum—a temple of the water goddesses—situated beside a spring. There is a theory that this feature attracted many travellers, and the villa may have functioned as a hotel for them. The ruins were discovered in 1864, and the Victorian museum housing artefacts is an attraction in itself, for it is one of the earliest purpose-built, on-site museums in the world.

Corinium (Cirencester) E5

Of the second-largest city in Roman Britain little remains. Small parts of the stone wall that enclosed it may be seen in the Abbey Grounds, and on the western side of town is a 2nd-century amphitheatre, now grassed over. The Corinium Museum, closed until Spring 2004, has displays on the prehistory of the area and the Roman era, including outstanding mosaics.

Great Witcombe Roman Villa C4

Built round three sides of a courtyard and with walls standing over five feet high, this 2nd-century AD villa was repeatedly rebuilt and rebuttressed owing to the unstable ground on which it stood. Occupied until

the 4th century, the villa has many tessellated pavements and a bath wing.

Hetty Pegler's Tump and Uley Bury Hill-Fort near Nailsworth C6

Hetty Pegler was a 17th-century landowner, but the Neolithic long barrow that takes his name dates from 3000 BC. It has a central dry-stone passage with three burial chambers and extends for 180 feet; its entrance is recessed between two

protruding horns of masonry at the mound's wider end. A short walk away, Uley Bury hill-fort has yielded copious evidence of its Iron Age settlers, including pottery and coins.

Nan Tow's Tump near Wotton-under-Edge B6

Prominent beside the A46 is a long barrow, approximately 5,000 years old and 100 feet across: legend tells of Nan Tow, a local witch, whose upright skeleton is said to be buried inside.

North Leigh Roman Villa near Woodstock I4
First occupied in the 1st century AD, this large villa by the verdant banks of the Evenlode was remodelled in the 4th century. Living quarters displaying mosaics and baths are arranged around a central courtyard.

Rollright Stones near Chipping Norton G3
At the hub of the striking Bronze Age monument is a stone circle, 100 feet across and comprising some 70 stones known as the King's Men; it may have been used for ceremonial purposes. Close by is a taller stone group, part of a burial chamber, known as the Whispering Knights, while east of the main circle is a lone standing monolith known as the King's Stone. The stones are said to represent an invader king and his army who were turned to stone by a witch.

Woodchester Roman Villa B5
Once the grandest of the Cotswolds' Roman villas, Woodchester had more than two acres of rooms, whose floors were covered in mosaics. The finest of these depicts the Orpheus legend; the largest Roman mosaic in northern Europe, it was composed of around 1½ million *tesserae*, or cubes. It has now been reburied; a replica exists but is rarely displayed.

ROMAN VILLAS IN THE COTSWOLDS

LEFT *The remains of a plunge bath at Great Witcombe Roman villa, destroyed when a new bath complex was built in the 4th century AD.*

ABOVE *The sophisticated underfloor heating system in the caldarium, or hot room, at Chedworth Roman villa.*

BELOW *A mosaic at Chedworth Roman villa depicts spring as a figure with a basket of flowers and a small bird in her hands.*

THERE IS MORE THAN a grain of truth in the local saying 'Scratch Gloucestershire and find Rome'. For, of the 250 or so Roman villas discovered in Southwest England, the majority are clustered in the Cotswolds, especially around Corinium (Cirencester). Sites such as Withington, Great Witcombe and—one of the grandest—Chedworth show that the Romans found the area as attractive as modern visitors do today.

There were various reasons for this. The land was suitable for growing wheat and barley and for grazing sheep, and it had plenty of rivers and streams to supply water. The indigenous Dobunni tribe were relatively sophisticated and perhaps more easily Romanised than some of their fellow Britons. And Corinium itself was an important factor: the town had become the province's second largest after Londinium and provided a range of services and utilitarian and luxury items to the dozen or so villas that lay within a 10-mile radius.

Roman villas were essentially country farmhouses, varying in size and sumptuousness. Some stood near towns and major roads, others were tucked away in secluded valleys and on wooded hillsides. The villa was typically one storey high, sometimes built round a courtyard, and, with its pigs, sheep, cattle and fields of grain, virtually self-sufficient in food. Interiors could be highly luxurious: hypocaust systems brought hot air from outside furnaces beneath the floors to warm the rooms; baths consisted of a series of progressively hotter rooms ending with a cold plunge; and dining rooms were furnished with bronze and wooden chairs and couches, and marvellous mosaic floors.

WALKS

THE INTIMATE SCALE *of the Cotswolds makes much of the area ideal for exploring on foot. Field paths and quiet lanes connect classic villages and expansive country estates. In the far south the Thames towpath offers uncomplicated waterside strolls. And on the west side the escarpment has the most varied walking and finest views of all.*

Paths are generally well maintained and many are waymarked, with the national system of yellow arrows denoting public footpaths and blue arrows for public bridleways (along which you may also ride a horse or cycle); maps at 1:25,000 scale, which show field boundaries, greatly assist route-finding.

THE COTSWOLD WAY

With its far-ranging views encompassing the Severn estuary, the jagged outline of the Malvern Hills, the low-lying Vale of Evesham and the distant uplands of the Welsh border, the Cotswolds' western escarpment provides sustained drama.

Much of the best of this terrain is traversed by the Cotswold Way, a 100-mile route along footpaths, bridleways and lanes from Chipping Campden to Bath.

Fit walkers could complete the route in a week, but may have to walk up to 20 miles on some days; many prefer to take longer, as there is much to be seen. Many parts of the Way make excellent short walks.

A particular feature of the Cotswold Way is the abundance of ancient sites. Uley Bury is one of the most impressive Iron Age forts, lying close to Hetty Pegler's Tump, and by using other paths it can be included in a circular walk incorporating Peaked Down, Cam Long Down, Uley and Owlpen Manor.

The folding landscapes around Painswick rise to fine viewpoints at the ancient ramparts on Haresfield Beacon, a part of which, at Ring Hill, is designated a geological Site of Special Scientific Interest.

The village of Birdlip can be a starting point for a rewarding sample of the Way as it leads through Witcombe Wood and passes close to Great Witcombe Roman Villa. Further northeast, the Way encounters the Devil's Chimney, a precarious-looking pinnacle of rock in the abandoned quarries on Leckhampton Hill, high above Cheltenham.

Cleeve Hill is the highest point in the Cotswolds, rising to 1,083 feet, and is popular for kite-flying. From here

ABOVE *Atop Leckhampton Hill stands the Devil's Chimney, a dramatic limestone pinnacle left behind by quarry workers but reputed locally to rise straight from Hell.*

the Way heads past the remarkable Stone Age long barrow of Belas Knap before dropping into Winchcombe, where it meets the Gloucestershire Way and Wychavon Way and then gives a glimpse of the romantic ruins of Hailes Abbey.

The final section takes in some of the most attractive villages of all, including Stanway, Stanton and Broadway, with Buckland and Snowshill attainable on short detours from the route. Just before dropping into Chipping Campden, it skirts the top of the delightful Dover's Hill estate (site of the annual Cotswold Olimpick Games), acquired by the National Trust in 1928. The site includes Lynches Wood, an

ancient woodland bright with bluebells in spring and rich in birdlife, including greater spotted woodpeckers (*above*), tawny owls and tree-creepers.

BELOW *Hikers follow the Cotswold Way across Crickley Hill, an area of grassland and woods giving fine views over the countryside spread out below.*

THE FAME OF THE COTSWOLDS

OTHER WALKS

Away from the escarpment, some of the larger estates, such as Cirencester Park, are open to walkers (although many others are strictly private). Rights of way from Woodstock crisscross the northern part of the magnificent parkland of Blenheim Palace, passing the lake and the Column of Victory. A track leads northwest to reach the ancient earthwork of Grim's Ditch, crossed by a part of Akeman Street Roman road. This stretch is a field path followed by the long-distance Oxfordshire Way, a 65-mile route from Bourton-on-the-Water to Henley-on-Thames.

Woodchester Park, near Stroud, is a wooded National Trust estate sprinkled with lakes and with marked trails up to seven miles long. The National Trust also owns Minchinhampton and Rodborough Commons, which together comprise an open pasture dotted with archaeological sites and grazed by cattle, horses and sheep; the rich flora, which includes cowslips, and pyramidal and common spotted orchids, attracts chalkhill blue, dark green fritillary and other butterflies.

The gentle scenery of such valleys as the Coln, between Bibury and Quenington for instance, the Eye in the vicinity of Lower and Upper Slaughter and the Windrush near Burford makes for pleasant village-to-village walking. Eastwards from Lechlade, the Thames Path gives the opportunity for a more sustained wander along the water. The derelict Thames and Severn Canal in the Stroud valley has not seen a boat since its closure in 1911. Built in 1789, it was never a great success because of its large number of locks, but it remains a strongly atmospheric backwater, with ruined locks and lush undergrowth. Partly bordering a local nature reserve, the towpath ends at the grandiose entrance to the two-mile Sapperton Tunnel, the longest in Britain when it was built, in the same year as the canal. Beyond the eastern tunnel entrance, another worthwhile portion of the canal can be followed south of Coates, passing close to Thames Head, where a granite obelisk claims this to be the source of the Thames.

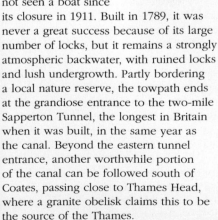

THAMES PATH

Public Footpath

SPORTING HEROES, *musical legends and literary geniuses populate the Cotswold hall of fame. This small corner of England has been, and continues to be, home to an array of talented men and women who were either born with the fresh Cotswold air in their lungs—such as Laurie Lee, whose writings captured Britain's pastoral charm—or have since been attracted to the region's unique and sublime beauty.*

Fred Archer
Jockey
(1857–86, born in Prestbury) Born into the world of racing near Cheltenham's racing ground, Fred Archer and his brothers all became jockeys, but only Fred took to the flat. At the tender age of 12 he rode his first winner, and by 17 he had earned the title of Champion Jockey. A master of his sport, he won most of the major flat races of his time on more than one occasion, and in 1885 alone he won 246 races. Tragically, Archer committed suicide when he was only 29 while suffering from typhoid; two years previously both his wife and a son had died.

Jilly Cooper
Novelist
(Born 1937 in Essex) The fresh-faced looks of this best-selling author beam from the covers of all her steamy paperbacks. Her raunchy writings on the love lives of the upper-middle classes have made Jilly Cooper one of the most famous female novelists in Britain today. Cooper is a fervent animal-lover, and keeps a veritable menagerie at her home in Bisley; she is also an active campaigner for animal rights.

W. H. Davies
Writer
(1871–1940, born in Newport) This distinguished writer spent much of his life wandering around America, where he claimed he was thoroughly educated by the numerous down-and-outs he met. It was during these years that he gained the material to write *The Autobiography of a Super Tramp* (1907), his most famous work. On a trip to the Klondike, he had to have his lower leg amputated following an accident sustained while trying to jump a freight train. Davies spent the last years of his life quietly—almost reclusively—in Nailsworth, Gloucestershire, happily married to his young wife, Helen.

Eddie 'The Eagle' Edwards
Olympic ski-jumper
(Born 1963 in Cheltenham) Eddie Edwards is Britain's most famous, best-loved—and only—ski-jumper. In 1988 Edwards (by day a plasterer in Cheltenham) burst onto our television screens as the British ski-jump competitor in the Winter Olympics at Calgary. Edwards had become obsessed with skiing after a school trip, but took his passion further than most and entered the Olympics. His courage, which to many seemed more like madness considering his meagre experience and training, had the nation gripped. Although he came last in his event Edwards immediately became a celebrity. Despite being notoriously clumsy and shortsighted, Edwards considers himself a serious sportsman, but has never again participated in the Olympics.

Thomas Hobbes
Philosopher
(1588–1679, born in Malmesbury) Hobbes was one of the most influential thinkers of the 17th century, and his works laid the foundations of the doctrine of materialism. His belief in the priority of the material world over the spiritual world would not be so shocking in today's secular society, but at the time it reeked of atheism, egoism and heresy, and led to his being nicknamed the Beast of Malmesbury. As a young man he was employed by the third Earl of Devonshire, in whose company he toured Europe. On these travels he met other contemporary philosophers, such as Descartes and Galileo. Hobbes was a Royalist and was caught in the political turbulence preceding the English Civil War. His writings frequently succeeded in alienating both Royalists and Parliamentarians, and in 1640 he fled to France. In later years Hobbes returned to England, where he was recognised as a venerable academic and lived to the grand old age of 92.

THE FAME OF THE COTSWOLDS (CONTINUED)

Gustav Holst
Composer

(1874–1934, born in Cheltenham) The name Gustav Holst is universally synonymous with *The Planets*, which this prolific composer wrote in 1917. At 17, Holst was

conducting Cotswold village choirs, and while studying he supplemented his income by playing the trombone with seaside brass bands. After leaving the Royal College of Music, Holst joined an orchestra and gained invaluable experience for his future career as a composer. His work was eclectic, including hymns and choral music alongside operas based on Indian folklore. He loved composing, but eschewed the fame that came with success. He had always endured ill health, despite being a fanatical walker, and he met an early death at the age of 59 following an operation.

Brian Jones
Musician

(1942–69, born in Cheltenham) An often forgotten member of the rock 'n' roll band the Rolling Stones, Jones was, in fact, one of the founder members of this hugely successful group. In 1962 Jones met Mick Jagger and Keith Richards at a gig in London, and within a year they had been signed to a record company. It was Jones, a fan of blues music, who came up with the name the Rolling Stones, taking it from a song by one of his favourite singers, Muddy Waters. Jones had been a teenage rebel, and the Stones were renowned for their bad behaviour. But the high life that came with stardom didn't do Jones any

good: he took drugs and drank heavily. In 1969, only a few weeks after quitting the Stones, he drowned in the swimming pool of his home in Sussex. His death was officially recorded as being by misadventure, but some believe it was suicide, while others still claim it may even have been murder.

Laurie Lee
Author

(1914–97, born in Slad) Lee was never a prolific writer, but all four of the semi-autobiographical novels he wrote were successes; his poetry, on the other hand, failed to win the same acclaim. Lee's nostalgic reminiscences of childhood in rural England in *Cider with Rosie* made his home village of Slad in the Cotswolds famous. In 1959 he confidently wrote 'should become a classic' on *Cider with Rosie*'s dust-jacket blurb, and he has since been proved right. When he was 19, Lee left Slad and made the long walk to London, where he worked as a labourer for a year. In 1935 he went to Spain, living off only his wits and his violin playing. He later returned to Spain to fight for the Republican forces in the Spanish Civil War. In his later years Lee, with his wife and daughter, made Slad his home once again. He was a regular at the local pub, the Woolpack, until his death at 82.

William Morris
Designer, writer and social reformer

(1834–96, born in Walthamstow) A master of creativity, Morris excelled in everything he put his hand to. Along with Dante Gabriel Rossetti and Sir Edward Burne-Jones, he was a leading light in the circle known as the Pre-Raphaelite Brotherhood. Morris is probably best known for his designs and prints, which have been reproduced in many forms, from fabrics and wallpapers to writing paper. A pivotal figure in the Arts and Crafts Movement of the late 19th century (*see feature on pages 96–7*), he was interested in reviving the dying skills of craftsmanship. When he moved to Kelmscott Manor in the Cotswolds in 1871, Morris established a number of important craft workshops in the area. In the 1880s he became increasingly drawn to socialism, and was active in establishing guilds of craftsmen. In 1891 he established the Kelmscott Press, which produced exquisite printed works. For Morris, beauty and art were the essence of life.

Joanna Trollope
Novelist

(Born 1943 in Minchinhampton) A multitude of novels have issued from this great-niece of the Victorian novelist Anthony Trollope. She is known as the 'Queen of the Aga Saga', as her novels tend to deal with the trials and tribulations of middle-class country folk who would typically have an Aga in their kitchen. But Trollope also writes historical novels under the pseudonym Caroline Harvey. Several of her successes, such as *The Rector's Wife* and *The Choir* have been adapted for television and filmed in her native Cotswolds.

William Tyndale
Translator

(*c.* 1490–1536, born in the west Cotswolds) Where exactly in Gloucestershire this Protestant martyr was born is unknown, but there is a tower commemorating him at Wotton-under-Edge. Tyndale was martyred for translating the Bible into English. He decided to carry out this mammoth task after becoming disillusioned with the Roman Catholic Church; this disenchantment compounded his belief that all Christians should be able to read the Bible in their own language. Forbidden to undertake this work in England, Tyndale moved to Germany. The first edition of his New Testament reached London in 1526 and caused uproar within the Catholic community, forcing Tyndale to prolong his exile. He was finally captured in Antwerp, where he was working on the translation of the Old Testament, and was burnt at the stake as a heretic.

Ralph Vaughan Williams
Composer

(1872–1958, born in Down Ampney) Vaughan Williams, one of the greatest 20th-century composers, left the village of his birth as a toddler. But he never forgot his roots and was very active in the Three Choirs Festival, composing works especially for it and conducting there on several occasions. Vaughan Williams also immortalised Down Ampney by naming a hymn tune after it. The strong influences of English hymnody and folksong imbued his music with a quintessential Englishness.

Rosemary Verey
Horticulturist and garden designer

(1918–2003, born in Kent) Rosemary Verey (*pictured right*) created beautiful gardens

LOVE AND WAR: THE MITFORD SISTERS

ABOVE *The Mitfords in 1934 at a family gathering at Swinbrook: left to right are Lady Redesdale, Nancy, Diana, Tom, Pamela, Lord Redesdale; seated in front are Unity, Jessica and Deborah.*

RIGHT *Jessica's life in the American Communist Party is described in the second part of her autobiography, A Fine Old Conflict.*

LORD AND LADY REDESDALE, better known as the Mitfords, of Swinbrook in Oxfordshire had a family of seven children—six girls and a boy. Endowed with striking good looks and diverse talents, the children all went on to achieve some measure of fame or notoriety.

Their father did not believe in formal education, so the sisters were never sent to school but were taught at home by a succession of governesses. They grew up in an intimate world of private jokes and nicknames and fierce sibling rivalry, acting just as they pleased. Their aristocratic childhood is recalled in Jessica's autobiography, *Hons and Rebels*. The sisters' beauty and unconventional behaviour ensured that they were much talked about, sought after and admired in English society.

The Mitfords were also famous for their widely differing political views. Nancy, the eldest, wrote novels depicting England's upper classes in the final years of empire, immortalising her family in her highly successful works *The Pursuit of Love* and *Love in a Cold Climate*. A socialist, she denounced her fascist sisters to the wartime authorities, and after the war moved to France where she died in 1973. Diana married the fascist leader Oswald Mosley; Unity fell in love with Hitler and shot herself in the head when war was declared between the two countries she so loved. She died eight years later from her injuries. The one Mitford brother, Tom, was killed fighting in Burma in the war that Hitler started.

Since childhood Jessica had saved 'running-away money', which she used to abscond to the Spanish Civil War when she was just 18; she then went to live in the USA, where she joined the Communist Party. Her extreme left-wing affiliations estranged her from her sisters and she barely spoke to Diana for over 40 years. Pamela married the son of a tabloid newspaper magnate, and Deborah wedded the Duke of Devonshire.

The family dominated high-society gossip for much of the 20th century. But, more than that, their lives and obsessions reflect the shaping forces of the century that produced such an astonishing brood.

across Britain, and those at her own home, Barnsley House, remain the show-piece of this talented woman's craftsmanship. She wrote numerous books on garden design and deployed her talents to the benefit of both friends and clients, including the Prince of Wales. Her extensive knowledge of gardening history informed much of her work, and is beautifully expressed in the Tudor knot garden at Barnsley House.

Evelyn Waugh
Author
(1903–66, born in London) Waugh is widely regarded as a master of satirical prose. While at Oxford, he spent more time socialising than studying, only later realising his talents as a writer. He wrote some of his most famous works while living at Piers Court in Stinchcombe, where he brought up, with his second wife Laura, six children. Waugh's first marriage had failed after his wife (also called Evelyn) was unfaithful. One of his best-known works, *Brideshead Revisited* (1945), was memorably produced for television.

HISTORIC INNS AND HOTELS

Bibury Court Bibury E5

Bibury Court is said to have been immortalised by Charles Dickens in *Bleak House*. But if this is true, it was only a legal dispute over a will and years of litigation that connected the house to Dickens's book, as it is anything but bleak. It has a wonderful location in the beautiful

Cotswold countryside, while the interior is a feast for the eyes of antique collectors. Over the centuries Bibury Court has entertained personages as great as Charles II, when he attended the renowned Bibury races, and, in later years, the Prince Regent. It is only since 1968 that the public have been able to enjoy the charms of this impressive country-house hotel.

Buckland Manor near Broadway E2

There has been a country house on the site of Buckland Manor since at least the 7th century AD, when the property was gifted to Gloucester Abbey. The manor remained in the hands of the abbey until the Dissolution of the Monasteries in the 16th century. Buckland was then a private house, passing through numerous families before becoming a hotel in 1981.

Calcot Manor near Tetbury C6

This relatively new hotel stands on land that was farmed by the monks of the Cistercian abbey at nearby Kingswood in the 14th century. Part of this monastic heritage is a tithe barn which still stands (but only just) on the property. The whole hotel is a conversion of various outbuildings from the farmstead that developed on the land between the late 17th and early 19th centuries. Since 1983 Calcot Manor has grown from a seven-bedroom hotel to winner of the *Which?* Family Hotel of the Year in 1998.

The Lamb Inn Great Rissington F4

Originally converted from a farmhouse, some parts of this mellow Cotswold stone building are 300 years old. In 1942 a Wellington Bomber crashed into the orchard of the inn. A propeller blade from the ill-fated plane is on display in one of the two bars, along with a photograph of the plane's crew, of whom only one survived.

Ye Olde Hobnails Inn
Little Washbourne D2

Until its sale in 1999 this inn was in the Shurey family for over 250 years—in 1743 Timothy Shurey rented the property for £25 a year. But Hobnails was an inn before this family's time, and once accommodated Catherine Parr when bad weather delayed her journey to Sudeley Castle. Considering the antiquity of the inn, it is not surprising that there is a ghost: 12-year-old Harry, from the days of Queen Victoria, who reportedly likes nothing better than to engage in poltergeist pranks.

Lower Slaughter Manor
Lower Slaughter F3

Since pre-Norman times Lower Slaughter Manor has been an important building in the locality. Today the Grade II listed building entertains holidaymakers who appreciate a bit of luxury, but in the past it was home to lords and ladies, and, for a period, nuns: from 1443 to the mid 16th century the house was a convent. It was largely rebuilt in the 1650s, with numerous additions over the following centuries.

The Lygon Arms Broadway E2

The inn was first recorded in parish ledgers in 1532, when it was a resting place for travelling wool merchants and was known as the White Hart Inn. During the English Civil War the Lygon Arms must have taken a neutral stance: it played host to Oliver Cromwell on the eve of the decisive Battle of Worcester, while Charles I had once used the inn to meet his own supporters. Located on the main coaching route between England and Wales, the inn prospered in the 18th century. In the mid 19th century it took the name the Lygon Arms from its then owner General William Lygon. Today the award-winning inn successfully combines its ancient tradition of being a welcome haven for travellers with the

provision of every 20th-century comfort. The 17th century Minstrel Gallery can still be seen in the Great Hall.

The New Inn at Coln Coln St Aldwyns F5

When Elizabeth I decreed that there should be a coaching inn within a day's travel of every major centre of population, the New Inn was one of the hostelries that fulfilled the royal order. For nearly 400 years it has been Coln St Aldwyns' only pub and the local entertainment and social hub. In 1988 the inn was threatened with conversion into flats, but the villagers battled to keep it as their local, their victory proving the New Inn's undiminished purpose in serving the Cotswolds.

The Old Bell Malmesbury D7

This beautiful inn (*pictured below*) on the southern edge of the Cotswolds is the oldest hostelry in Wiltshire, and is also reputed to be the oldest in England. Its surroundings, too, are ancient, with the fascinating Malmesbury Abbey situated right next door. The inn would not, in fact, have existed without the abbey, as it was Walter Loring, Abbot of Malmesbury, who founded it in 1220 as a guesthouse for visitors to the abbey's library. The abbey at that time was one of the most important seats of learning in England. The inn was greatly extended in Edwardian times, but many elements of the original building remain. The Great Hall is a restaurant, while the rest of the building is a rather luxurious hotel.

CALENDAR OF FESTIVALS AND EVENTS A SELECTION

THE COTSWOLDS' *annual calendar includes many traditions of great antiquity, as well as lively arts festivals and small-scale village fairs. Tourist Information Centres have further details of these and numerous other events (addresses and telephone numbers are listed below).*

MARCH

CHELTENHAM THE FESTIVAL The major racing event of the year, featuring the Gold Cup and the Smurfit Champion Hurdle.

APRIL

NAILSWORTH FESTIVAL The last week of April sees authors, musicians and poets visit the town.

MAY

BISLEY WELL-DRESSING A tradition of laying flowers on local wells, begun in the 19th century and held on Ascension Day.

BROCKWORTH CHEESE-ROLLING A massive wooden 'cheese' is rolled down steep Cooper's Hill, pursued by local daredevils.

CHIPPING CAMPDEN SCUTTLEBROOK WAKE Whitsuntide celebration featuring the 'Cotswold Olimpick Games', the crowning of the May Queen, bands and a torchlit procession.

GREAT BADMINTON BADMINTON HORSE TRIALS

RANDWICK CHEESE-ROLLING Three cheeses are blessed after a church service: one is rolled round the church three times and shared out, the others are rolled down a slope the next Saturday to herald the opening of Randwick Wap, a medieval fair and carnival.

STROUD STROUD AND DISTRICT ARTS FESTIVAL Classical music, opera, dance and drama.

TETBURY FESTIVAL AND WOOLSACK RACE Originally a trial of strength for young drovers keen to impress the womenfolk, the race features teams carrying bales of wool up and down Gumstool Hill, the town's steepest street. Day-long medieval-style market.

JULY

CHELTENHAM INTERNATIONAL FESTIVAL OF MUSIC

CIRENCESTER EARLY MUSIC FESTIVAL Singing and music concerts

CIRENCESTER PARK COTSWOLD COUNTRY FAIR

FAIRFORD ROYAL INTERNATIONAL AIR TATTOO Huge military air show at RAF Fairford.

GUITING POWER FESTIVAL OF MUSIC AND ARTS Classical music, jazz, opera and art exhibitions in a village setting.

STROUD INTERNATIONAL BRICK AND ROLLING-PIN THROWING CONTEST Feats of fun; both men and women join in the contest.

AUGUST

FAIRFORD STEAM RALLY AND SHOW Vintage steam vehicles in Fairford Park.

GLOUCESTER, HEREFORD AND WORCESTER THREE CHOIRS FESTIVAL The three cathedrals take turns to host this festival of choral music.

MINCHINHAMPTON GATCOMBE PARK HORSE TRIALS

SEPTEMBER

PAINSWICK CLYPPING CEREMONY Revived in 1897 but of unknown origins. Parishioners link hands to surround the church while singing the Clypping Hymn to the accompaniment of a band, and children wear circlets of flowers in their hair.

WOODSTOCK BLENHEIM INTERNATIONAL HORSE TRIALS In the park of Blenheim Palace.

ABOVE *Morris dancers escort the wake queen through the streets of Chipping Campden to celebrate Whitsun.*

OCTOBER

CHELTENHAM LITERATURE FESTIVAL Authors' talks, book signings and events.

NOVEMBER

CHELTENHAM THE OPEN Three-days at Cheltenham Race Course of steeplechasing and hurdle racing.

DECEMBER

CHELTENHAM FESTIVAL OF CHRISTMAS LIGHTS Procession and ceremonial switching-on of lights by Father Christmas.

MARSHFIELD MUMMING PLAY Performed on Boxing Day.

TETBURY SOUTH COTSWOLDS CHRISTMAS ANTIQUES FAIR Held at Westonbirt School.

USEFUL INFORMATION

Listed below are the details of Tourist Information Centres for a selection of popular Cotswold destinations. Please note that these details may be subject to change.

BROADWAY
1 Cotswold Court,
The Green, Broadway
WR12 7AA
Tel: (01386) 852937

CHELTENHAM
77 Promenade,
Cheltenham
GL50 1PP
Tel: (01242) 522878

CHIPPING CAMPDEN
The Old Police Station,
High Street, Chipping Campden
GL55 6HB
Tel: (01386) 841206

CIRENCESTER
Corn Hall,
Market Place, Cirencester
GL7 2NW
Tel: (01285) 654180

STOW-ON-THE-WOLD
Hollis House,
The Square, Stow-on-the-Wold
GL54 1AF
Tel: (01451) 831082

For general information, contact:

Cotswold District Council Offices,
High Street, Moreton-in-Marsh
GL56 0AZ

The following websites may also be of interest (NB website addresses can change):

The Cotswold HyperGuide
http://www.digital-brilliance.com/
hyperg/towns/index.htm

Cheltenham, Centre for the
Cotswolds
http://www.cheltweb.co.uk/
cotswold.htm

Cotswolds Country
http://www.cotswoldcountry.co.uk

Gloucestershire Tourism
http://www.visit-glos.org.uk/

INDEX

and acknowledgments

Note: page numbers in **bold** refer to captions for illustrations

ACKNOWLEDGMENTS

The editors gratefully acknowledge the use of information taken from the following publications during the preparation of this volume:

AA Essential Explorer: Britain by Tim Locke, AA Publishing 1994

The Arts and Crafts Movement by Steven Adams, Grange Books 1996

The Arts and Crafts Movement in the Cotswolds by Mary Greensted, Alan Sutton Publishing Ltd 1993

Book of British Villages, The Reader's Digest Association Ltd 1990

Britain: A Lonely Planet Travel Survival Kit by Richard Everist, Bryn Thomas and Tony Wheeler, Lonely Planet Publications 1995

The Buildings of England: Gloucestershire, The Cotswolds by David Verey, Penguin 1970

Cheltenham Races by Peter Gill, Sutton Publishing Ltd 1997

The Cotswolds by Brian Smith, Sutton Publishing Ltd 1992

The Cotswolds by Geoffrey N. Wright, David and Charles 1992

The Cotswolds: A New Study edited by Charles and Alice Mary Hadfield, David and Charles 1973

The Cotswolds: Landranger Guidebook by Peter and Helen Titchmarsh, The Ordnance Survey and Jarrold Publishing 1991

The Cotswolds, Life & Traditions by June Lewis, Weidenfeld & Nicolson 1996

Coughton Court, Coughton Court and Jarrold Publishing 1997

Country Eye: A Walker's Guide to Britain's Traditional Countryside by Geoffrey Young, George Philip 1991

The Countryside Companion edited by Robert Hardy, Michael O'Mara 1989

The Daily Telegraph: The Cotswolds in a Week by Gabrielle Macphedran, Headway 1993

The Dictionary of Festivals by J. C. Cooper, Thorsons 1990

The Gypsies: Waggon-time and After by Denis Harvey, Batsford 1979

The History of Croquet by D. M. C. Prichard, Cassell 1981

Jane Austen's England by Maggie Lane, Robert Hale Ltd 1986

Landmark Visitors Guide: Cotswolds and Shakespeare Country by Richard Sale, Landmark 1997

Life in the Villa in Roman Britain by John Burke, Batsford 1978

Meet the Ancestors by Julian Richards, BBC Books 1998

Old Cotswold by Edith Brill, David and Charles 1968

On The Verge: the Gypsies of England by Donald Kenrick and Sian Bakewell, University of Hertfordshire Press 1995

Ordnance Survey Leisure Guide: Cotswolds, The Automobile Association and the Ordnance Survey 1992

The Oxford Companion to English Literature edited by Margaret Drabble, Oxford University Press 1985

The Rise and Development of the Sunday School Movement in England, 1780–1980 by Philip B. Cliff, National Christian Education Council 1986

The Rise and Fall of Merry England by Ronald Hutton, Oxford University Press 1994

The Roman Villa in South-West England by Keith Branigan, Moonraker Press 1976

The Shell Book of Rural Britain by Keith Mossman, David and Charles 1978

Stratford-upon-Avon and the Cotswolds by Michael Hall, Pevensey Heritage Guides 1993

The World of Jane Austen by Nigel Nicolson, Weidenfeld & Nicolson 1991